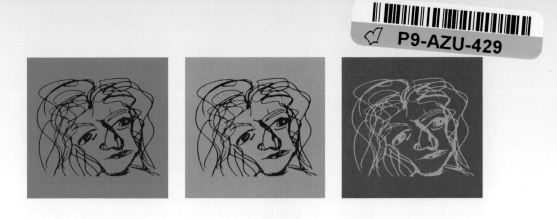

Finding the *Artist*

Within

Creating and Reading Visual Texts in the English Language Arts Classroom

Peggy Albers

INTERNATIONAL
Reading Association
800 BARKSDALE ROAD, PO BOX 8139
NEWARK, DE 19714-8139, USA
www.reading.org

The International Reading Association attempts, through its publications, to provide a forum for a wide spectrum of opinions on reading. This policy permits divergent viewpoints without implying the endorsement of the Association.

Executive Editor, Books   Corinne M. Mooney
Developmental Editor   Charlene M. Nichols
Developmental Editor   Tori Mello Bachman
Developmental Editor   Stacey Lynn Sharp
Editorial Production Manager   Shannon T. Fortner
Production Manager   Iona Muscella
Supervisor, Electronic Publishing   Anette Schuetz

Project Editors   Tori Mello Bachman and Christina Lambert

Cover   Design, Linda Steere; Illustration, Peggy Albers

The publisher would appreciate notification where errors occur so that they may be corrected in subsequent printings and/or editions.

Library of Congress Cataloging-in-Publication Data

Albers, Peggy.

 Finding the artist within : creating and reading visual texts in the English language arts classroom / Peggy Albers.

     p. cm.

 Includes bibliographical references and index.

 ISBN 978-0-87207-613-6

 1. Language arts (Middle school)--United States. 2. Language arts (Middle school)--Activity programs. 3. Language arts (Secondary)--United States. 4. Art--Study and teaching (Middle school)--United States. 5. Art--Study and teaching (Secondary)--United States. I. Title.

 LB1631.A363 2007

 428.0071'2--dc22   2007012049

This book is dedicated to the Manthey Meadowlarks, my mother's childhood family band: Tony Manthey, Mary Manthey, Genevieve Tomscha, Bob Manthey, Carolyn Bower, Pauline Popek, Jane Archer, and Pat Anawski. Their love of the musical arts and continued performances, even while they are all now in their 80s, strongly exemplify why the arts are essential in our lives.

CONTENTS

ABOUT THE AUTHOR

Peggy Albers is an associate professor at Georgia State University in Atlanta, Georgia, USA, where she works with preservice teachers preparing for careers in English education and inservice teachers in literacy and English education. Her current interests are semiotics, children's literature, English education, and the integration of multimedia into instruction.

Originally from South Dakota, USA, Peggy's interest in the arts was fostered by her mother, a musician in her family dance band. Peggy studied at Dakota State University, Madison, South Dakota, where she earned her B.S. in English and Speech and Drama. For 15 years, Peggy taught in these areas and also directed more than 40 full-length and one-act plays, coached oral interpretation, and acted in community plays. She earned her master's degree in curriculum and instruction at the University of South Dakota, Vermillion, South Dakota, and then received her doctorate in language education from Indiana University, Bloomington, Indiana, USA.

Peggy has published widely in such journals as *Language Arts*, *English Education*, *Talking Points*, and *The Reading Teacher*, and she has co-authored with Sharon Murphy a book titled *Telling Pieces: Art as Literacy in Middle Grades Classes* (Erlbaum, 2000), which focuses on the exploration of literacy practices in art classes, as well as a critique of visual arts texts that students create.

When she's not teaching, Peggy enjoys studying pottery and art at Callanwolde Fine Arts Center in Atlanta. Her work has been shown and sold at local and state pottery shows. Peggy also combines her interest in writing and making video documentary short films in her study of pottery. She has written for *Clay Times*, a national journal for ceramicists, and documents the processes of local and international potters through video. Two of her documentary short films premiered at the 2006 annual conference of the National Council on Education for the Ceramic Arts.

FOREWORD

As an advocate of a critical, inquiry-based, multiple-ways-of-knowing curriculum, I like to envision the reading language arts curriculum as being made up of meaning making, language study, and inquiry, all done from a critical perspective. By *meaning making*, I mean offering lots and lots of opportunities to make sense of all kinds of text using all of the resources the humanities provide (such as language, art, music, dance, drama). My goal is to help students unpack the systems of meaning that are operating in text to position them as readers and endow them with identities they may or may not wish to take on. A second component of curriculum is language study, the goal of which is to create readers who are agents of text rather than victims of text. In short, I want students who know how texts work as well as students who are able to read and create powerful texts that do important work in the world. The third component of curriculum is inquiry, which I see as the opportunity to pursue one's own inquiry questions using reading, writing, and other sign systems as tools for learning. Said differently, I want to produce learners who know how to use art, music, drama, etc. to reposition themselves, gather information, change perspectives, re-theorize issues, and take thoughtful new social action.

Because I want meaning making, language study, and inquiry done from a critical perspective, the question I, as a teacher, have to ask myself is, "What kinds of social practices do I need to put in place so that I and my students can live the kind of curriculum I envision for the 21st century?" Notice the emphasis on *social practices*. One of the things critical theorists have taught us is that the forms of literacy are sustained and maintained because of the social practices that surround them. From this perspective, literacy can be thought of as a particular set of social practices valued by a particular set of people. In order to change anyone's definition of literacy, the social practices that keep particular (and often older) definitions of literacy in place have to change. What we do in our classrooms and how we think about the work we do in our classrooms is important. And this is where *Finding the Artist Within: Creating and Reading Visual Texts in the English Language Arts Classroom* comes in: Peggy Albers addresses what new social practices we need to put in place in order to think about literacy differently, as well as what new social practices we have to put in place in our classrooms in order for students to live the kind of curriculum they need to experience as 21st-century citizens.

Like theory and curriculum, the function of a good foreword is to give perspective. Theoretically, the framework underlying this book is transmediation. Psychologically, transmediation is the process of moving what you know from one sign system (language) to another sign system (art). Because the units of meaning in various sign systems are not the same ("love," for example, can be expressed very differently in art than it can be expressed in writing), moving across sign systems (transmediating one's knowing) can be very generative in that it unfreezes what was thought known and opens up new spaces for discovery.

While the psychological effects of transmediation are significant, even more significant may be the fact that as a function of seeing the world differently social relationships are changed; there is in this sense a very important sociological aspect to the process of transmediation. Not only does transmediation cause one to be positioned differently in the world, but as a result of that positioning one's identity is altered. Said differently, others begin to "read" you differently.

In these ways transmediation plays a significant role in literacy learning by supporting students in engaging in the social practices we associate with being critically literate:

- conscious engagement (which transmediation heightens by calling attention),
- entertaining alternate ways of being (which the move across sign systems assures),
- inquiry (facts are only beliefs at rest, so unfreezing beliefs raises doubt, which is the impetus for learning), and
- reflexivity (the process of using yourself and others to outgrow yourself).

Curricularly, Albers believes that moving within, across, and between sign systems (art, music, language, drama, etc.) revitalizes teaching, more accurately reflects the multimodal nature of literacy events in the real word, and enhances learning by making learning more relevant (accomplished in part by tapping into the literacy practices in which young people are already engaged). But (and this is a big BUT), in order to reap these benefits, Albers argues that teachers and students need to know something about the systems of meaning that operate in the visual arts for the purpose of more effective production (she has included chapters that cover the basics of drawing, painting, three-dimensional work such as sculpture, and technology) as well as interpretation (she has included chapters on how you read art critically as well as how knowing something about the grammar of visual design enhances meaning making).

Her first chapter frames the book, while her last chapter explores the potential of curriculum when the arts are kept front and center. Throughout, readers are invited to try their own hand at creating art forms. They hear testimonials from a variety of educational stakeholders on how the arts have affected their thinking as well as how "messing around" with the arts has affected the stances and identities they have taken on. (I use "messing around" purposefully as Albers sees the arts as both a tool and toy for learning.) To support teachers in exploring the arts in their classrooms, Albers has recommended key curricular engagements and linked these to the International Reading Association and the National Council of Teachers of English *Standards for the English Language Arts* (1996). Given that the intent of this book is to invite teachers of the English language arts to play with the discipline of art while at the same time learn about that discipline and how the arts can be made an integral part of literacy learning, linkages of this sort are important.

I see *Finding the Artist Within* as filling a unique niche in the reading/language arts textbook market. It expands our notions of "reading" as well as our notions of literacy. While Albers charitably gives those of us who have advocated for the arts much credit, her contributions to our understanding of the discipline of art, as well as how to read it critically and use it strategically in instruction, constitute significant contributions to our understanding of the potential and possibility of English language arts curriculum and instruction for the 21st century.

Jerome C. Harste
Bloomington, Indiana, USA
June 2006

PREFACE

We are all artists, every one of us. As we grow, the impetus for the creative often wanes. Each visual text that is drawn, painted, constructed, or fashioned in classrooms proves the existence of the power and desire of humans to create. Within visual texts done by children, adolescents, and teachers exists a spark of creativity that communicates, at once, an aesthetic object and an object that tells a story of their life and school experiences. For some, this spark of creativity is nurtured and extended through formal art study. Yet for the majority of children and adults, their visual texts emerge from their experience with art in the world and from self-taught knowledge–untutored, spontaneous, and sometimes irrational; in essence, these visual texts are raw creations worthy of significant study, both as immediate responses to literature and/or language study and as ongoing understanding of learners' literacy practices. I use the term *visual texts* to differentiate from the often-used term *artworks*. *Artwork* connotes that learners draw upon knowledge of art as a knowledge domain or discipline; however, I have found that learners have little experience in art (approximately an hour a week) and, over time, they grow to dislike art as a communicative form largely due to their inability to realistically represent the object they wish to represent (Albers, 1996). Yet visual texts are continuously integrated into English language arts (ELA) instruction and, more often than not, tied in to learners' responses to literature. Thus, to call students' representations *visual texts* more closely aligns with how students work with art in ELA classes; they draw upon their understanding of written texts and apply what they learn by reading public art or the art in their own homes.

At a time in which federal funding for the arts in school is being cut, and teachers and administrators face the daunting challenge of meeting Adequate Yearly Progress (AYP), the visual arts are in jeopardy of losing visibility in public schools. However, with the discovery that the arts present something else, something that demonstrates students' learning and achievement, teachers can be assured that making art in ELA classes is indeed worthwhile and informative. When educators delve more deeply into the potential of the visual arts and technology to communicate complex and telling messages, their worry about meeting AYP can be lessened, and they can reason with administrators, school boards, and state boards about the arts' significance to literacy learning.

Accepting the visual arts into ELA instruction continues to be an uphill battle that spans recent decades. Educators cannot know the many visual texts their students have created that may have been deemed great, but have been tossed in trash cans or destroyed. When we hold on to our visual texts for years, as I have done, we know the significance that art plays in our lives. After 40 years, I still hold on to the cartoon, now browned with age and colors dulled, shown in Figure P.1. The visual texts that students create in today's classrooms should hold similar significance to them.

Figure P.1 Albers's cartoon drawing, age 7; crayon.

As a literacy educator for nearly 25 years, I am continually surprised by the range and complexity of texts that students create, especially when their teachers support visual expression. Figure P.2 is a collaborative cartoon designed, developed, and created by a small group of 11th-grade students during their study of transcendentalism. The cartoon reads as follows:

Frame 1: (Daughter) Mom! What are Daddy's bags doing by the door?

Frame 2: (Daughter points to luggage)

Frame 3: (Mother) Well honey...

Frame 4: ...I read Thoreau today & I've decided to make your father leave.

Frame 5: (Daughter) Why?

Frame 6: (Mother) To simplify!

These students' ELA teacher, Alli, has now just begun to learn about the potential of the visual arts to support students' conceptual understanding of complex content.

Both Figures P.1 and P.2 are raw creations. They are visual texts created from self-taught knowledge about art; they are untutored and spontaneous texts in response to class assignments. Figure P.1 was created in my second-grade classroom and inspired by one of my favorite cartoons at the time. My second-grade teacher, a Catholic nun, had no formal art training and asked us to draw a cartoon that we liked. Although

Figure P.2 Eleventh-grade students' cartoon image of their understanding of transcendentalism.

collectively conceived, Figure P.2 was produced by one of the group members who morphed his self-taught knowledge about and interest in Japanese anime. As ELA educators, we can continue to encourage such raw creations, and we should also find space in our classrooms to support students' interest in and desire to learn tools and techniques for creating visual and media-rich expressions that more closely fit students' intentions and interpretations.

For years, the visual arts have been recognized as developing only the affective, or emotional, side in learners. However, because of an increasing number of studies, both formal and anecdotal (Berghoff, Borgmann, & Parr, 2003; Cowan, 2001b; Eisner, 2002a), the visual arts must be acknowledged not only for their aesthetic contributions to learning but also for their cognitive contributions, as demonstrated in Alli's students' cartoon drawing. For instance, Alli's students demonstrate their cognitive connection and understanding of transcendentalism through their visual text. The time has come for ELA educators to commit to classrooms in which languages such as art, technology, music, and written and oral communication are valued for what each contributes to knowledge about students' learning.

Purpose of This Book

Finding the Artist Within: Creating and Reading Visual Texts in the English Language Arts Classroom is an introduction, a guidebook, to support middle and high school English teachers' learning—raw and untutored, perhaps—in designing and creating visual arts and technology-rich texts, as well as reading and interpreting students' visual texts. The breadth of this book is such that only basic concepts and techniques that artists use when creating visual texts can be introduced. Yet I hope you will continue an inquiry into the visual arts and technology media that will inspire you to establish a media-rich classroom.

How to Use This Book

Conceptually this book is divided into two parts. The first section introduces you to basic art techniques, principles, and concepts in drawing, color, and three dimension (3-D). Built into this section are art engagements for you to practice and build your knowledge about the visual arts. In these chapters, teachers' recounts of their journeys in the arts, as well as examples of student- and teacher-generated visual texts, contextualize the visual arts and technology within ELA instruction. The second section of chapters introduces you to the basics of reading visual texts, both artistically and critically, and helps you design curriculum with the visual arts and technology in mind.

Chapter 1 lays the foundation for linking art and language by presenting semiotic theory, a framework that theorizes representation. Chapters 2, 3, 4, and 5 address basic techniques and tools for learning the visual arts and technology: drawing, color, 3-D, and technology, respectively. In chapter 2, you will learn about the basics of drawing, from cartoon images to realistic figure drawings. Chapter 3 introduces you to color, and you will learn how to work with media such as colored pencils, colored paper, and paints. In chapter 4, you will learn the basics of building 3-D texts, especially with paper, papier-mâché, and clay. Chapter 5 introduces you to the basics of Microsoft PowerPoint, Microsoft Publisher, and Windows Movie Maker to support your work in creating media-rich presentations and engagements.

In chapter 6, you will learn how to read and interpret visual texts and photographs, especially in terms of how, where, and why elements are placed on a canvas. Chapter 7 teaches you to read visual texts from a critical literacy perspective—a view that offers insights on the underpinning beliefs and values that emerge in students' creations. Chapter 8 describes the Focused Study, a curricular framework in which the visual arts and technology become valuable components of ELA instruction.

Included in the Appendixes are more than 20 arts-based ELA strategy lessons that you can implement in your curricula, and which are linked to the International Reading Association and National Council of Teachers of English *Standards for the English Language Arts* (IRA/NCTE, 1996). Also included are examples of two media-rich curricula that you will find valuable when (re)designing your own curricula and text sets that will help you inquire more deeply into the visual arts. And a list of art terms and definitions will support your own ongoing knowledge about the visual arts.

Unique Qualities of This Book

One unique feature of *Finding the Artist Within*, found in no other language arts trade book that addresses the role of the arts, is the importance this book places on ELA educators' need to study the discipline of art. To encourage and support strong and complex literacy learning in their students, ELA educators must have basic knowledge of the visual arts. A second unique feature is a framework by which to read and analyze your students' visual texts in a way you might not have considered. Such readings offer educators yet another tool for assessment of, as well as insight on, students' literacy learning. With their interactive design, these chapters will engage you joyfully in the visual arts and technology and inspire you to continue your inquiry into the visual arts and technology.

ACKNOWLEDGMENTS

A number of people have supported me throughout this work, and I would like to thank them here. First, I want to thank all of the English language arts (ELA) teachers and preservice teachers with whom I have worked over the past 16 years, especially Allen, Michael, Kay, Kathy, Mark, Tammy, and Nicole, who wrote their own stories about art. They integrate arts-based projects into their practice and continue to demonstrate the significance of the visual arts and technology in urban classrooms. I also thank their students for allowing me to include their artworks in this book; they continue to surprise and enlighten me with their visual creations.

My pottery community in Atlanta, Georgia, USA, and the surrounding area has nurtured my intellectual, creative, and aesthetic evolution as a potter and artist. Glenn Dair, the pottery director at Atlanta's Callanwolde Fine Arts Center, has encouraged my work in clay, my professional writings for clay trade journals, and my video production. Many thanks to Atlanta potters Bill Buckner and Rick Berman for allowing me to videotape their soda and raku firing workshops, respectively—experiences that taught me about the essential role of video technology in classrooms. Another big thank you to the Callanwolde Clay Guild, especially David Robinson, Ingrid Weishofer, Sandy Culp, and Earl Baum, for their contributions to this book. This art community continues to nourish and support my creativity.

Thank you to my Indiana University (Bloomington, Indiana, USA) friends who unceasingly offer me encouragement and guidance for my work with the visual arts: Carolyn Burke, Jerry Harste, Kathy Egawa, Dorothy Menosky, and Mitzi Lewison. Not only have they appreciated my personal development in the visual arts but they inspired new insights on future creations. I especially want to thank Carolyn Burke for the many conversations we have had regarding semiotics, the arts, and critical literacy. Many ideas developed from these discussions.

Many thanks to Tama Robertson, my first art teacher, who taught me, while I was in graduate school, techniques associated with visual art forms, as well as art philosophy and critique.

The editorial and production staff at IRA have been most helpful in completing this project. Corinne Mooney, Executive Editor of Books, initially worked with this manuscript, and her enthusiasm for this project and encouragement gave me confidence that the ideas presented here are important to educators. Thanks also to

Christina Lambert, my copy editor and production editor, and Becky Fetterolf, who painstakingly checked my references. A special and heartfelt thanks goes to Tori Bachman, my developmental editor, whose negotiation made it possible for this book to be printed in color. She recognized the significance that color plays in the reading, interpretation, and analysis of visual texts.

I would also like to acknowledge the following permissions to include artwork:

- Charles M. Russell (1864–1926), *The Scout* (1907). Sid Richardson Museum Collection of Western Art.

- Cover of *Night of the Gargoyles* by Eve Bunting, illustrated by David Wiesner. Jacket illustration copyright 1994 by David Wiesner. Reprinted by permission of Clarion Books, an imprint of Houghton Mifflin Company. All rights reserved.

- Paul Cezanne (1839–1906), *Apples, Peaches, Pears, and Grapes* (1879–1880). State Hermitage Museum, St. Petersburg, Russia.

- Formerly attributed to Vincent van Gogh (1853–1890), *Still Life With Mackerels, Lemons and Tomatoes* (1886). The Oskar Reinhart Collection "Am Römerholz," Winterthur, Switzerland.

- Edward Hopper (1882–1967), *House by the Sea* and *Studies of Cows*. The Whitney Museum of American Art, New York, USA.

- Mary Cassatt (1844–1926), *Italian Girl*. Reprinted with permission by The Spencer Museum of Art, The University of Kansas, Lawrence, Kansas, USA.

- *A Country Far Away*, reprinted with permission by Anderson Press; author Nigel Gray, illustrator Philippe Dupasquier.

- Microsoft product screen shot(s) reprinted with permission from Microsoft Corporation.

Most of all, I would like to thank members of my family. My mother, Genevieve, inspired my own work in the visual and dramatic arts. Her early experiences with music and her talent in sewing and crafts were the impetus for me and many of my 11 brothers and sisters to engage in some aspect of the arts. Thanks also to Rose Mary, my sister who studied art education and is a quiltmaker, and Greg, her husband, both of whom critique my work and offer their perspectives on how to continue building a stronger understanding of visual texts.

Finally, I would like to thank Andy, my long-time partner, who continues to support my ongoing commitment to the arts.

To all of the people and organizations mentioned above, I am humbly grateful.

CHAPTER 1

Finding Purpose and Meaning In and Through the Arts

- *What is art?*
- *Why do we fear the making and reading of art?*
- *What is semiotics and why is it important to ELA instruction?*
- *Why should we study and create visual texts in ELA classes?*

Finding the Artist Within Through Drawing and Sculpture: A Teacher's Story
by Jerome C. Harste

One of the sketches I drew that I particularly liked was a back-end view of a man and his dog walking down a beach, and while in real life the man had on a swimming suit and the dog wore a collar and leash, I drew both him and the dog stark naked, both in midst of the same stride, both with the same shaped butts. Despite being convinced that I was only doodling, I managed to capture something more—tranquility, bliss, freedom, defiance—in the sense of the real world, be damned—and peace.

This sketch hung in my office for a long time and reflects the kind of guy I am. Basically I play with art and then accidentally do something that forces me to outgrow my current self as an artist, albeit a self-made one (see Figure 1.1).

Figure 1.1 *Jerry paints on pottery.*

I probably would be an artist today had I not grown up in a religious household. Doodling was the mind at rest, "the devil's workshop," and my sketches of people were all the proof that was needed to confirm my parents' concern for my misguided soul. What they didn't know, but what I learned the easy way, is that through drawing you begin to observe your world more closely. Over the years I've become more and more convinced that all new knowledge—even writing—begins in observation. If a writer doesn't have something new to say, he or she isn't going to have much of a career.

My wife maintains that during the first 20 years of our marriage I never took a "real" vacation. I'd take a speaking engagement or agree to do a workshop and in between "gigs" we vacationed. This changed the year we went to Myrtle Beach, South Carolina, USA, and I discovered two things: I could only vacation if I had something to do, and wet sand is a perfect art medium. Even better, my son joined in, and more recently, his wife. Together we sculpted sand castles, Neptunes, octopuses, rhinoceroses, black bears, polar bears, grizzly bears, koalas, Volkswagens, readers, sunbathers, elephants, wolves, sheep, hippopotamuses, frogs, cats, dogs, turtles, whales, owls, and the list goes on and on. Our lions are famous. We make our objects big and invite anyone with a passion to participate to join in. More often than not we attract a crowd of people who stop to admire and do what we never do–lament the fact that by morning our handiwork would be washed away. We like starting over.

So what have I learned from my involvement with art that is useful for understanding literacy learning? First, it is useful to work in a medium in which you are not expert. It makes you humble as well as reflective–painting on ceramic plates (see Figure 1.2) is a recent endeavor of mine, and I am always surprised at how the colors change from the initial application to the final firing. Second, art is generative–full of surprises, and I like surprises. Third, art can expand one's world. I now have whole sets of friends whose fingers reside in a different paint can than the one in which mine typically reside. Each of us has a communication potential that includes language as well as other ways of knowing, and we are richer personally and as a nation when all of these communication capabilities are developed, honored, and respected. In short, art is why I see a good language arts program as expanding the communication potential of every student and why I continue to call for a much expanded definition of what it means to be literate.

Figure 1.2 *Jerry's Picasso-inspired painting of a goat, on ceramic plate.*

ow often have you looked at an artwork and wondered about its making or what it meant? Or wished that you could draw, or paint, or sculpt like the artists whose work lives in your home? How many cups of coffee have you drunk out of that handmade ceramic mug because it felt just right? How often have you gone to an arts festival and seen the artist, but had little to say because you did not know what to say? In her book, *Art Objects: Essays on Ecstasy and Effrontery*, Winterson (1995) states, "and in the moment of passing [I] saw a painting that had more power to stop me than I had power to walk on. The quality of the draughtsmanship, the brush strokes in thin oils, had a Renaissance beauty" (p. 3). The arts push us into wonderment; they stop us, as Winterson suggests, by nature of the craft or of the composition. They also stop our tongue, and at times, we turn away from art because we may not know how to read, speak, or write in its language.

The desire to make images and to communicate something that is beyond words is part of the human desire to create. Few of us can deny that we drew as children, whether using materials supplied by adults or by scratching marks in the sand or in the ground. *Finding the Artist Within: Creating and Reading Visual Texts in the English Language Arts Classroom* is designed to recapture some of that childhood wonderment that revolves around the visual arts, to imagine what it is like to draw, paint, and sculpt images once thought unimaginable. To do so necessitates a shift from a teacher's stance to a learner's stance that, at once, is fearful but also compelling.

This chapter presents semiotic theory, a framework that theorizes representation, to lay the foundation for linking art and language. Further, it discusses research that documents the cognitive role that the arts play in learning, accountability, and standards, and how to actively inquire into the visual arts.

Representation of Meaning: Semiotics as a Theoretical Framework

Early in our lives, we made marks, patterns, and representations with anything that was at hand, unconsciously exploring their significance. In this way, we began to discover the creative relationship between us and a world that went beyond practicality. We enjoyed scribbling on paper and showing pictures that we made to family members. As small children we learned that art was a language through which we could communicate and be understood. Although some adults continue this creative relationship by becoming professional image-makers, few develop their creative impulses beyond adolescence. Picasso once remarked that "Every child is an artist, the problem is how to remain an artist once he grows up" (cited in Evans et al., 2003, p. 281). His words encourage us to recall those moments in which art was our everyday language as children, and to consider art's significance in adulthood, especially now that our world is so visually oriented (Kress, 2003).

As a child, my sisters encouraged me to participate in drama and art; I acted and performed in plays. Later, as a high school English teacher, I designed, built, and painted sets for plays I directed. When the curtain rose, I communicated time, atmosphere, and mood through painted backdrops, furniture and its arrangement, and lighting. As an actress, I communicated messages of surprise, denial, or deceit with my eyes, voice, and body. My mother's talent as a musician enabled her to communicate through the piano and saxophone. Today, I continue to be surprised at her ability to "play the ivories," although she has no piano at home. As a literacy teacher educator, I now see that these early experiences were unconscious explorations into the potential of communication systems (written language, art, music, drama, and movement) to say something that the other could not. My graduate work at Indiana University with Jerry Harste and Carolyn Burke helped me put a name to this exploration: *semiotics*. Simply defined, semiotics is a study of how meanings get communicated and how they are constructed to maintain a sense of reality. Humans communicate not only through written and oral language but, as semioticians suggest, through *languages* such as: art, music, math, dance, and written/oral language. In ELA classes, semiotics is significant because teachers often ask students to communicate their interpretations of texts in ways other than through written and oral communication, such as art, drama, music, and movement. So teachers must be aware both of the potential of these languages to communicate as well as how to read interpretations created from them.

At its basic level, semiotics involves the study of signs. According to Charles Peirce (as cited in Thayer, 1981, 1982), signs take the form of words, images, sounds, gestures, and objects. A sign has no intrinsic value until someone brings meaning to it. And signs are interpreted in association with other signs. Peirce understood signs as part of a triadic relationship among the *object*, the *representamen*, and the *interpretant*. Peirce referred to the interaction among these three elements as *semiosis* (see Figure 1.3). A sign in the form of a *representamen* is something that stands for something to somebody in some respect or capacity. The *interpretant* is the sense made from the sign. The *object* is what the sign stands for. For example, in Figure 1.3, the sign *dog* makes sense for me as I relate it to my dog, Bailey (interpretant). Bailey is the object of this sign. The representamen is

the form the sign takes, or how we represent visually our interpretation of the sign. In Figure 1.3, it takes on the form of contour line drawings of dogs and photographs done by graduate students who interpreted the sign *dog* (and the photograph). This suggests that a range of interpretations can be made from the sign *dog*.

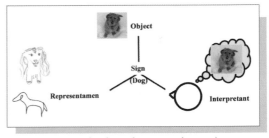

Figure 1.3 *Triadic relationship in signs (semiosis).*

The object of the sign can never be represented in its entirety. Only aspects of the object can be represented. Kress and van Leeuwen (1996) call these aspects an object's "criterial aspects" (p. 6). Criterial aspects that humans choose to represent their interpretation directly relate to their social, psychological, literary, etc. experiences with dogs. Observe how, in Figure 1.3, both graduate students represented their experiences with *dog*. One is more artistic with graceful contour lines, while the other is more realistic. One dog faces left while the other faces the viewer. (In chapter 6, you will learn more about the significance of these criterial aspects.)

Signs make up semiotic systems, or a collection of elements used in relation to other elements to represent meaning (Albers & Murphy, 2000). Bailey, as the sign *dog*, must be viewed in relation both to the element of sitting and the element of snow. Together, these elements create a system, and the meaning of the system does not reside in any one element. Bailey sitting in the snow means something different than Bailey swimming in water, for example. To make sense of signs (which have no entity) in relation to one another, humans *represent* in a variety of forms. *Representation* is a process in which humans express their idea of an object or entity. Writing, visual art, music, and photography are among the forms through which humans make meaning with the intent to be understood by others (Langer, 1957). Representation occurs across and within forms, and expression of meaning is *semiotic*. Expressions that are created, such as artworks, musical scores, dramatic performances, and photographs, are semiotic and draw upon several sign systems. For example, artists may draw upon what they know in art and written language (history, geography) to paint a more realistic image of a time period. *How* and *what* humans represent is driven by their interest in the object or entity at a particular moment, and which arises out of their knowledge and experiences with that object or entity (Kress & van Leeuwen, 1996).

The significance of semiotics as a theoretical framework for inquiry into the visual arts and media-rich classes lies in supporting students' expressions of meaning, and an ability to interpret these expressions. That is, if teachers invite students to represent meaning in the visual arts, music, photography, and technology, teachers must be able to guide students' expressions so students express the meaning they wish to convey. Further, students who know what the signs they make mean (marks on their papers, canvas, or nonverbal presentations) become more critically aware of how to create and interpret the signs in their own and other expressions, or semiotic systems. Facility in the process of creating or interpreting the signs of one or more semiotic systems is how we define literacy (Albers & Murphy, 2000). Students' abilities to create and interpret through the visual arts, music, photography, and technology expand the potential of what students can say and how they can say it. For instance, students who can read and interpret a photograph will use this knowledge when using photography to express themselves; students who read and interpret areas of an artwork will use this knowledge when invited to express their interpretation through art. The open and generative nature of semiotic theory enables us to stretch our perception of what constitutes being literate in today's society. In his teacher story that opens this chapter, Harste explains the significance that the visual arts (in particular doodling) had in his imaginative explorations in a religious household. For him, actual experience working within and across different art media offered him insight on literacy, and the potential of these media to explain ideas that written/oral language could not.

The thinking and work in this book is guided by the work of a number of scholars whose work is located in semiotic theory, the arts, and inquiry: Albers and Murphy (2000); Berghoff et al. (2000, 2003); Eisner (2002a, 2002b);

Greene (1995, 2001); Halliday (1978); Kist (2005); Kress and Jewitt (2003); Kress and van Leeuwen (1996, 2001); Lankshear and Knobel (2003); Moxey (1994); Short and Burke (1991); and Short, Harste, and Burke (1996). From this work, I derived four principles:

1. Representation of meaning occurs through the use of semiotic systems.
2. Sign systems offer potential for a range of meanings and alternative perspectives.
3. Semiotic texts are culturally and personally situated.
4. Inquiry-based learning offers flexible opportunities for semiotic expression.

Representation of Meaning Occurs Through the Use of Semiotic Systems

Semiotic systems involve collections of elements used in relationship with other elements in a text. It is possible to imagine the innumerable texts that can be generated when learners are offered a range of resources through which to make meaning. Harste's description of his sand sculpture of a rhinoceros is one example of a semiotic system. The sand, space, water, color, and shape are elements that operate together to create the system. The meaning of this system, the rhinoceros, does not reside in any one element, but in how these elements are interpreted in relation to one another. In other semiotic systems, sand can be used to make glass and paintings, and can be used for traps in golf and in ceramic clay bodies. However, in this system, sand is an element that serves a particular purpose as sculptural material.

Semiotic systems can be visual, cultural, political, psychological, or other, and semiotic systems are informed by the expectations and beliefs of a larger social collective. Visual semiotic systems can include a person's choice of clothing, advertisements seen on buses or in subway stations, films viewed, or children's visual representations presented in your classes. For example, from reality shows that focus on fashion we learn which fabrics, textures, colors, and styles operate together to create an outfit that is pleasing. So we might not wear plaid polyester pants with a striped wool shirt; this is not a pleasing semiotic system. Furthermore, such visual semiotic systems are guided by the expectations and assumptions of a larger social collective. For example, a teacher probably cannot wear "hot pants" in a classroom, although this same article of clothing may be perfectly acceptable in the office of a fashion magazine. The social collectives that guide schools (school boards, state departments of education, school districts, etc.) often delineate expectations for teachers to wear professional clothing such as suits, dresses, or tailored pants. On the other hand, a magazine editor who defines fashion trends may be guided by a social collective that expects a less confining dress code. Semiotic systems, therefore, are informed, created, and interpreted by the expectations and beliefs set up by larger social collectives.

Sign Systems Offer Potential for a Range of Meanings and Alternative Perspectives

Within a semiotic perspective, an implicit assumption is that meaning is partial and communicates only a part of an overall message (Kress & Jewitt, 2003). Any one text consists of a number of elements that are involved in its meaning and collectively represent an overall message. Yet each element carries a different part of the overall message and expresses a part of the message that another element cannot. For example, Figure 1.4 shows a ceramic platter comprised of many elements (clay, paint, glaze, color, line, shape, written language), each of which carries a part of the overall message. The round shape explains the utilitarian aspect of the platter, yet the wooden stand that supports it suggests that the platter's function is as art, not as a serving dish. Another element, the title *FacetoFace*, spelled without hyphens and spaces, encourages viewers to interpret the two faces along with the other elements. All elements collectively operate to support viewers' interpretations.

Figure 1.4 FacetoFace, *painted platter, Albers.*

Sign systems are not redundant; that is, different systems communicate meaning uniquely. Eisner (2002a) argues that not everything knowable can be articulated in one particular form. Written language, for example, is not always the most apt form of representation. In the movie *Jaws*, Spielberg (1975) used music and visual elements to evoke a sense of fear in viewers. Certain phrases of music aptly communicated this message, and close-ups of the actors' faces, the opaque underwater scenes, and the frantic activity on the boat—the visual elements— enabled viewers to imagine what horror lay ahead. We experience sign systems and interpret signs in the world in many combinations because they are complementary systems (Shagoury, 1989). That is, when we express meaning, we do so as informed by several sign systems, expressions I call *semiotic texts*. For instance, when interpreting a text set on Latino experience that included music, artwork, and written texts, ELA teachers Heidi and Lydia responded visually through tempera paints. Heidi's semiotic text (see Figure 1.5a) is a colorful swirl of circular elements bordered by yellows and oranges. Her perspective is from above; she watches the twirling of the skirts of the females on a dance floor. Lydia's elements (see Figure 1.5b), on the other hand, are more easily recognizable to the viewer. Her perspective is frontal and her elements float, outlined in thick black strokes of paint, on a backdrop of red-orange. Although both Heidi and Lydia read the same text set and listened to the same music, they take on different visual perspectives and include different elements in their paintings.

Figure 1.5a *Heidi's response to Latino experience.*

Figure 1.5b *Lydia's response to Latino experience.*

Sign systems offer us different perspectives, as viewed or read from the various sign systems, while simultaneously offering us the potential to express meaning in a variety of ways.

Semiotic Texts Are Culturally and Personally Situated

Signs are inventions of our culture and reflect the social conventions and communication needs of a larger social collective. For example, national flags are symbols that, for many, immediately evoke feelings of patriotism and citizenship. At the Olympic Games, during medals ceremonies, the flag of the gold medalist is raised highest and the national anthem of that person's country is played. Over time, we recognize this part of the Olympics as a social convention. Semiotic texts are often informed by norms and conventions established by a social collective (Albers & Murphy, 2000; Kist, 2005; Lankshear & Knobel, 2003). For example, when we invite students to interpret their understanding of love, they probably create a heart, or two conjoined rings; to express envy, they use green. These are symbols and constructs that have been constructed over time, and as viewers, we personally internalize these symbols, and integrate these symbols in our semiotic texts. Michael's description of his watercolor (see Figure 1.6) illustrates both a personal and cultural connection to his sense of home:

> As a young boy growing up in the mountains of northeastern Georgia, I was surrounded by a variety of art forms that were a part of my everyday existence. My mother and I played the piano and sung, and...small, clapboard churches [were] tucked in lush valleys throughout the hill country....

Figure 1.6 *Michael's personal and cultural connections; watercolor.*

While Michael's painting is infused with personal experiences, this artwork is also informed by art conventions. His canvas has a fore-, middle-, and background, and his colors blend easily and expertly. Michael's watercolor is a semiotic text, situated within his cultural and personal experiences.

Inquiry-Based Learning Offers Flexible Opportunities for Semiotic Expression

When inquiry is a focus of ELA learning, several elements become important to learning (Short & Burke, 1991). First, inquiry is thinking about that which makes us curious. We each constantly search in many directions at one time to find answers to our questions. This desire to know more leads to intentionality behind our inquiry. We develop questions and hypotheses and go about trying to organize our learning to make sense and present a purpose. To find answers to our questions, we actively seek relationships with others who may have expertise or experiences in that which we want to explore. Inquiry becomes socially driven.

Inquiry-based curriculum has as one of its central tenets the importance of a learner's interests and experiences. Burke (2004) argues that personal inquiry drives one's interest in a subject or topic. Flexibility in how students investigate topics and their active engagement is essential if they are to be vested in their learning (Short & Burke, 1991). Within an inquiry-based curriculum that supports a semiotic perspective, learners investigate topics that interest them and they represent meaning across sign systems. Furthermore, all learners of varied experiences and language abilities can participate in ways that support their ongoing learning. Mei Lu, a Thai newcomer to Atlanta, Georgia, in fourth grade, was interested in the number of homeless people she saw in her neighborhood. Her interest led her to read picture books that addressed homelessness and news articles with statistics on the homeless. Mei Lu's semiotic text (see Figure 1.7) shows her learning: Homeless people reside in large cities and create shelter from discarded furniture, and those who have homes have a responsibility to give homeless people money or help.

Figure 1.7 *Mei Lu's visual representation of homelessness.*

This theoretical framework outlines the significance of learning about the tools, techniques, and materials, and the creation and interpretation of semiotic texts in ELA instruction. Next, I present the representational possibilities in ELA classrooms when the visual arts and technology media are intentionally integrated and read with intention and purpose. *How* students represent is only part of *what* they say (Eisner, 2002a). That is, when students' visual texts are created and read with an informed eye, educators can more completely understand their students' visual messages. In other words, all meanings matter.

Research Into Schoolwide Arts-Based Programs

Children often learn more literacy outside school than inside school. That is, children bring to the classroom knowledge about a variety of texts, whether music, art, technology, language, or movement. As educators, we must learn to value and honor these literacies. When we do, we can reach more populations effectively. In the United States, those making decisions about curriculum value efficiency and content which can be tested scientifically. This tacit view, so Eisner (2002a) argues, is intended to create an efficient system that will help our students achieve. The arts, because they cannot be encapsulated in a standardized test or measured scientifically, have little room in curriculum. Eisner's (1982, 1991, 1992, 2002a, 2002b, 2003a, 2003b) research studies in the arts indicate that the arts do not just teach students to feel about the world, or engage the *affective*, but they also teach students to see, notice, and critically interrogate the world, or engage the *cognitive*.

Eisner (2002a) articulates several forms of thinking that evolve when the arts are part of teaching and learning. First, the arts require that learners pay attention to the relationships that exist within any text, whether it be a story, poem, artwork, or musical composition. The arts help learners notice what is subtle in text, from a simple and single statement made by a character to the shades of a single color used in a landscape to a subtle introduction of horns or strings in a musical piece. The arts teach that paying attention to such subtleties matters when interpreting and creating texts (Eisner, 2002a). Second, the arts, by nature, invite problem-solving and complex thinking. Although schools would argue that they want learning to be divergent, imaginative, or creative, standardized testing promotes convergent or single-track thinking (Arts Education Partnership, 2005; Eisner, 2002b). Finding the one theme in a play or story, or coming up with a single answer to a math problem, is valued in such testing. The arts, however, promote thinking beyond rules and regulations. Complex thinking revolves around searching out many possible solutions or interpretations rather than looking solely for a right answer. Third, the arts promote paying attention to the way a text is configured. Focusing on how a story is written, how the words in a poem are chosen, how an artwork is presented, or how an argument is expressed through speech encourages learners to pay attention not only to what someone is expressing, but how what is being expressed is constructed.

Other recent formal and anecdotal research indicates that the arts, indeed, do have an impact on how well students do in schools (see Albers, 1996, 1997, 2001; da Silva, 2001; DuCharme, 1991; Ernst, 1994, 1997; Flynn, 2002; Graves, 1975, 1983; Greenway, 1996; Igoa, 1995; Katzive, 1997; Noden & Moss, 1995; Siegel, 1984, 1995). Carger (2004) reported on the positive influence that the visual arts have on bilingual children. In a response to the events of September 11, 2001, children were encouraged to bring their own culture and experiences to the reading and creating of visual texts. As a result, children developed stronger literacy practices. They were better able to visually communicate their intended messages across sign systems, and engage in critical discussions. Using reader response theory, Piro (2002) invited students to explore the reading of artworks as they learned the interdependent nature of the visual arts and language. They were better able to translate what they learned from artworks (such as observed detail, focus, critical thinking, and analysis) into their writing. Murata (1997) integrated the arts into an English curriculum to demonstrate the link between genre in written language and genre in art. Her students reported that when the visual arts were a part of learning, they were more effectively able to deal with language. Olshansky's (1994, 1995, 1997) and Dyson's (1988, 2001) works indicate a significant relationship between students' study of the arts and strong writing. They found that when students learn to read elements within artworks, they are better able to translate these elements into their writing, and their writing becomes more vivid and descriptive.

The Arts Education Partnership (2005) has found significant gains in achievement, especially in struggling learners, in its study of an arts-integrated approach to learning in 10 urban schools. Rabkin and Redmond (2005) report on arts-based research conducted in the United States in Chicago and Minneapolis:

> It is fall. Fourth-graders in a Chicago school in a low-income neighborhood are focused and coiled with excitement. They are drawing portraits of each other in a lesson that is part of a unit on descriptive writing. They are deeply engaged, and the rich writing and art on the walls are evidence of real learning and accomplishment. Most other classrooms in the building also integrate the arts with other subjects and buzz with the intensity of discovery. The same day, in another low-income Chicago school, fourth-graders slump in their chairs, waiting to read a bit of advice to their classmates. They mumble, "Don't hit your sister," and "Do your homework." There is no children's work on the walls, no evidence of learning. Instead, posters remind students of rules they must follow. One asks, "What is freedom?" The answers suggest freedom is a reward for self-control. (n.p.)

These two journalists discovered that even though today's society requires higher-order skills such as creativity, adaptability, and teamwork, most schools in low-income areas focus narrowly on basic academic skills, testing, and discipline. The student boredom and academic failure that result prompt more testing and discipline. The principal of Edgebrook, Chicago's highest-scoring nonselective elementary school, attributes her school's success to the arts, stating, "We were concerned that we would see a negative impact on test scores. But actually, the opposite happened." A study of 23 arts-integrated schools in Chicago showed test scores that were rising up to two times faster. In Minneapolis, programs that were arts integrated show substantial effects on all learners, but the greatest impact is evident among disadvantaged learners. Gains go far beyond basic skills, and students in these programs become better thinkers, develop higher order skills, and heighten their interest in learning (Rabkin & Redmond, 2005).

Cowan (2001a, 2001b), working in northern Georgia, USA, with grades 1–6, found that when she integrates the arts in all disciplines, students learn concepts in much more complex ways. Her study of the composing processes of fifth-grade students concluded that when the arts are part of literacy instruction (1) students write with force and interest; (2) art and language operate as reciprocal processes, both dependent on the other for clarity in and extension of meaning making; (3) students learn to pay attention to details in both written and artistic texts, and understand how to use language and art to create shades of meaning; and (4) students "feel on fire" (Cowan, 2001b, p. 122) when the visual arts are part of literacy learning. Furthermore, Cowan's students met and exceeded state and national standards in literacy. In subsequent work, Cowan studied in depth the relationship among the arts, literacy, and achievement:

> I realized that the visual and performing arts, by their very nature, connect the student to both affect and cognition, and there is an increased energy in the learning experience. The experience takes on an emotive quality and the student easily moves to higher-order thinking processes, and remembers the content long after it has been taught. Beyond this *major advantage* of an integrated approach...assessment ranging from vocabulary development to comprehension of text to writing in a meaningful way cuts across many standards. This often is not the case when skills are taught in isolation. (Cowan & Albers, 2006, pp. 134–135)

Addressing Local, State, and National Standards in the English Language Arts

Accountability is in the foreground of many of teachers' minds in language learning, and the question "Why art when my students need to know how to read and write?" often arises in my conversations with teachers. From the research previously cited, we learn that art strengthens learning skills, increases a learner's attention to detail, incites the imagination, and encourages new perspectives on the world. Politicians across the United States have loudly, visibly, and with certainty suggested that the arts are not important to learning (Steiner, 1995) and, as a consequence, have suggested that when "funding difficulties arise, the arts are easy to cut" (Miller, 2006, p. 2). This sends the message that the arts have no place in our students' learning.

In contrast, the importance of the arts, literacy, and multimedia is immediately of interest to professional organizations such as the National Council of Teachers of English (NCTE) and the International Reading Association (IRA). NCTE executive committee members named multimodal literacy, or the production of meaning across multiple forms or modes, as one of the three most important areas of investigation in ELA instruction (Lambert-Stock, 2004). Several NCTE commissions, such as the Commission on Arts and Literacy (COAL), have been set up to explain and research the multimodal nature of learning and to promote the arts as integral to ELA learning and teaching. Further, both NCTE and IRA developed standards that include the arts as an essential component of literacy learning. The committee that drafted these standards suggests that a quality language arts program must include reading, writing, speaking, and listening, but must also recognize the potential of art, music, drama, mathematics, and movement to communicate complex messages (IRA/NCTE, 1996). In particular, these standards state that uses and expressions of language have changed with the times and, especially today, the visual aspect of communication is significant to literacy and education, in general. Teachers, therefore, must integrate opportunities for students to critically analyze the texts they create and view in relation to knowledge in other forms.

State standards such as those in the state of Georgia support the integration of the arts and resemble closely the IRA/NCTE standards as well. Students in the state are expected to respond creatively to literature, drama, art, and multimedia projects, and be knowledgeable about multimedia texts, be able to evaluate and read multimedia texts, and use multimedia in their presentations and representations. Further, preservice ELA teachers in Georgia must demonstrate knowledge of the influence of media on culture and on people's actions and communications and demonstrate appropriate reading strategies that permit access to and understanding of a wide range of print and nonprint texts. Such standards for students and teachers demonstrate the importance that the arts, multimedia, and technology play in students' learning.

Getting Ready for Art

Releasing the Fears to Experience the Joys of Art

Along with new learning comes fears and joys. When my preservice and inservice teachers are asked to create texts using art, many of their eyes widen and they become uneasy. When I ask them to show their visual texts, again, they panic. Why do so many teachers (and students) fear sharing their artistic responses to literature and language? In 1998, Kay Cowan and I conducted a study that addressed to what extent elementary teachers did or did not integrate the visual arts into ELA instruction. Two significant findings emerged: (1) Teachers who had limited knowledge about the arts tended to limit their integration of art, and (2) teachers limited their integration of the visual arts because visual art projects are messy and time consuming.

Artmaking, like writing, involves skills that can be learned. Bayles and Orland (1993) suggest that while conventional wisdom states that craft can be taught and art remains a magical gift bestowed by the gods, this is not so. Becoming an artist and learning to do art better consists of learning art as a discipline, not hiding from it. How often have we seen an artist's visual talent and learned through his or her stories that he or she works hard at mastering techniques? If you believe that only talented people can make art, your art will never get done, and you may deny yourself the pleasures that art elicits. If I continually compared my own pottery to that of accomplished potters, I would retreat and not make art. However, art for me means I am always in a state of becoming an artist. Such a belief keeps me taking classes, reading about pottery, and publishing ideas for other potters (Albers, 2002, 2004b, 2006b). Furthermore, learning to become an artist means learning to accept yourself, those elements of your life that make your work unique and personal, and in following your own voice. In the opening teacher story, Jerry Harste relates that he found that art enabled him to speak in ways that language cannot, and he continues to learn how art supports his personal and professional inquiries. Artistic qualities can be nurtured in yourself and you can nurture them in your students through strategy instruction in the discipline of art, and a strong desire to continue learning.

Ordinary art means that any of us can do art; however, we manufacture difficulties that often stop us from studying and making art. First, art involves taking risks with representation, and people who need certainty or control in their lives are less likely to make art. All that is needed to make art is a broad sense of what you are looking for, some strategies on how to find it, and a true willingness to embrace mistakes and surprises along the way. Art is chancy—it doesn't mix well with control or predictability. Uncertainty is inevitable in art, and artists learn from the unexpected, the surprises, and apply these surprises to future situations. A second difficulty we encounter is our negative perception of others' perceptions of our visual expressions. For instance, we *pretend* to do art because we doubt ourselves and our abilities. Our fear is that we have nothing really to say visually, and we believe that only real artists know what they're doing and that only they— not us—are entitled to feel good about themselves and their art. However, from my work in the ceramic arts and my friendships with various artists, I know that art is a process of becoming, both in terms of confidence and ability. So if as teachers we truly want to value the *arts* in English language *arts* instruction, we need to begin with what we know is essential to learning, and release our fears and our imagination, and inquire into the secrets of the visual arts.

Collecting Everyday Items

Like writers who love to read others' work and collect books for their own libraries, artists, too, are invariably avid collectors of many things that, to others, appear to be junk. Accumulating anything and everything that interests you is fascinating and may come in handy as you begin your exploration of various arts-based media: rice, newspapers, noodles, toilet paper or paper towel cardboard rolls, beans, shredded paper, newspaper, boxes, and so on. After the holiday season, I go to places like fabric stores and discount stores to buy tinsel, holiday lights, miniature ornaments, masks, and others such things at a 75–90% discount. I go to thrift shops where materials, glassware, and other items are inexpensive. I have boxes of materials under and alongside my office desk, on top of my bookshelves, and in any space available. So, although storage is an issue, I believe it is important to have such materials on hand when working in the visual arts. You never know what creations students will construct when they have access to a variety of materials.

Acquiring Traditional Art Materials and Resources

Art, like any communication form, has its own materials traditionally used to express meaning. You will want to have available several types of pencils, a set of watercolors, tempera paints, pastel chalks, crayons, various types of brushes and papers, and a good well-lighted place to work. Materials range from inexpensive to very expensive; however, I suggest that you buy the best you can afford from an art supply store so that you can experience each medium introduced in this book more fully and with all the potential the medium affords. Watercolors from an art supply store, for example, are extremely good value because their life span is often much greater than watercolors bought from discount centers, and they respond well on good paper. Consider using potters' clay rather than play dough when you work in 3-D. You will notice how different the feel of clay is and how it more easily allows you to build sculptures. Throughout the book, you will be asked to explore how various media play on various papers; you will learn which materials are more suitable in making the meaning that you desire.

As you learn about art as a discipline, consider building a library of art books. My collection of art books has grown substantially since I started my study in clay. These resources contain information on drawing, painting, and sculpting, and all, interestingly, become part of the work I do as a potter. As you and your students build more knowledge about the visual arts, your students will want to do further inquiry into particular media they find engaging, and a strong library will support this inquiry.

Sketchbooks: Audit Trails of Art Learning

While exploring art when reading this book, I encourage you to buy an unlined sketchbook that can be used for drawing and painting, preferably a large one, 8$\frac{1}{2}$ x 11 inches. Artists such as Leonardo da Vinci, Pablo Picasso, and Edward Hopper kept journals in which they sketched ideas, did *studies*, or variations, of objects or ideas, and kept track of their thinking. Many potters I know also keep journals. You can purchase an inexpensive sketchbook at a bookstore or art supply store, and it will last for a long time.

An artist's sketchbook, like a writer's journal, is varied in nature. This sketchbook can be an exploration of your sketches, or it can be a recording of your impressions, reflections, and paintings. It can be a recording of various materials that you use and ideas that you discover while exploring a *medium* (a material used to construct meaning). It can be a collection of notes about how you might apply your learning to projects within your own classes and curriculum . It can be a scrapbook of images that you notice for their line, shape, and composition, or a collection of cut-out images that you want to explore in various media. It can also be a space where you collect the work of your students as they try a technique. My early sketchbooks were little more than notes and a few sketches, but now they are more complex, full of sketches, written reflections on my art, and photos, postcards, and flyers. My current sketchbooks also include my notes on demonstrations and art shows in which I participate. (Most recently, I have begun *video audit trails* in which I record pottery demonstrations and create short documentary-type movies using Windows Movie Maker and Adobe Premiere Pro.)

Creating and Learning From Your First Artwork

Before you begin to study art as a discipline, open your sketchbook and create an example of your best artwork. You can use any medium you like and any composition that you like. What did you create? Why do you think this is an example of your best artwork? What elements of the artwork do you like? What would you like to do better?

The purpose of this initial engagement is to see where you are currently in your ability to work in the visual arts. On the first day of the first pottery class I ever took, my instructor Glenn Dair told the class, "Always keep your first piece of pottery so that you know how far you have come." To this day, I return to this piece of pottery (see Figure 1.8a) to see just how far I have come in nine years of study (see Figure 1.8b). Reflection on your process is key; you will learn to notice what you like and what you would like to do better and this learning will drive your inquiry into the visual arts and their connection to ELA instruction. As you

Figure 1.8a *Albers's first piece of pottery.*

Figure 1.8b *A recent work by Albers.*

work through this book, continue to reflect upon each of the art engagements that you experience, your process of meaning making, how various media help you construct different and multimedia representations, and how working in the arts enables you to understand literacy processes differently. You will find that the more you learn about the disciplines of visual arts, the more you will see the potential for their integration into your ELA classes.

Your sketchbook will be an audit trail (Harste & Vasquez, 1998; Vasquez, 2004) of your experiences, frustrations, fears, and the joys of learning this new language of art. After you have worked through this entire book, return to your first artwork and notice your progress in making art. I hope that by the time you finish this book, you will see impressive changes in your beliefs about art, yourself as an artist, and your commitment to integrating the visual arts into your ELA instruction.

Inquiry Into Drawing

- *Of what basic elements are images comprised?*

- *How does someone become better at drawing?*

- *How can I engage learners in more complex literacy practices through knowledge about drawing?*

- *How is drawing important to the teaching of the English language arts?*

Self-Identity and Art: A Teacher's Story
by Allen Koshewa

Lumbering down the hallway, with his oversized head, freakish haircut, and black overcoat, Jonathan at first resembled Frankenstein. Upon closer look, he did not look so ghoulish, but both Jonathan and the tall gaunt mother at his side looked glum. They seemed lost, and since the school day had ended two hours earlier and few teachers were around, I approached them.

"May I help you?" I asked, and was informed that they had just moved into the neighborhood and were looking around the school. I showed the two of them around and ascertained that Jonathan wouldn't register until August, since it was the last week of the school year. During the tour, Jonathan spoke as little as possible and avoided eye contact. His mother, on the other hand, babbled nervously, and her anxious anticipation of hypothetical problems for the school year ahead did not augur well.

Over two months later, while preparing for the new school year, I noticed that a Jonathan was on my fifth-grade class list and wondered if it would be the same child. My answer came on the first day of school when I again spotted the trudging walk and big black overcoat, as out of season in September as it had been in June.

"Jonathan!" I yelled down the hall. "You're in my class!" Months later, I learned from Jonathan's mother that my indiscreet announcement had been a good thing, as Jonathan had told his mother that same day I'd remembered his name and, for the first time, he had responded positively to a teacher.

As the school year began, Jonathan's responses to me didn't seem positive, however. One-word grunts usually served as answers to questions, Jonathan's participation in group work was minimal, and he never volunteered to speak in front of the group. He did, however, follow directions and, for the most part, get his work done. For weeks I searched in vain for a spark of interest, a flash of talent, or a measure of accomplishment, but Jonathan was usually resistant or lethargic. I began to notice his classmates giving up after earnest efforts to include him in group activities, as well.

About a week after meeting with his parents—who displayed obvious tension while we discussed Jonathan's behavior—I noticed Jonathan's attempt to use a cross-hatching technique to shade in a drawing. I had already noticed Jonathan's engagement in our "blind drawing" activity, and his splendid freehand drawing of a Picasso figure had earned him several compliments from classmates. Now I suddenly realized that Jonathan not only loved art, but was committed to exploring it. I vowed to introduce more art techniques during my weekly art lessons, despite my weak background in art. I researched books on drawing, composition, and color. I bought more art materials and began introducing media I hadn't used in teaching before, such as clay and pastels. I established an "artist of the week" bulletin board that students helped research and create. Art became a favorite subject of nearly all the students, and when Jonathan grudgingly gave me permission to use his artwork as examples, I could tell he was actually pleased I'd noticed his deft application of concepts I'd introduced.

Jonathan's success in art gradually brought him out of his shell. I'm sure that other factors influenced his emergence as a salient, contributing class member, but I am convinced that nurturing Jonathan's passion for art and my public recognition of his explorations provided the most significant boon to his success. Soon, many class members asked Jonathan to draw for them, or consulted him when encountering roadblocks in their own artwork. By the end of the school year, Jonathan had become more responsible, more interactive, and more confident.

A year after Jonathan left fifth grade for middle school, I became the co-editor of a National Council of Teachers of English (NCTE) professional journal. It occurred to me that I could perhaps commission Jonathan to design the first cover. I phoned to speak to Jonathan and his parents about my idea.

"Bert," I said when his father answered the phone. Our numerous conversations during Jonathan's fifth-grade school year had resulted in our first-name relationship. "I have a question for you: Is Jonathan still pursuing art?"

"Is he still pursuing art?" he answered. "You should see him! His drawings are fantastic and he's always doing extra art projects for school. His artwork is great!"

Figure 2.1 *Jonathan's drawing for journal cover. Copyright 2002, National Council of Teachers of English. Reprinted with permission.*

Jonathan's subsequent drawing for the NCTE journal, a tongue-in-cheek interpretation of literacy mandates (see Figure 2.1), was perfect and received kudos in its published form. More importantly, in his father's eyes, Jonathan was OK. In fact, he was even more than OK: He was an artist.

*L*ike a magician, an artist uses tricks to convince us of the reality of his or her creations. Artists want the viewer to envision a world that may or may not have been seen before. In some ways, artists want us to reconsider what we already know as art and view it in new ways. Allen Koshewa's story tells us of his insight and diligence in searching for just the right connection that makes students like Jonathan engage in life and learning. Jonathan's life, at best, seemed challenging, yet his exploration into drawing, using techniques that he learned on his own and those which Allen introduced, enabled him to find that niche, that inquiry, that continues to drive his interest in school and life today. Inspired by students like Jonathan, Allen began to inquire into the arts more passionately because he knew they were important to his students. Rather than leave them with few or no strategies for making art, Allen brought in ideas, books, media, and techniques to support artistic growth in his students.

From childhood we have used pencils to scribble, make notes, and record our responses to things that we have seen, heard, and imagined. Pencils offer the most direct, and the most versatile, means of allowing our thoughts to flow from the mind through the fingertips to a sheet of paper. We often see our students doodle or create colorful and energetic images on their folders and notebooks.

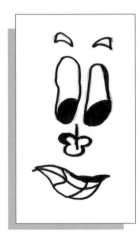

Figure 2.2 *Sixth-grade student doodle.*

The student who doodled Figure 2.2 is playing with shape, eye position, and open forms for the nose, mouth, and ears. Such play demonstrates a student's interest in and desire to draw. However, as students get older, they hesitate to share their visual expressions in ELA classes often because their art knowledge is self-taught, and they are embarrassed by the visual meanings they are able to construct. But, when given short and quick art strategy lessons, students will be able to express the meanings they desire and share these meanings willingly.

For example, Yadira Gonzalez invited me in to present a lesson on drawing to her freshman reading class, then work with the students as they visually interpreted one of the main characters from a novel they were reading independently. José had chosen to draw Alice from *Go Ask Alice* (Anonymous, 1998), and I had to coax him into showing me his drawing. The facial and bodily features in José's initial drawing were out of proportion, from high placement of the eyes to the thin cylindrical arms. He told me that he wanted to show Alice during the time that she was using drugs and was hardened by street life. Seated next to José, I demonstrated a short five-minute strategy lesson on drawing curved and angled lines, especially with eyebrows and eyes. I asked him to tell me what he saw and how he interpreted these two line shapes. The angled lines, to José, seemed to show anger, while curved lines were softer. José now wanted to edit his initial image to reflect these changes. He erased the facial features, and redrew Alice's eyes in a diamond shape, with pupils that looked directly at the viewer (see Figure 2.3). José then called Ms. Gonzalez over and proudly showed her his visual revision of Alice.

Figure 2.3 Jose's drawing of Alice.

Many students (and adults) become frustrated at their lack of expertise in drawing. They hold up their artwork very briefly or hide it. As teachers, we want to encourage and support students as they create a range of expressions—drawn, written, or performed. Furthermore, we want to challenge students not only to respond to texts through art, but to think through and interpret through visual expressions. In this chapter, you will learn to read art elements and principles associated with drawing, a medium through which many ELA students share what they know or understand about a written text. Additionally, you will learn five basic drawing techniques to help you artistically represent meaning more realistically. You will learn to draw and practice techniques in the elements of shape, contour line drawings, basic shapes, 3-D drawing, and figure drawing—all in the context of the English language arts. While you read this chapter, I hope you will find the artist within you who can support students like José and Jonathan in their desire to visually represent their interpretations more accurately.

Paper and Drawing Materials

The materials that you will need for working through demonstrations in this chapter include different types of paper, pencils, charcoal, chalk, drawing paper, and colored markers. Various types of sketch paper can be found in art stores, office supply stores, and discount superstores. Different papers have different *grips* and allow various textures to emerge. All drawing materials are made of particles of color, or *pigment*, bound together with a different kind of gum, to perform different jobs. Graphite pencils are the basic drawing implement, and you can produce all sorts of marks with a few pencils. The pencil that you are most familiar is the HB #2, perhaps the most common tool in school. This pencil works great for most purposes, in particular in showing *gradation*, or the shades from black to near white. David Macaulay and Tom Feelings, Caldecott Award–winning artists, use gradation and line to create realistic depth and detail. *Cathedral* (1981), *Motel of the Mysteries* (1979), *City* (1983), and *Pyramid* (1982) provide wonderful examples of how Macaulay uses these techniques to illustrate buildings of the past, while *The Middle Passage* (1995) or *Jambo Means Hello* (1974) show the powerful, dream-like drawings Feelings creates.

There are a variety of other drawing tools that will support your inquiry into art. Colored pencils are one of the most basic coloring tools. Artist Stephen Gammell, who was not formally trained in art, started out with lots of paper and pencils to develop his own talent at using color. *Song and Dance Man* (Ackerman, 1992) is illustrated using a combination of pencils and watercolor. Charcoal, another favorite drawing tool of many students and artists, comes in both black and white. It is available in sticks of varying thickness or in pencil form. David Wiesner's striking charcoal illustrations in *Night of the Gargoyles* (Bunting, 1999; see Figure 2.4) provide a wonderful example of this medium and capture the immense heaviness of the stone figures and their gloomy malevolence as they come to life during the night. Another important drawing tool, the eraser, comes in many different varieties and can be used to remove graphite as well as to add texture or create mood through smudging. Ordinary pencil erasers will work fine for the graphite pencils. For chalk or charcoal drawing, it is best to use a kneaded eraser, a soft gray eraser that you can squeeze like clay into any shape you want.

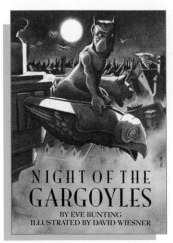

Figure 2.4 *Wiesner's charcoal illustration,* Night of the Gargoyles *cover. Copyright 1999, Clarion Books. Reprinted with permission.*

Practice Playing With Pencil

In your sketchbook, use several different pencils, graphite and/or colored, or charcoal, and play with gradation (see Figure 2.5 for an example). Notice what happens when you press and move the pencil firmly and then softly against the paper. Notice how the gradation, or shading of black to gray, changes. Now, explore line and pencil by cross-hatching, or criss-crossing lines to build pattern and texture. Hold the pencil at an open angle (pencil tip touches paper) and then at a severe angle (pencil close to paper). Notice how the intensity of shading changes with each decision you make. Now, with a tissue, soft cloth, or your finger, try smudging the graphite. Notice how much softer the effect becomes. Bang

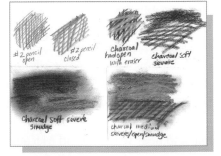

Figure 2.5 *Drawing techniques, gradation.*

(2000) writes that lines invoke emotions: What emotions are invoked when thick lines are made? Thin lines? Tight lines and loose lines? Erased lines? Smudged lines? Jot these interpretations of line next to your own textures.

Figure 2.6 is a line drawing of a teapot drawn by Atlanta, Georgia, teacher Bill Buckner. Notice how the lines take shape, and how he draws two types of lines: tight and close together, and loose and far apart. Notice also how he cross-hatches in three distinct places: at the bottom, to define the foot of the teapot; at the base of the spout and up the side of spout; and at the top and bottom of the handle, where it is attached to the teapot. Cross-hatching is often used to separate one part from another and to give shape and depth.

Figure 2.6 *Teapot using lines, drawn by Bill Buckner.*

Hogrogian's picture book, *Always Room for One More* (Leodhas, 1965), provides a lovely example of using cross-hatching in black-and-white illustrations, and blending some color to create interest and emotion. Brian Selznick also effectively uses pencil to illustrate the stories of Amelia Earhart and Eleanor Roosevelt in *Amelia and Eleanor Go for a Ride* (Muñoz Ryan, 1999). ■

Building Knowledge of Composition and Line

Molly Bang (see www.mollybang.com/picture.html) explains the important relationship between disciplinary knowledge—how elements in a picture relate—and practice with the discipline's tools—the structural elements and how they inform interpretation and production of visual images:

> I tried to figure out what elements were making the pictures scarier or less scary, tried to figure out how all the elements related to each other. Gradually, I began to understand something about how the structural elements of pictures affect our emotions. (n.p.)

The study of how meaning is made across semiotic systems, like art and language, will help you and your students read and interpret, as well as create, messages from a number of media sources (political cartoons, advertisements, paintings, and drawings, and so on). In this section, you will learn to read, interpret, and create your own compositions.

Composition

Composition is basic to all productions of meaning whether they be in writing, speech-making, art, or music; people compose pieces. Composition in art and other semiotic systems is about rearranging elements and ordering them in a way that seems more balanced and harmonious. Holistic readings of art provide a foundation from which learners can apply ELA concepts of understanding narratives, writing process, and analysis.

Choose and arrange five small objects in your house or in your classroom that you feel might go well together in a picture. Add one or more to see how the composition changes. Take away one or two. How does the composition change?

Arrange them in different ways by height, space, color, and shape. Notice the differences in each of the arrangements. Figure 2.7 shows *still life* compositions, one by Paul Cezanne (left) and one formerly attributed to Vincent van Gogh (right). What is the "feel" that you get for each painting? Which one do you like

Figure 2.7 *Still life paintings:* Apples, Peaches, Pears, and Grapes *(Paul Cezanne, 1879-1880), State Hermitage Museum, St. Petersburg, Russia;* Still Life with Mackerels, Lemons and Tomatoes *(formerly attributed to Vincent van Gogh, 1886), The Oskar Reinhart Collection "Am Römerholz," Winterthur, Switzerland. Reprinted with permission.*

better? What qualities of one appeal to you more than the other? Think about what you like about the arrangement and the spacing. These are elements associated with one's *aesthetic*, or pleasure when viewing spaces, images, and objects. ■

Reading Line and Composition in Students' Visual Texts

Artists use various types of line to evoke emotions. Read Figure 2.8 (Cowan, 2001b): What feeling do you get when you read this composition? How does this young artist achieve this response? Now, look specifically at the types of lines he uses. What effects does he achieve? Is he successful at conveying the meaning of the word *militant*?

Figure 2.8 *Fifth grader's pencil drawing of militant.*

In Kay Cowan's ELA classes, students visually compose to support their study of descriptive language. Cowan teaches her students to read techniques that artists use to convey emotion and intention. Students learn that thick black lines direct viewers' attention, and the shape of the line informs interpretation. Thick straight or angular lines convey anger, tension, frustration, and fear, while curved lines are more organic and soft and evoke a friendlier emotion. Read Figure 2.8 again: Notice this student's use of thick, inwardly turned triangular lines for the eyebrows, and a curved, thick line on the right side of the face to represent a scar. Cross-hatched lines in the hair and explosion in the background add to the interest and reality to this image. The curved lines in the smile that end in a sharp angle and the curved lines at the top of composition and in the face indicate this student's use of visual irony. At once, we understand that this figure is full of anger—but it is just this anger in which he finds some pleasure and comfort. This young artist uses art to convey an understanding of irony, both visually and linguistically, and offers insight on the complexity of such understanding. Knowledge of line enables learners to read images in picture books, anthologies, and popular culture texts. Furthermore, they can make deliberate and informed choices about the effects of line when creating their own representations, and how they want their viewers to interpret their characters or compositions.

Building Knowledge of Elements of Drawing

I have come to learn in my work with ELA students of all ages that nearly all of them want to know how to draw realistically. To do so, they must understand that, like language, art has a graphic cueing system, an "alphabet" of basic elements that compose all images (Albers, 2006c). When students recognize the alphabet of drawing and identify the elements in images, they will use this concept as they draw their own images.

There are five basic elements that make up all objects: dot, line, circle, curve, and angle (see Figure 2.9). Practice drawing these elements in your sketchbook to get a feel for them.

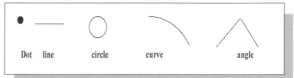

Dot   line   circle   curve   angle

Figure 2.9 *Basic elements of drawing.*

Reading Elements of Drawing

Cartoon characters in comics or picture books offer wonderful examples of using basic elements of drawing to create characters. Mickey Mouse, Daffy Duck, the popular television show *The Simpsons*, and Japanese anime cartoons often influence students' own cartoon stories. Review Figure P.1 in the preface (see page xiv): What basic elements of drawing do you notice? What do you think these elements say about this female character?

Let's look at a female character that a teacher created for a fictional narrative (see Figure 2.10). Notice how this teacher uses the basic elements of drawing—dots, circles, curves, angles, and lines—to create this character. Try drawing this character's portrait in your sketchbook. Get a good feel for each of the elements. What did you notice about your own ability to draw this figure? Now, using these basic elements create a portrait of your own original character. Reflect upon this exercise in your sketchbook next to your drawn figure.

Figure 2.10 *Teacher's female cartoon character.*

27

Illustrators of picture books offer strong examples for study when one is learning to read the basic elements of drawing. Bahti illustrated the deities known as Kokopellis and birds on the cover of *When Clay Sings* (Baylor, 1987)

predominantly with curved lines that move upward and curl into a wave. Curves also appear on the tops of the birds' heads, they make the shape of the birds' bodies and beaks, and they shape the Kokopellis' bodies and hair. According to Bang (2000), curved lines embrace us and protect us. We associate curved surfaces with nature such as hills, waves in water, and the shape of mothers' bodies. Figure 2.11 shows a high school student's use of curved lines to express Romeo's extreme grief when he encounters whom he believes is his dead Juliet. Notice how these curved lines embrace readers and pull us into Romeo's grief.

Figure 2.11 *High school student's use of elements of drawing, Romeo.*

In *Anansi the Spider* (1986), McDermott uses the same elements in the cover design, but these elements operate quite differently. McDermott draws thick black diagonal lines. When artists use thick black lines, they often intend to create a sense of foreboding and gloom, and when drawn diagonally, these lines are dynamic because they imply movement (Bang, 2000). McDermott's spider could be menacing, but he uses bright yellow circles and bright blue angles for the eyes, as well as red angled lines for the lips, moving upward—all of which combine to make this spider inviting. Note Figure 2.12, drawn by a fifth-grade girl. Her spider could be frightening, but she chooses to draw curved lines for the arachnid's legs, swirls of lines for the body, and circular eyes to generate a friendlier image. Encouraging students to read the basic elements in illustrators' images supports prediction about the story. What does the illustrator intend with his or her lines? Shapes? Colors? Such discussions support students' choices when they draw their own illustrations, as well. Students begin to build knowledge about art as a discipline, and they begin to read and create visual texts with intention.

Figure 2.12 *Fifth grader's use of elements of drawing, spider.*

Practice Reading Basic Elements of Drawing

Gather several picture books, illustrations, textbooks, or other artworks that you have in your home or classroom. Look for and read the relationships among the elements of drawing. Reflect on the overall message that each artist conveys through these elements: Does the artist's interpretation relate to your own? To the author's? This practice will build your confidence in reading these basic elements. ■

Practice Drawing Basic Elements of Drawing

In this exercise, you will practice drawing a cartoon of a lion in a setting, then generate ideas for a short narrative. Before you begin drawing, think about your image of lions: What do they look like? How are female lions physically different from males? Cubs? In what settings do you see them? Gather several photos or illustrations of lions. What basic elements can be seen in the figure of a lion? Its environment? If there is a mountain in the setting, what elements seem appropriate to represent it? Angles? Curves? These decisions will depend on your experience with mountains. What element would you use for the ground? A line? A curve? A combination of both? What you are doing by thinking about these images is creating a context for the lion; this will later become part of your *composition*, or what the image is about.

Figure 2.13a *ELA teacher's lion in composition using elements of shape.*

Now look at Figures 2.13a and 2.13b, cartoon lions drawn by ELA teachers in an arts-based literacy seminar. Notice the elements that make up each drawing, think about how you will draw your lion, and move it into a composition. Start with the eyes. Place two dots where you think the lion's eyes will be in this setting. Next, place circles around the eyes. Notice how these two elements in relation take on meaning. Now, draw a straight line downward between the eyes to create the bridge of the lion's nose. Next, make a triangle for the nose. Draw one more straight line down from the triangle, and add two curved lines that move upward to delineate the upper part of the mouth. Draw a big circle around all these elements to frame the lion's head. To add details, draw curved lines for the eyebrows.

Figure 2.13b *Another ELA teacher's lion in composition using elements of shape.*

Next, add the body by drawing a long rectangle and placing it along the right or left side of the head. Draw four shorter rectangles for the legs. Add two parallel, curved lines for the tail. Depending on the attitude of your lion, the tail can be up or down. To draw the tuft of hair for the tail and the lion's toes, draw curved lines. Now, draw curved lines that move around the lion's head for his mane, and add two curved lines for the ears (one is inside the other). Voilà! You have just drawn a lion! Using the elements of shape, draw the setting for your lion.

Read and study closely Figures 2.13a and 2.13b once more: How have these artists used elements of drawing to create a particular mood? Which is richer in detail? Which do you like more? Continue to work on your own lion drawing, and fill in as much white space as possible using the basic elements. Draft a story in which this lion might exist. How does your illustration help you consider the elements of narrative writing: who, what, where, when, why, and how of this story? How does your story encourage you to consider adding more elements to your illustration? Writing and drawing are reciprocal in the composition process. Reflect upon this reciprocity and the composition process in your sketchbook. ■

Contour Drawing: Seeing Objects in Lines

Can you imagine what life would be like without textures, colors, and shapes? We would have a very different world, and our imaginations would likely be very

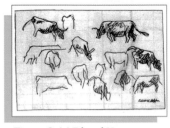

Figure 2.14 *Edward Hopper, contour line drawings. Reprinted with permission, Whitney Museum of American Art.*

strange! When a person begins to draw, one of the best ways to look at objects is to see nothing but the outside lines, the *contour* of the object. Paul Klee, a Swiss painter, once told his students, "Take a walk with a line" (MacMillan, 2000, p. 1361). He wanted them to explore what could be done with simple line drawings, with little attention to texture, depth, shadow, or other aspects that make a drawing come alive. Pablo Picasso did a number of *contour line drawings*, or simple, continuous line drawings, of animals, birds, and people. Edward Hopper (Lyons, 1997, p. 103) also did a series, or a *study*, of cows using contour lines (shown in Figure 2.14).

How does Hopper capture the essence of cows? Notice how he uses line sparingly, yet captures the essence of cows in different positions and perspectives.

   Contour drawing, or drawing in one continuous line, helps an artist *look* at the outside lines of an object and teaches the viewer to *see*. Every object in our world has an outline, so contour lines are all around us. This looking and seeing is part of what artists do when they work with contour lines. They look at the

Figure 2.15 *Mary Cassatt, line drawing. Reprinted with permission, Spencer Museum of Art.*

outside lines and imagine the details—just like when we look up at clouds and see objects, or read a floor plan of a dream home, or develop outlines on the whiteboard or overhead transparency to explain ideas. Consider simple contour line drawings such as Charles Schulz's endearing characters of Snoopy, Charlie Brown, or Lucy, or more complicated contour line drawings such as Mary Cassatt's *Italian Girl* (see Figure 2.15). Contour drawing can help to reveal humor, moods, and ideas, especially with the use of *blind contour drawing* in which the artist does not look at her or his paper when drawing the outline of an object. Working with contour line drawings allows a learner to imagine possibilities through line and shape.

Reading Contour Lines

When you read the contour drawing in Figure 2.16, what do you see? You may have immediately recognized this as the outline of da Vinci's *The Last Supper*. When an outline is drawn, your brain always attempts to fill in details left out. Harste (1994) says that making meaning is just human nature. The reason that you are able to make sense of this

Figure 2.16 *Contour drawing,* The Last Supper.

line drawing is that you have experience with this painting, whether it be through the bestselling novel *The Da Vinci Code* (Brown, 2003); your knowledge of art history; a visit to Santa Maria delle Grazie in Milan, Italy, where this painting resides; or your knowledge of Christianity.

Pablo Picasso appreciated works that felt unfinished; for him, they were on fire: "Unfinished, a picture remains alive, dangerous. A finished work is a dead work, killed" (Picasso, cited in Ashton, 1972, p. 38). Picasso's sketchbook was filled with many contour line drawings of images that he wanted to recast in painting or clay (see www.picasso.com/gallery/index.html for examples). Like Picasso, our students often doodle using contour lines in their notebooks. As teachers, we may misinterpret these doodles as students' inattention to class discussions or as merely insignificant sketches. However, doodles often reveal students' visual imaginings and can be likened to contour line images drawn by Picasso or Hopper. Through their doodles, students visually brainstorm and capture the essence of a story, the imagined characters, and the flow of events. Sometimes, as Cowan (2001b) found in her study, writing was too slow for her students, and they often doodled or did *quick draws,* or short uninterrupted drawings, as part of the composing process. Figure 2.17 shows a student's simple but elegant contour drawing of a giraffe. This illustration accompanied a story that she wrote on African animals and the need to preserve grasslands.

Figure 2.17 *Student's contour drawing of giraffe.*

Practice Blind Contour Drawing—Common Objects

In this exercise, you will create a blind contour drawing of a common object and focus only on the outline or the shape of the object. Blind contour drawing requires concentration and should be done quite slowly and deliberately as you observe and draw. Look at the blind contour drawings of a banana and a pear in Figure 2.18. These drawings are not realistic, but outlines that suggest these objects. The goal of this exercise is to look closely at the outline of an object—really study it—and without looking

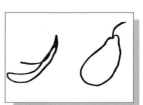

Figure 2.18 *Blind contour drawings of a banana and a pear.*

down at your paper, draw it. You are learning to see the essence of objects. Before you draw, place an object on a table in front of you. Open up your sketchbook and place your pencil on the paper, but do not look down at your paper as you draw the object's contour lines; focus only on the outside lines of the object. Let your brain guide your eye and hand. ▪

Practice Blind Contour Drawing—People

As I mentioned earlier, blind contour drawings can be humorous, especially when the drawing is representative of people you know and care about! In this exercise,

create a blind contour of your friends (this is a favorite art engagement of students). You can use a photograph, unless you want to use your friends as models on the sly. Place your pencil on your paper, and without looking down, force your eyes and brain to help you draw the outlines of your friends. (See Figure 2.19 for an example.) When you are finished, reflect upon your drawing. Notice how the blind contour drawing often looks more like the composition of the photo or group

Figure 2.19 *Blind contour drawings of friends in a photograph.*

of friends than you anticipated. Your brain fills in many of the details, and you recognize the people in the drawing. ▪

Practice Contour Line Drawing

Now do contour line drawings of the same objects and people. Study the outlines of the objects or people in your blind contour drawings, look down at your paper, and draw, transferring your gaze between the objects or people and your drawing. Did you notice a difference in how you drew your lines? Was this technique more comfortable than blind contour drawing? Which was more humorous? Contour line drawing encourages attention to the line of an object, which often transfers

into other work. When you see contour line drawings, you learn to fill in details that may not be apparent, and learn to infer aspects of a text that are not visibly noticeable.

Once you are comfortable with contour line drawing, draw contour line sketches of famous images and faces, or faces of your students. Figure 2.20 shows three contour

Figure 2.20 *Contour line drawings: Self-portrait, John Lennon, student.*

line drawings, one a self-portrait and the second of John Lennon (which later became a study for a vase that I made and painted), and one drawn by Bill Buckner of one of his students.

Many books covers, such as Creech's *Love That Dog* (2003), Williams's *The Glass Menagerie* (1999), and Silverstein's *The Giving Tree* (1964) and *Where the Sidewalk Ends* (2004), are illustrated with contour line drawings. Line drawings immediately invite readers and viewers to imagine and wonder about the characters, people, animals, and objects and ask, "What do these line drawings suggest about this text?" "Why a line drawing on the cover of *Love That Dog* instead of a painting or a photograph?" Line drawings may suggest simplicity, whether it be in the theme, moral, or in the events in a character's life. In *The Glass Menagerie*, the contour line drawings on the cover position the reader of this play to consider the frailty of both the glass figurines, the glass menagerie, and the emotional lives of the characters. Engaging students in conversations about the type of illustrations, such as contour line drawings, can be likened to a discussion of the significance of the title of a literary work and may add to the depth of the overall analysis of the work. ■

Basic Shapes and Forms

Shapes and forms are all around us. Although the terms are often used interchangeably, shapes and forms are quite different. A triangle is an example of a *shape*; it is flat and two-dimensional (2-D). It has height and width, but not depth. A prism is an example of a *form*; it has height, width, and depth, which makes it three-dimensional (3-D).

Compare the images in Figure 2.21: The left-hand image shows a stylized shape, a 2-D autobiographical representation created by Carolyn, an elementary teacher; the right-hand image shows a 3-D form, a papier-mâché representation of Carolyn, complete with accessories. The 3-D image allows Carolyn to work more completely with details. Consider how shapes and forms are metaphors for such ELA instruction concepts as summary and interpretation. Shapes contain basic information, equivalent to summaries of stories, while forms contain

Figure 2.21 *Shape and form in autobiographical artworks.*

more details and encourage rich interpretation. The writing adage "Show, don't tell" may become more comprehensible for students when they learn about the distinction between shape and form.

Four Basic Shapes

There are four basic shapes that make up nearly all things that we see in world: circle, square, triangle, and rectangle (see Figure 2.22). Look around the room in which you are sitting and notice that the common objects that surround you are indeed made up of these shapes. Basic shapes are not often true shapes. That is,

Figure 2.22 Four basic shapes: circle, square, triangle, and rectangle.

sometimes the circle becomes an oval, or the triangle is rounded, or the square and rectangle do not have sides that are equal. An object may comprise several shapes. For instance, look at your couch. What shapes do you see? Rectangular seats? Arms in the shape of circles?

Similar to contour line drawings, basic shapes are outlines of an object viewed.

Shapes inform and mold our thinking. Angular shapes like squares, rectangles, and triangles are the foundations of our everyday objects: buildings, flat-screen monitors, picture frames, students' desks, etc. The sense and spirit of the clean lines of angular shapes are associated with logic, science, religion, and progress, as well as honesty, straightness, and order. We relate angularity with inorganic objects and technology. Values attached to angled images can imply technology in a positive way, as in progress, or negatively, as a source of oppression, as in clichés like "feeling boxed in."

On the other hand, basic shapes that are curved, such as circles and ovals, indicate warmth, protection, and endlessness; traditionally, circles also symbolize eternity and the heavens. We tend to see relationships in circles, as in Venn diagrams, and collaboration, as represented by expressions and symbols such as the Circle of Life, Olympic rings, or wedding rings. Look again at the objects around the rooms in your home or your classroom: What basic shapes do you see? Do these shapes represent order and logic or warmth and endlessness? Or, do you see an equal representation of both?

Reading Basic Shapes in Building Structures

Architects, such as Frank Lloyd Wright, design buildings with the intent to evoke particular feelings. Wright's design of The Solomon R. Guggenheim Museum in New York, for example, has wide sweeping curves that move upward, while a house he designed in Florence, Alabama, USA, has a wide flat roof and strong angular shapes. Figure 2.23 contains images of well-known buildings from around the world. How do you read the basic shapes in these buildings? Which one(s) seem more logical, scientific, or ordered? Which one(s) feel more inviting? How do these shapes influence our interpretation of these designs? How do the rectangular shapes

Figure 2.23 Well-known buildings: New York City skyline; Eiffel Tower, Paris; Royal Albert Hall of Arts and Sciences, London.

of the New York City skyline (shown in the far left photograph in Figure 2.23) represent logic, progress, and centrality? How does the triangular shape of the Eiffel Tower in Paris (shown in the center photograph in Figure 2.23) suggest logic and science? How does the circular and curved shape of the Royal Albert Hall of Arts and Sciences (shown in the far right photograph in Figure 2.23), a music venue in London, represent the organic warmth of classical music? Record your thoughts about these buildings in your sketchbook. Then, in your sketchbook, record the design of your own classroom, your school, or your campus. What shapes are the buildings? How are your desks organized? How does building design and arrangement of your classroom shape the perception we have about schooling? In his photo-picture book *Alphabet City*, Johnson (1999) invites young and old readers to consider the shapes in everyday objects. Consider introducing this book in your classroom and inviting students to study the shapes that Johnson presents, and ask them to speculate as to what these shapes or objects connote. Such an exercise invites readers to learn how shapes inform our perceptions of objects.

Reading Basic Shapes in Artworks and Illustrations

Like architects, artists also use basic shapes to draw or paint images and characters. Figure 2.24 shows three different artists' images created with basic shapes. How do these artworks make you feel? Are some more inviting than others? If so, why do you think so? Record these notes into your sketchbook.

Let's now practice reading and thinking about basic shapes in illustrations. Wiesner's cover illustration in *Night of the Gargoyles* (Bunting, 1999; see Figure 2.4 on page 24) appears to be complex, but when we look for basic shapes in the gargoyle, the image is less daunting and more achievable (see Figure 2.25).

Figure 2.24 Artists' work with basic shapes: David Robinson, Earl Baum, and Peggy Albers.

Figure 2.25 *Wiesner's gargoyle sketched in basic shapes.*

Notice Wiesner's use of shapes to create interest and intrigue. For example, the bright white circular moon against the gradated shadows of the clouds, the round white penetrating eyes of the gargoyle against the dark shadows of the face, and the strong triangular shapes of the bird work together to create mood, or atmosphere. Bang (2000) suggests that various shapes, like triangles, make an image "feel scary" (p. 24), especially in conjunction with sharp lines as seen in the gargoyle's ears, nose, and buildings. Yet the strong round and curved shapes of the gargoyle's and bird's bodies and the upturned mouth work against this scariness, adding intrigue and inviting the viewer and reader into this story.

Students enjoy drawing animals and likenesses of their favorite characters; by drawing such likenesses, they bring their own interpretation to the image. When we draw from an illustration, it is helpful to first read the illustration for basic shapes, then retranslate these shapes onto the page.

Figure 2.26 *Two versions of a rabbit sketched in basic shapes.*

Figure 2.26 shows two drawings of well-known characters focusing on basic shapes: On the left is a hand-drawn likeness of Willems's (2004) *Knuffle Bunny* and on the right is a computer-generated version of Potter's Peter Rabbit. How do the basic shapes in the rabbit based on Willems's illustrations look and feel different than those of Potter's? The left-hand rabbit flops backwards, looks like it is carried around by a child, and is comfortable. The shapes of the right-hand rabbit are upright and appear prim and proper. Both of the characters contain ovals, yet both convey quite different meanings. In the first rabbit, the softness of the ovals, the overall curve of the rabbit, and the movement of the eye from left to right create a narrative, a story. The viewer senses that this rabbit has been carried around like a good friend for a long time. From the shapes, it is a passive object, while the second rabbit, which walks upright, is active and shows a sense of intention and purpose. What types of stories can you imagine with rabbits who have these two postures?

Practice Drawing Basic Shapes in Animals

Let's practice drawing animals—perhaps your own pet or an animal in the wild. Before you start your drawing, look for basic shapes in the two photographs of a dog and a cat presented in Figure 2.27, and convert these images to loose and free basic shapes, as in the drawings in the figure. Challenge yourself to draw these shapes several times, exploring size. Draw these shapes small (quarter page), midsize (half page), and large (whole page). How do your drawings take on different meanings when size of the basic shapes is altered?

Now find a photo or illustration of your favorite animal and, in your sketchbook, draw it in basic shapes only; remember to draw light, loose lines at first. Reflect on your drawings: Was it difficult to see and draw the various shapes, or did you surprise yourself by drawing a likeness of this animal? Did you notice how the size of your shapes varied? This is your initial impulse to put your sense of proportion to work! ■

Figure 2.27 *Looking for basic shapes in photographs of animals.*

Practice Drawing a Favorite Character From a Picture Book

Picture book illustrations provide wonderful resources when working with basic shapes. One of my favorites is the Caldecott award–winning book *Olivia* (Falconer, 2000). When I draw the character of Olivia (see Figure 2.28), I first study the basic shapes that make her full image. I draw these shapes in a variety of sizes and organize them according to how I read her image. Once I draw my basic shapes, I use my knowledge of contour lines to connect the shapes and create Olivia's outline. I then use curved lines, or basic elements of drawing, to give Olivia's dress some sense of movement, and I use gradation to define the pattern in her tights. When I combine the knowledge from all three techniques, I am more able to draw a realistic image of this delightful character.

Figure 2.28 *Olivia sketched in basic shapes and contour lines, then shading and gradation.*

Find a picture book character that you really like and draw it using what you have learned about the basic elements, contour line drawing, and basic shapes. Work with a simple image at first, and once you have practiced and are satisfied with your drawing, choose one that is a bit more complicated. What are you learning about these art techniques? Is art as mystifying as you might have once thought? Record your thoughts in your sketchbook. ■

Value Scale: A Study of Light and Dark

In the last three sections, you have learned how to develop techniques for drawing more realistically. Yet our drawings remain two dimensional in their appearance. In order to create more realism in our drawings, it is necessary to know something about *value*, or the study of light and dark. Knowledge about techniques that show value will help you create the illusion of depth and move 2-D shapes into 3-D forms.

Light and dark are not merely black and white. There are countless shades or values in between. Artists use gradation to make basic shapes appear 3-D–to have height, width, and depth. The part of an object closest to the light source has the lightest value and the part furthest away has the darkest values. Notice in Figure 2.29 that the light comes from the right side of the objects pictured. Therefore, the closer a side of an object is to the light, the lighter that side will be; the further away from the light source, the darker the side is. In the figure, the right sides of the objects receive the greatest amount of light while the left sides receive little or no light, so the value graduates from light to dark and casts a black shadow behind the objects pictured.

Figure 2.29 *Effects of light on value.*

Reading Illusion and 3-D Created With Value and Line

Artists depend on their knowledge of value and line to capture depth, and curved lines give the illusion of depth to 2-D artworks. Da Vinci was a master in creating the illusion of depth and used value to study *highlights*, or where the light hits strongest, and *lowlights*, or where the light hits least (for examples, visit www.visi.com/~reuteler/leonardo.html). In the piece shown in Figure 2.30, *Closet*, artist David Robinson takes an everyday scene and gives depth to his shirts, pants, and leather jacket using gradual changes in shade, or *value*. If he did not incorporate value, these clothes would appear flat and unrealistic, much like a contour line drawing. Look again at David Wiesner's cover illustration on *Night of the Gargoyles* (Bunting, 1999; see Figure 2.4 on page 24). Notice where the light source is and how Wiesner uses gradation to create highlights and lowlights to define and accent various features of the gargoyles.

Figure 2.30 *David Robinson,* Closet.

Practice Working With Value and Line

Let's practice working with value and line by drawing a common, simple object: a lemon. When you read the images of a lemon seen in Figure 2.31, consider how the light value affects interpretation. Which of these lemons is most appealing to you?

Now you will practice changing a 2-D shape to a 3-D by working with curved lines. Draw loose contour lines of a basic oval shape to create an outline of a lemon.

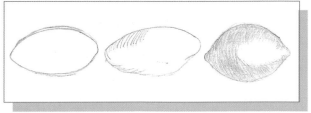

Figure 2.31 Creating the illusion of 3-D with curved lines and light source.

Remove, or erase, the lines you do not want. Let's say the light source comes from the front of the lemon. Draw short lines curved inwardly and close together towards the center on both the top and bottom of the lemon. Continue until you reach the nub on the right side of the lemon. Then layer more inwardly curved lines onto existing lines. Move these lines across the top and bottom of the fruit until the lines are less visible individually, always mindful of the light source. Now, cross-hatch lines over your curved lines to create even more depth. If you want, you can smudge or blend the lines to create a soft and warm impression. ■

Practice Creating a Still-Life Composition

Using curved lines and cross-hatching, create a still-life composition with several objects. Place a small lamp where you want the light source to be, and turn out any overhead lights so the major light comes from the lamp. Now, look at the still life, draw basic shapes, and create 3-D with curved lines and cross-hatching. As you fill in the light value, if there are areas that you want blurred or softened in your image, smudge the pencil with a tissue, your finger, or a soft cloth. After you are finished with drawing, practice other basic forms. How does practice enable you to draw more realistically? What difference do you see between your contour line drawings, and the drawings with additional curved and cross-hatched lines? Which do you prefer? ■

Practice: Revision of Favorite Character

Like writing, artworks can be revisited and revised. Return to the drawing you made of your favorite picture book character in the previous section. Look at your character—it is probably more two-dimensional than you want it to be. Try to make it three-dimensional by adding curved lines, cross-hatched lines, and smudging. Study my drawing of Olivia again (see Figure 2.28 on page 37). Do you notice the light source? The smudging? These are aspects of the drawing that may have gone unnoticed earlier. To create an illusion of depth in Olivia's chin and underside of her dress, I used light, curved, and cross-hatched inward lines. I then smudged these lines to create a gradation that moves from light to middle gray. To create depth in Olivia's ears, I again used curved and cross-hatched lines, but I did not go to the edge of the ear, just the inside. Again, I smudged these lines together to show the distinction between the inner ear and the outer ear (which receives more light). Next, I used curved lines to create the tights and dark lines to make her legs and stomach area distinct. I then used a dark value and a light value to show Olivia's striped tights.

Take your own character drawing and play with it, and give it life and three-dimensionality as shown in my sketch of Olivia. Once you are finished, think about how both versions of your character drawing have distinct differences and inspire quite different responses. What details in your second rendition did you add that were not present in your first attempt? ▪

Figure Drawing

Students and teachers with whom I have worked have a strong desire to draw the human figure more realistically—to create figures that have depth, shape, and interest. You can support this interest as you learn how to work with visual details in your own artistic inquiry. In Figure 2.32, Vickie, a teacher of English-language learners (ELLs), draws two autobiographical images, one stylized and the other more realistic. When you read these two images, how does each reveal details about Vickie that the other does not? How do you interpret Vickie's two perceptions of herself? Students often play with exaggeration in image, yet many want to know how to draw more realistically. This requires knowledge of proportion, perspective, and movement.

Figure 2.32 *Stylized and more realistic autobiographical drawings.*

Reading Proportion

Study Figure 2.33. The left-side image is ninth-grader Miguel's drawing of a character from a novel; the right-side image is a proportionate representation of a human form. You can immediately appreciate the creativity and the complexity of

Miquel's interpretation. However, you can also notice that something about the actual figure itself is not quite right. When compared to the proportionate image, Miguel's figure's arms appear too short, the legs too long, and the head too big. Because many ELA teachers and their students have little experience with art principles such as proportion, we are willing to accept this image and our brain recasts this image as acceptable. However, teaching students how to create more realistic drawings of human figures offers them confidence in their ability to interpret and represent characters or figures in their writing as they imagine them.

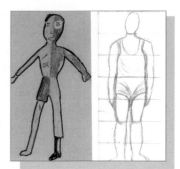

Figure 2.33 *Student's figure drawing and a figure in proportion.*

One of the important aspects of drawing realistic figures is understanding *proportion*. To many artists, proportion revolves around comparing the size of one thing to another and showing different sizes as accurately as possible on any media. To support students' more accurate representation of the human figure, you need to teach them about proportion, perspective, size, and shape. Let's return to Miguel's self-portrait for a moment (see Figure 2.33). The human form is approximately seven head-lengths high, and the grid in the right-side image marks equal approximations of one head size. A common element in drawings that is often out of proportion is the length of a figure's arms. Miguel's character's arms are too short; they fall around his waist when, realistically, hands fall at the thighs. Second, realistically, shoulders are about three heads wide, but Miguel's head is slightly too large, and his shoulders are about one head wide. Interestingly, many students across ages (even adults) represent the human figure in much the same way as Miguel, so students welcome information about proportion, incorporate it into their final artworks, and develop confidence about their ability to represent the human form.

To help you conceptualize key relationships among parts of the human form, Figure 2.34 shows a proportionate drawing of a standing human figure. It's simplest to measure body parts in relation to the head. Here are some interesting relationships to keep in mind when drawing human figures:

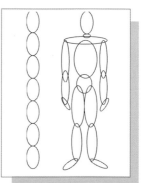

Figure 2.34 *Human proportion.*

- The average adult human is seven and a half heads tall.
- Shoulders are three heads wide.
- When arms are outstretched, the distance from fingertip to fingertip equals the figure's height.
- Arms and hands at the side fall halfway between knees and hips.
- Arms and legs bend at the halfway point.
- Hips are halfway down the body; a person can fold in half.

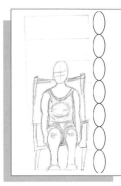

Figure 2.35
Foreshortening.

Of course, not all of the human figures are drawn as standing. Many actions require that humans sit, lie down, or move around. This is where drawing becomes a bit complicated. Proportions seem to change as humans move around. Parts of the body appear larger or smaller, depending on whether they are near or far from the person looking at them. For instance, if your figure's arm or leg is pointing directly at you, part of its length will be hidden. This is known as *foreshortening*. Notice that in the form pictured in Figure 2.35, two head lengths have been lost because the figure is in the sitting position. The space from the hips to the knees has become foreshortened and the figure's thighs are hidden from view.

Practice Reading and Drawing Basic Shapes in Human Figure Drawing

This set of exercises will shed light on the process of drawing the human figure. Stand in front of a full-length mirror (or look at a photo in which you are standing) and study the proportions of your own figure. Is your head one-seventh the size of the rest of your body? Is your torso three heads in length? Look at where your arms fall. Where does the upper arm fall in relation to the body? The lower arms? The hands? Now, to study foreshortening, sit in a chair in front of the mirror. Notice the spaces that are foreshortened and parts of the body slightly hidden. Let your hands fall to the side. Where do the hands fall? Point a finger at the mirror. Does the finger appear larger?

Now, in your sketchbook, draw a proportionate human figure by sketching a series of ovals as shown in Figure 2.34 on page 41. (I suggest that you draw grid lines of one inch in thickness or stacked ovals at first to help you gauge proportion.) As you practice, study where the parts of the figure fall. Also, use what you've learned about basic shapes to think about and sketch the various parts of the body: What shape is the head? Is it a circle or an oval? If it is an oval, is it a thin and long oval or a short and rounder oval? What shapes form the arms? The legs? The torso? After you have done one drawing, reflect upon the process: What did you learn about proportion and foreshortening? Practice drawing your students as they read, or stand, or write, people moving in the mall, or in other places. ■

Practice Gesture Drawing

Humans are rarely still; we are always moving. Now that you have practiced studying and drawing the human form standing, try to free your mind and draw the human figure in motion. *Gesture drawings* are loose line drawings of basic shapes (see, for example, Figure 2.36) meant to convey movement, not necessarily proportion. Practicing gesture drawings will help you to loosen up and will give life to your figures. Although your aesthetic may tell you that humans must be represented realistically, gesture drawings, like studies, help you conceive the many positions that the human figure can take in final drawings.

Figure 2.36 Teacher's gesture drawings.

To practice gesture drawings, you will need someone to be your model—a child, parents, spouse, partner, or your students. Or, if this is not possible, sit at table in your cafeteria, on a bench at the mall, or at a coffee shop, and capture people as they move across your space. To do gesture drawing, call upon what you learned about basic shapes, and your knowledge of proportion and foreshortening. If you have a live model, let her or him know that you are going to ask her or him to take on a pose for no more than one minute. During that time, you will make quick short and loose drawings in your sketchbook that are composed of basic shapes. The model should have at least five poses in mind before you start so this exercise is continuous. If you are in another place, like a mall or a cafeteria, draw the figure in motion and imagine how your model might look when he or she stops.

Now you need to visually define the human figure by connecting the ovals with contour lines as you did with your favorite character drawing. Figure 2.37 shows a sixth-grade student's gesture drawing. After about ten different sketches, she chooses one and connects the basic shapes with contour lines to indicate clothing. She then plays with the figure's personality with multiple loosely curved lines. Choose one of your gesture drawings; add contour lines to give the figure a more realistic look, and erase the lines of the ovals that are no longer necessary to visually represent the human form. Record your insights on this process in your journal. ■

Figure 2.37 Gesture drawing, basic shapes connected.

Drawing Faces

Nearly all students with whom I have worked want to know how to draw the human face accurately. If you think about your own students' renditions of characters' faces, nearly all have eyes placed near the top of the head with the mouth near the bottom of the chin. Although no two faces are the same, the same proportions and basic shapes make up a face. Read and study the facial features of family and friends in your photo albums or your students' faces, or look at facial features of characters in some of your favorite picture books. How are the eyes shaped? Oval? Almond? Also note where the eyes are in relation to other facial features.

There are a number of different head shapes (square, oval, triangular, pear); however, you will work with only the oval for now. Our heads, like our bodies, are symmetrical; the basic proportions for the head are as follows:

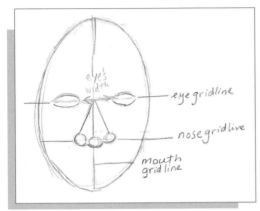

- The eyes are halfway between the top of the head and the bottom of the chin.
- The nose is halfway between the eyes and the chin.
- The mouth is halfway between the nose and the chin.
- The ears are the length of the space between the eyes and the nose.

After reading the proportions in Figure 2.38, practice drawing heads using grid marks and basic shapes to help you internalize these proportions.

Figure 2.38 *Head and face proportions.*

Practice Drawing Eyes

It has been said that the eyes are the windows to the soul. They express a range of emotions and expressions. On the face, the distance between the eyes measures one eye length. Eyes have many different shapes, but an easy shape to draw is an almond shape. Look at how artists and illustrators paint or draw eyes to connect

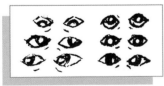

Figure 2.39 *Drawing eyes.*

with the viewer or others in the image. Where are the pupils? How wide are the eyes? How do such decisions inform interpretation? In your sketchbook, play with this shape and place the pupils in various positions. (See Figure 2.39 for examples.) How does each eye placement, and the shape of the eyebrows, convey a different expression? ■

Practice Drawing Noses

Like eyes, noses inform viewers about a character's personality and emotions. Consider how Cyrano de Bergerac outwitted his critics, especially when he responded to a fan who insulted the size of his nose: "A great nose is the banner of

a great man, a generous heart, a towering spirit..."
(Rostand, 1950, Act I, p. 34). Noses are basically
rounded triangles. To practice learning to draw a
realistic nose, start with a triangle with a *symmetrical
guideline*, or a line the divides the nose into two equal
parts. Round the bottom of the triangle, and then
round the point at the middle. On the right and left
sides of the bottom triangles, add curved lines to give

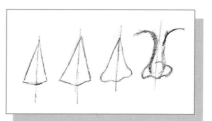

Figure 2.40 Drawing noses.

shape to the nostrils. Lightly draw in a circle to give depth to the rounded part of
the nose. Draw in curved lines at the top of the bridge of the nose to indicate
eyebrows. With your experience with lines, gradation, and lowlights and
highlights, add more depth with shading to give the illusion of three dimensions.
(See Figure 2.40 for examples.) ■

Practice Drawing Mouths

Mouths convey a range of emotions with simple upward or downward curved lines.
Examine various mouths of characters in paintings, illustrated books, or your
literature anthology. How do these painters and illustrators use curved lines to help
us interpret the characters' happiness, sadness, suspicion, and fear? Consider which
emotion you want your face to convey before you draw. To practice drawing mouths,
you need only remember that mouths are simply three curved lines. To start, draw a
flattened *m*-shaped line to define the upper part of the mouth. Below that, draw the
lower line of the bottom lip with an upside-down but
flatter *m* shape. To complete the mouth, draw a third
flattened *m*- line; this line separates the upper from the
lower lip and indicates the emotion you want to create
with its upward or downward sweep. Figure 2.41
presents a basic sketch of a mouth. ■

Figure 2.41 Simple curved lines for mouth.

Practice Drawing Ears

Ears are quite easy to draw, especially when you consider them in basic shapes.
Ears can create a humorous element to a character, such as Pinocchio, whose ears
change from human to donkey, or Hirshfeld's caricatures of famous people, who
are drawn with exaggerated facial features, including the now famous ears of
Prince Charles (for examples of his work, see www.alhirschfeld.com/artwork/
originals.html). Ears consist of two ovals—a larger oval for the top part of the ear, or

Figure 2.42
Drawing ears.

the outer ear flap, and a smaller one for the lobe (see Figure 2.42). Erase the line between the lobe and upper ear. Add an inside curved line that moves alongside the larger oval to about halfway. Draw in another curved line from the middle of the last line that extends to where the lobe starts. Finally, add a small curve to define the small protrusion, and some shadowing to give the ear depth. ■

Practice Drawing Self-Portraits

Now, to put it all together, practice drawing your self-portrait. Look in the mirror and notice the basic shape of your head. Practice drawing your head shape, others' head shapes, and then head shapes with the grid lines. Draw your own head shape using a gridline to guide proportion.

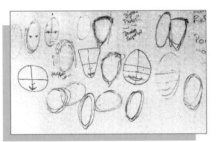

Figure 2.43 *Practice drawing head shapes with grid lines.*

Figure 2.44 *Initial and revised autobiographical drawing.*

Now you are ready to add the basic shapes that make up your facial features. While looking in the mirror, study your eyes, ears, and nose, and think about the basic shapes and loose lines of your features. Use gridlines to guide your proportions, as in Figure 2.43. Think about the pupils of the eyes. Where do you want them to focus? Draw them onto the eye lines of the grid. Now draw a triangle on the dividing line in the middle. Add the pointed oval for the mouth, the curved *m*-lines to define the lips. Add a few contour lines to smooth out your facial features. Add lines to represent your hairstyle image. How does knowledge of proportion and basic shapes help to create a more realistic self-portrait? Figure 2.44 shows fourth-grader Nancy's initial (left) and revised (right) self-portrait after practicing these same techniques. ■

Reflection on Inquiry Into Drawing

I have found that when students and teachers learn basic art techniques, they realize that art is not so daunting:

Ellen: I like drawing, now.

Peggy: You do?

Ellen: I do, I really do. I really did tell my students, "Don't laugh at me when I draw on the blackboard because I can't draw." And they would laugh and say, "What's that's supposed to be?" I would laugh with them, and it was fun. But now that I'm aware about basic shapes and proportion, I know that images are nothing but a line, a dot, a curve, a circle, and an angle. That's it.

By studying drawing as a language, Ellen has now learned that images, like written language, are comprised of conventions and structures. Like language, art has cueing systems, and Ellen begins to notice graphic information in basic elements, "a line, a dot, a curve, a circle, and an angle," which helps her to read and produce a range of visual texts. Art is demystified for her, and her fear of working with art diminished.

When teachers like Ellen are given opportunities to study the visual arts, they see many possibilities for its use in their ELA classes. English-language learner teacher Vickie states in an interview, "I want to include an art workshop into the literacy learning of my English learners. Art allows them to show me what they know, and they will not struggle with written language. Art will become for them their mother tongue, initially, in school." For Ellen and Vickie, the visual arts are in dialogue with written and spoken language, rather than in opposition or alongside. Together, they become integrally related in the semiotic expression.

Eisner (2002a) argues that art helps to build students' imagination and encourages symbolic and metaphorical thinking. Art pushes learners to become problem-solvers. They learn about value to create an illusion of 3-D. They study proportion and are able to draw more realistic figures. They notice relationships among and between details in an image, and apply this conceptual understanding to texts written in various language systems.

When given opportunities to explore drawing with technique and with study and knowledge of line, shape, and form, as artists do, students can and do apply this knowledge across language systems. Figure 2.45 shows ninth-grade student Larry's drawing of Verona, based upon his reading of *Romeo and Juliet*. Notice how Larry used contour lines, shading, and shape, and consciously showed relationships among these elements. The sharp angular lines and perspective suggest orderliness, yet the arc in the background suggests warmth and unity. His

Figure 2.45 *Student's drawing of Verona, based on a reading of Romeo and Juliet.*

use of shape artistically demonstrates strong interpretation of themes that run through *Romeo and Juliet.*

Learning the basics of drawing will help you support your students' drawings. Your ability to read lines and shapes gives you two languages through which you can talk with your students about their visual and written texts. Rather than say, "That's a lovely drawing," you may say instead, "Tell me why you chose to draw a curved line or arc in the background?" By asking such questions, you teach your students to look at and see their representations with new eyes, and you will encourage them to see relationships among and between the texts they read and the texts they produce.

Inquiry Into Color

- *What is color?*

- *What are some of the terms associated with color?*

- *What emotions are conveyed through color?*

- *What do the colors you choose for your environment say about your personality?*

- *Why is color important to ELA instruction?*

- *What does color tell us about our learners?*

Art Is a Part of Life: A Teacher's Story
by Michael Shirley

Art has always been an integral part of my life. As a young boy growing up in the mountains of northeastern Georgia, USA, I was surrounded by a variety of art forms and artists, like painters on the beach, that were a part of my everyday existence; I just didn't recognize them as being art at the time. My love for drawing developed into an interest in painting, and I was soon buying an assortment of brushes and a range of paint colors with which I could express myself. In school I was notorious for drawing both in colored pencil and graphite, when I should have been taking notes. I made colorful greeting cards, decorated book covers, and became a renowned artist in my own mind. The combinations and mixing of colors fascinated me, and I soon realized that these shades of color helped me to re-create those wonderful memories from my youth.

My landscape watercolor scenes express my love of my community. I can speak of my heritage and culture through my works of art because art is an extension of my personality. At times, my creativity surfaces with little effort, but there are times I struggle. I value my art because it is my own personal way of saying something that cannot truly be duplicated by another medium. The color palette I use for each of my paintings helps me to create the mood of the piece, which, in most cases, is a reflection of my own feelings. Even the manner by which I apply paint to paper or canvas—vibrant brush strokes or soft, flowing shapes—serves as a statement to the viewer.

Figure 3.1 *Michael's watercolor landscape.*

The visual arts have helped me understand my own literacy learning in several ways. I better recognize the need humans have for understanding one another. I tend to look at my environment through a variety of lenses of various colors that allow me to see nuanced differences in my personal and professional worlds. I have begun to realize a sense of freedom that artistic expression supplies. My watercolor paintings detail my own life. The painting in Figure 3.1 is simple but highlights the significance of the curved road that led to my house, the beautiful blue sky, and the dark green pine trees that graced the land.

Art was a strategy for creating a framework for understanding in school as well. I illustrated concepts in several colors, which helped visually when it came time to remember and study these concepts. Art also encouraged me to observe and think more closely and more critically. Art begs me to slow down and see things from different perspectives. Just as a good piece of writing gets a point across to a reader using descriptive words, so do the shades of color I use in a painting get my point across to viewers. Art is multilingual and multicultural, and gives us power to understand and to be understood despite language barriers. I cannot imagine my life without it.

Michael's story indicates the role that the arts played in his early life. For him, the arts represent enjoyable family experiences, beachside artists, representing conceptual understanding of content, and expression of self through his own inquiry. Now, as a county resource literacy consultant, Michael demonstrates to teachers how the arts support strong literacy practices. Both Jerry Harste's story in chapter 1 and Michael's story here remind us that single events or everyday experiences are often the impetus for further study in a discipline. Figure 3.2 shows a page from a book written collaboratively by ELA and art students from Fresno, California, USA, a project designed by teacher Marc Patterson. These students' illustrated story is based upon their interpretation of family vacations gone wrong, and inspired by Edvard Munch's painting *The Scream*. Their use of line, shapes, and color bring energy and life to this illustration. In this chapter, you will learn about color, explore its purpose, study color theory, and discover how color supports intended meanings in created texts and how color shapes interpretations in a range of texts.

Figure 3.2 *Collaborative ELA-art project, illustration based on Munch's* The Scream.

To begin, read and study Figure 3.3, painted by Kendra, a sixth-grade student. What comes to mind? What do you think of Kendra's juxtaposition of blue, black, and red-orange, horizontally positioned? How does meaning change when the painting is inversed? What texts might be generated from these two images? The first image reminds me of a landscape under a bright blue sky, while its inverse reminds me of a waterscape against a setting sun. Both remind me of

Figure 3.3 *Kendra's three-color perspective.*

the work of Mark Rothko, a renowned abstract painter who wanted his viewers to experience a range of emotions and thoughts as they read his work. Rothko often resisted talking about his work. "Silence is so accurate," he said (quoted from www.nga.gov/feature/rothko/classic2a.shtm), fearing that words would only stifle the viewer's mind and imagination. After studying Rothko's use of color, sixth-grade students were asked to generate an artwork using three colors (separate or blended) to create the atmosphere of a setting they imagined while reading a self-selected novel. The art in Figure 3.3 conveys Kendra's interpretation of the snowy landscape of *Woodsong* (2002), Paulsen's autobiographical recount of his participation in the Iditarod, an Alaskan dogsled race. For viewers of Figure 3.3, color and expression, as well as art as a sign system, offer the potential for many meanings.

Reading Color

Color is life and a world without colors appears lifeless. Nothing affects the human mind more dramatically than spectacular rainbows, breathless sunrises and sunsets, or the beautiful ranges of blues in lakes, rivers, and oceans. An element of design, color is central to our daily lives. Color permeates our lives from the colors in our clothing, to the paint or wallpaper in our homes, to the colors of the sky that inform our moods and actions, to the food we choose. Color also is important to our reading of literature. Like artists, authors use color to express ideas, convey messages, evoke feelings, and accentuate areas of interest in their texts. Think about classic titles such as *A Fine White Dust* (Rylant, 1996), *The Scarlet Letter* (Hawthorne, 1991), *Black Like Me* (Griffin, 2003), *The Red Badge of Courage* (Crane, 1990), and *The Color Purple* (Walker, 1992), or short stories such as "The Scarlet Ibis" (Hurst, 1988), or picture books such as *Brown Angels* (Myers, 1993) and *My Man Blue* (Grimes, 1999). For example, the fine white dust of Rylant's book is a crumbled white ceramic cross, which symbolizes disillusionment of faith. The scarlet letter on Hawthorne's Hester Prynne identifies her as a sexual being whose impure actions incite her community. Authors intentionally position readers to immediately associate what they know about a color and make interpretations about what these colors may signify before entering the book.

Knowledge of the use of primary, complementary, and triad colors can help you and your students choose and interpret colors that are appropriate for intended ideas and messages across a range of texts. To give another example, color captures the energy of the Harlem Renaissance. In a focused study on the Harlem Renaissance, middle and high school teachers studied a range of texts and music, as well as the techniques, colors, and expressions of artists and photographers (see Text Set for the Harlem Renaissance). They created their own interpretation of their learning. High school teacher Alika studied Jacob Lawrence's technique and use of bold colors and William Johnson's painting entitled *Street Life–Harlem*, and captured the energy of Harlem's nightlife (see Figure 3.4). For teachers like Alika, learning to express meaning across sign systems is essential in their own teaching and learning. Alika explains, "Visual representation is a freeing experience.

Figure 3.4 *Alika's interpretation of the Harlem Renaissance.*

My high school students learn to think symbolically, and at the same time, they learn about the potential of art to say something that their words cannot."

Materials and Tools for Working in Color

Common Tools

You have probably had a great deal of experience working with colored pencils, crayons, or colored markers in school or at home. These common art materials come in a large range of colors and offer you unlimited choices. Gather some of these materials as well as tempera, watercolor, and/or acrylic paints. When you select paints, choose basic colors such as yellow, blue, red, white, black, as these will enable you to produce a wide range of *hues*, or another name for colors. A *palette*, or a set of colors, of red, blue, and yellow—the primary colors—will help you learn about and understand color theory and how colors blend. Black and white will help you understand *intensity* and *value*, concepts introduced a bit later. Have ready inexpensive synthetic brushes of all shapes and sizes; they will allow you to work with the smallest of details and the widest of brush strokes.

Supports Needed

A *support* is any surface—paper, canvas, bricks, board, or even walls—an artist uses for painting or drawing. The support for painting is often canvas or paper, but paper is more common in the classroom. The range of papers is overwhelming and they vary in weight, texture, size, and color. The quality of the paper you use is important as it affects the way the paint is accepted by the paper. For instance, your sketchbook paper will work well with pencil, marker, and crayons. However, when working with tempera, acrylic, or watercolor paints, use a more absorbent paper. All of these materials can be purchased at art supply or discount stores.

You have learned how your sketchbook paper takes, or accepts, pencil. Now study how your sketchbook paper takes color using colored pencils, crayons, and tempera or acrylic paints. Choose one colored pencil and crayon, and create a gradation of color, moving from light to dark or dark to light, as you did in the previous chapter with graphite pencil. How does your sketchbook paper take colored pencil? Crayon? Now, with tempera or acrylic paints, paint on several different supports: a sketchbook page, typing paper, watercolor paper, newspaper, construction paper, drawing paper, etc. What do you notice about how different supports take color in different ways? Is one paper better than another for each medium? Does one paper feel better than another as you draw or paint? Which one(s) do you think your students would enjoy using? Cut out portions of these experiments and paste them into your sketchbook. Jot down notes about how different supports accepted each medium to help you remember how color and media respond to these supports. ■

Color Theory, in Brief

Contemporary color theory draws from the work of Sir Isaac Newton. In 1676, using a triangular prism, Newton analyzed white sunlight into a spectrum of colors, made up of seven colored rays: violet, indigo, blue, green, yellow, orange, and red. He organized these colors onto a *color wheel*, which is an arrangement of colors in a circular format. Johannes Itten is considered to be one of the foremost authorities of color theory. His 12-hue color wheel represents colors moving from *warm* (yellows, reds) to *cool* (blues, greens) (for an example of Itten's color wheel, visit www.siteprocentral.com/color_tutor.html). Color results from light waves, but the light waves are not in themselves colored. Nor does the object itself have color; the color is generated by light. For instance, when we say an object is red, what we really mean is that the surface of the object absorbs all light rays but those of red. A quick example might clarify this theory. A red bowl looks bright red in the afternoon sun; however, it may look a darker red in the evening. The light has modified the color of the bowl. Our attention is drawn to the way things appear under certain light and at a particular time of day. How light plays on colors can signify the difference between a romantic evening and a business meeting.

Colors are often divided into two categories: warm or cool. In general, warm colors—yellows, bright yellow-greens, and oranges—evoke warm images like the sun, love, relationships, and summer. Cool colors—blue, green, and violet—remind viewers of cool images like ice, grass, winter, and water. In art compositions, warm colors give the impression of movement toward a viewer's eye, while cool colors appear to move back and away.

As you learn about concepts associated with color, consider how color theory can be applied to literacy learning, especially writing. Knowing how to blend colors to create subtle differences is conceptually the same as understanding the importance of diction, or word choice, and shades of meaning in written text. The shades of difference between the words *stroll* and *skip* in written language are like those of pink and hot pink in color theory; both have similar qualities but encourage different meanings.

Three Traits of Color

To discover and express their sensations and emotions and achieve particular results, artists must understand three properties, or traits, of color: hue, value, and intensity. *Hue* is a color's name. *Primary hues* are red, yellow, and blue, and are termed *primary* because they can be mixed to create all other colors, but they themselves cannot be made by mixing other colors (see Figure 3.5a). *Secondary hues* are green, orange, and violet (see Figure 3.5b). They are placed on the color wheel between the primary hues, which can be mixed to make them. For example, blue and red make purple, blue and yellow make green, and red and yellow make orange. *Intermediate hues* can be made by mixing primary and secondary hues together. For example, primary blue mixed with secondary violet makes the hue blue-violet. An endless number of hues can be mixed to create new hues. Just think of the vast number of hues represented on paint chips at your local home improvement or hardware store. How do "Sunburst Yellow" and "Desert Sun" differ in your mind? *Complementary hues* are pairs of pure color that reside across from each other on the color wheel: red and green, purple and yellow, blue and orange (see Figure 3.5c). Complementary hues contrast the most and create excitement when placed side by side. They also enhance or complement each other—red looks redder next to green, and green looks greener next to red—and are visually appealing and harmonious. Triad hues are a set of three colors that appear

Figure 3.5a *Primary hues.*

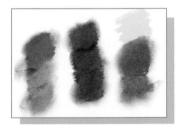

Figure 3.5b *Secondary hues.*

Figure 3.5c *Complementary hues.*

equidistant on the color wheel, and are considered to be a pleasing combination when placed alongside or in a group. The triad color schemes that you may recognize include the primary colors–red, yellow, and blue–and secondary colors–orange, green and violet. Combinations of triad colors are limitless.

Value is the lightness or darkness of a hue. When you look at a 12-hue color wheel (e.g., www.siteprocentral.com/color_tutor.html) some colors appear to be lighter and some colors are darker. In other words, pink is light in value while deep green is dark in value. The value of a hue can be changed by mixing it with white or black. When lighter values are mixed, or white is added, artists call these *tints*; light yellow could be considered a tint of yellow. When a hue's value is made darker, this is called a *shade*; plum is created by mixing red and violet and could be called a shade of purple.

Some hues appear bright and energetic, while others appear dull and sluggish. *Intensity* refers to the brightness or dullness of a hue. A bright color may be considered high in intensity while a dull color is considered low in intensity; "Sunburst Yellow" is high in intensity while "Desert Sun" is low in intensity. When you look at the color wheel, notice how there is higher intensity of hues as your eye travels from blue to yellow. When your eye moves from green to red, the intensity is lower.

The Color Spectrum

Part of studying color entails learning to see variations in the *spectrum*, or the range of colors. Look again at the color wheel and notice how yellow moves to green, green to blue, blue to violet, violet to red, red to orange, and orange back to yellow. Knowing the spectrum of colors is like having a visual thesaurus at hand; the shades and tints of hues that are used within a visual text invite viewers and readers alike to consider the shades of meaning. For example, consider this sentence: "Lady Lavender in the indigo house by a purple wood, cobwebbed by spiders in magic magenta" (Nordine, 2000). How does Nordine capture Lady Lavender's character through his distinctions between, purple, lavender, magenta, and indigo? Each of these hues has a slightly different shade of meaning when viewed in artworks as well as in written language.

Variation Through Color Media and Paper

Colored pencils, markers, crayons, and colored paper (such as construction paper or tissue paper) are common in your classroom and offer a good start when exploring color. Color carries meaning and visually cues the viewer where to look in the image, and each medium offers different ways to explore meaning. For instance, you can use colored pencils to create textures, blend colors, smudge, or add other effects. You can change the intensity of a color by layering another color on top of it. Colored pencil markings range from very bold hues to the lightest pastel, with every value in between, each carrying a different

Figure 3.6 *Anya (colored markers), Kim (colored markers), and Conrad (colored pencil) use color to emphasize attention and express meaning.*

meaning. Figure 3.6 shows three student artworks, those of Anya and Kim, fourth graders, and of Conrad, a ninth grader. Notice how Anya's use of colored markers enables her to create a strong and vibrant Easter egg. Her use of line, elements of shape, and contrasting colors helps viewers to notice each section as separate and beautiful, but together as a lively composition. Kim's use of hot pink marker, against the wide sweeps of yellow for her character's hair and dress, defines and highlights her barrettes and smile in her self-portrait. Conrad is able to convey evening with his use of yellow and orange in the lighted wall torches, against the blacks and grays of the stone wall. Anya and Kim use markers to create the bold solid colors that they like, while colored pencils offer Conrad more control with shading, light, and depth. Artists, like these students, intentionally use different color media to express particular ideas, emphasize features they want viewers to notice, and guide the viewer toward an intended meaning.

In the following exercise, you will learn the color spectrum by starting with one color on the color wheel and continue blending primary and secondary colors to create a composition that highlights the color spectrum.

Practice Exploring Color With Different Media

Choose one colored pencil and explore its values from light to dark. Notice how the force with which you press down on the paper changes the value of the color (as in chapter 2 when using graphite pencil). Also notice how the paper takes color when the colored pencil is pressed firmly or lightly against it. Now, take another hue—yellow, for example—and change the intensity. Brighten the intensity of yellow by layering a lighter hue of yellow. Lower the intensity by adding a darker hue of yellow onto the original yellow. How does intensity change your original hue? Now, hold the colored pencil at an open angle (pencil tip touches the paper) and then at a severe angle (pencil close to paper). How does each decision about the force and angle of the colored pencil change the texture, the line, and the meaning behind the lines you created? What emotions or ideas are evoked when you use thick colored lines? Thin? Smudge the lines you have drawn. Does the paper move color like it did with graphite pencil? Explore the qualities of colored markers and crayons. Which media offers more control? Which is more forgiving? More permanent? ■

Practice Composing With the Color Spectrum

To begin, use a pencil to create a simple composition that incorporates an artist's most important tool—your hands. Move your hand in any shape or anywhere on the paper. Outline your hand and then integrate and arrange other drawing tools like a pencil, scissors, paintbrush, or a protractor (see Figure 3.7) into a composition that fills the entire sketchbook page. Now, with your colored pencils, move from cool to warm colors and vice versa within each of the objects (see Figure 3.8). Blend the colors so they move smoothly from one color to another.

Figure 3.7 *Teacher's contour line drawings and initial color spectrum work.*

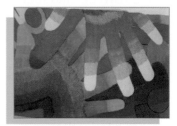

Figure 3.8 *High school student's study of color.*

What did you learn about moving from cool to warm colors or vice versa? How easy was it to blend colors, and how does the blending add interest to the pure color? What did you learn about a hue's value? ■

Andy Warhol: A Study in Color Spectrum and Autobiography

Andy Warhol was a well-known artist whose famous multiple color paintings of Marilyn Monroe, Jackie Onassis, and Campbell's tomato soup cans became synonymous with the type of art known as pop art. Warhol was fascinated with mass production and the public's obsession with it. As a result, he developed a silk-screen process by which he could convey his intended message of mass production by choosing a single subject and multiplying it in various colors. Warhol discussed his technique:

You pick a photograph, blow it up, transfer it in glue onto silk, and then roll ink across it so the ink goes through the silk but not through the glue. That way you get the same image, slightly different each time.... When Marilyn Monroe happened to die that month, I got the idea to make screens of her beautiful face, the first Marilyns. (http://webexhibits.org/colorart/marilyns.html)

Warhol applied color to various parts of an image—lips, hair, eyes. He used another color for the same features in an identical image.

To explore Andy Warhol's concepts of color, the shades of meaning that emerge in choices of hues, and the concept of multiplicity, teachers created their own visual texts using colored markers, colored pencils, crayons, glitter, and other color media with a focus on autobiography. Figure 3.9 shows teacher Ellen's rendition of her "colorful personality." Such exploration of color and autobiography enables learners as they try to imagine their lives, or even the characters about whom they read, in all of their complexity.

Figure 3.9 *Ellen's use of color and Andy Warhol technique.*

Practice Creating a Pop Art Autobiography

You will create your own Andy Warhol–like artwork self-portrait that encourages viewers to consider the many facets of your personality. Using a digital or film camera, have someone take several headshots of you and choose one that you like. Make nine photocopies of this image in black and white. Think about which features of your face you want to highlight with color. Choose colored pencils, markers, or crayons (or a combination, mixing media), and lay color onto these features. When you are finished with one image, move onto the other until all nine images have different colors. Using the floor as your frame, arrange the nine images into a composition that you like, thinking about which colors you want next to others.

Note the decisions you make about color and composition, and the relationship among each of these images. What hues from the spectrum did you choose? Which hues did you juxtapose? What shades of meaning did you want your viewers to notice? Also note your interpretation of this multiple presentation of yourself. How does viewing yourself nine times as opposed to one help you see yourself differently? What stories or metaphors come to mind? When you have completed your composition, tape the images together and hang the portrait on a wall. Take a photograph of it and put it in your sketchbook as part of your inquiry into color. Have family or friends read your image and write comments next to it in your sketchbook. What are their responses to your artwork? What did you learn about yourself that you may not have learned by just recording notes about your life? What else can you now say about yourself that you might not have been able to without the exploration of color and image? ■

Practice With Colored Pencil and Self-Portrait

You have just completed your first portrait composition using Andy Warhol's concepts of multiplicity and color. Now, consider all the portraits you have seen.

Figure 3.10 David Robinson, self-portrait; charcoal.

How are aspects of personality and mood conveyed by the artist? Read Figure 3.10, a self-portrait. What do you think David was thinking—or wanted his viewers to think he was thinking? How does he achieve this effect? David uses shades of black and white, smudging, eye placement, and gradation to convey his personality.

Adding color to your portrait can really liven it up, and also teaches you to observe how values change within one hue. This next engagement is designed to help you draw self-portraits or portraits in color that show personality.

Study the shape of your face as you did in chapter 2 (see page 43). In light blue pencil, lightly draw a contour line that defines this shape. Add in your features, keeping proportion in mind. Draw your eyes looking in some direction other than straight ahead (right or left, up or down; see Figure 3.11a).

Now, in light blue, draw in lines to indicate your hair and how it flows (Figure 3.11b). With a brown pencil, go over the blue contour lines. Add eyebrows drawn in brown. Draw dark brown lines above the eyes to show the eyelids. With sharp pencils, color in your eyes: the irises will be your own eye color and the pupils will be in black.

Lightly shade one side of your face in a value that matches your skin. If you have caramel-colored skin, begin with a light layer of brown and then add some yellow and white pencil. If you have pinkish skin, begin with a light layer of red and layer on some blue and white pencil. If you have a darker value, use a light brown pencil, and cross-hatch darker brown lines to give your face depth. Shade your lips in red or a combination of red-brown, and add some brown at the top to make it a brownish color.

Figure 3.11c shows an example of one teacher's colored pencil self-portrait. What do you think she was trying to capture in this image? What features does she highlight as significant in who she is? How does she want us, the viewers, to see her? Consider your pencil drawing in chapter 2. How would adding color change your viewing of this portrait? How easy or difficult was working through

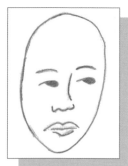

Figure 3.11a
Beginnings of a self-portrait in colored pencil.

Figure 3.11b *Self-portrait drawing in blue pencil with hair added.*

Figure 3.11c *A teacher's colored pencil self-portrait.*

this process? Do you like your final image? How does this self-portrait differ from your Andy Warhol–like artwork? Both use color, yet the effect is different. Reflect on these two techniques of using color in your sketchbook. ■

Colored Papers and Stylized Technique

As you have experienced, color invites exciting images through colored pencil, markers, and paints. Yet, another common way to add color in classrooms is with paper such as construction paper and tissue paper. Using color with these two media allows you the freedom to work with a swath of color to create a stylized image of yourself, a caricature, to show the essence of who you are.

Twentieth-century Italian artist Amedeo Modigliani's interest in African masks and sculpture inspired him to create stylized portraits in which the subject's faces are flat and mask-like, with almond eyes, twisted noses, pursed mouths, and elongated necks. They conveyed a sharp sense of the subject's personality. Al Hirschfeld, a well-known caricaturist whose portraits were published in *The New Yorker* and *Vanity Fair* magazines, captured the personalities of famous celebrities by exaggerating their features. Caricatures or stylized portraits (such as that in Figure 3.12) have been written, performed, and illustrated in literature including Italian *commedia dell'arte*, Greek and Roman theater, and Japanese Kabuki.

Figure 3.12
Albers's stylized portrait of friend.

Practice Creating a Stylized Self-Portrait

In this engagement, you will create a stylized image of yourself, or a caricature, using colored tissue paper. First, experiment with both colored and black-and-white tissue paper by cutting out shapes to change the value and the intensity of color. Lay red, orange, or yellow atop of a white sheet. Does the value lighten? Lay black underneath these colors. Notice how the value darkens. Now lay blue on top of a red or a green. How does the intensity change?

Next, to create a stylized self-portrait in colored tissue paper, you will draw upon what you have learned about portrait drawing. In pencil, draw an extended oval, circle, or rounded rectangle onto a large white sheet of paper to represent your face shape. Draw in very light quadrant guidelines to help you (see Figure 3.13). Draw your eyes and eyebrows in the upper part of the top quadrants. Draw a long, thin nose that extends from the upper quadrant to the lower quadrant. Add a small mouth below the nose. Draw in long, thin ears between the bottom and top quadrants. Add contour lines that represent your hair style. Erase the quadrant lines.

Figure 3.13 *Stylized features, with grid.*

Now gather various colors of tissue paper. Choose a color for your face, tear the size you need, and paste it over your stylized drawing. Edges of the paper do not have to be sharp or defined. In fact, allowing the paper to extend beyond the outlines of the lines creates an intriguing visual element to your image. Tear and paste colored tissue paper for your hair and other details (clothing, lips, etc.). You may want to work with just two or three colors and keep the image simple.

Figure 3.14 *Finished stylized self-portrait.*

When the glue is dry, go over the lines of your face and hair with a thin black marker. Notice how the colored tissue paper adds visual interest and intrigue and creates an atmosphere around the image unlike that of your colored pencil or complementary colors images. (See Figure 3.14 for an example of a finished work.) Look across your self-portraits and record how each of the media (colored pencil, crayons, and colored tissue paper) allows you to do and say something about yourself that the others do not. ■

To support students' study of literature and their connections to it, try to keep a variety of media in your classrooms as well as a range of color within each media. Different kinds of paints and papers can help students create a variety of images and also helps them tell unique stories about characters or about themselves.

Studying Skin Values and Autobiography

Marc Patterson is an art teacher in Fresno, California, who fully integrates writing and reading into his art classes. His students create a range of images and write corresponding texts including poetry, short stories, picture books (refer to Figure 3.2 on page 51), and narratives. In studying autobiography in art and language,

Marc invites his students to study skin values using the colored paper found in magazines (see Figure 3.15) and to create self-portraits in color.

ELA teachers with whom I worked study autobiography as a genre with their students, and paper collage self-portraits offer students a way to see how observation, attention to detail, and the relationship between image and word combine. Like the students in Marc's classes, these teachers created their own autobiographical paper collages. Using mirrors and referencing photos of themselves, the teachers study their own skin color and texture, jotting notes onto their contour line face drawings about colors. They search through magazines to find values and textures (matte or shiny) in colors that match their own skin. They tear out these colors and place them onto contour line head drawings, moving paper bits around to portray their highlights and lowlights. Once they are satisfied with their color blending, they paste down these paper bits onto their contour drawing. Some teachers add other objects, like flowers, to their autobiographical paper collages to create more visual interest.

Figure 3.15 *High school student's study of color and autobiography.*

This art engagement challenges teachers in terms of time, patience, and "getting it right." Kim reflects on this process:

> In doing this project, I thought about the times that my students get to a point when they say, "I'm done with this. I can't do this, or I can't figure it out." I got to that point. But when I put my portrait on the wall, I could see it coming together. But I could totally feel their frustration of...am I doing this right?

Although challenging, these teachers problem-solved their dilemma of "getting it right" and learned to see the qualitative relationships among art elements that Eisner (2002a) describes—colors, proportion, and composition. They also recognized that attention to detail is required to create a realistic self-portrait. Nicole states,

> I was thinking about my students' concept of skin color. They don't see black and white, but look at everybody's skin and say, "Well you're tan, and you're like coffee." Choosing the right values in skin is like finding the right words in language and writing, finding those shades of meaning.

As ELA teachers, we want students to study characters in literature and find the shades of meaning that the author intends. Character analysis takes time, patience, observation, and attention to an author's details. Studying relationships in art through color, especially skin color, challenges learners to pay attention to details, and engage in discussions that involve issues of identity, diversity and representation.

Working in Tempera and Acrylic Paint

Now that you have had some experience working with colored pencils, markers, crayons, and colored paper, you will begin to study color using paints. Tempera, acrylic, and watercolor are the most common in school classes. We will start with tempera and acrylic (you can use either) and later in the chapter you will learn how to work with watercolor.

Materials for Working With Tempera and Acrylic Paints

Tempera paints are the oldest of all paints, and are made by mixing dry colored pigments with egg yolks. Tempera paints dry quickly, so artists of the past had to apply it quickly with small brushstrokes. Tempera paints were used on prehistoric cave walls, Egyptian tombs, and cavern walls, but limited to red, brown, and black paints. You might recall seeing some of the simple but bold lines of the animals and hunting scenes in photographs of these walls. Tempera was the most popular paint until the 15th century when oils became a favorite medium. Today tempera is perhaps the most popular type of paint in school because it is one of the least expensive.

The pigments used for making acrylics are the same as for watercolors. The only difference is that the binder, or adhesive which holds the dry pigment together, is plastic. This is why acrylic paints dry darker than watercolors. Water is the solvent used to liquefy acrylics, and can be removed and worked while wet, but when it is dry acrylic is one of the most difficult of all paint mediums to move. Acrylics were developed in the 1920s and became the medium of choice for pop artists because of their brightness. David Hockney popularized acrylics in his representational or literal art.

When working with tempera and acrylics, consider working with supports (papers) designed for these wet media and good brushes. Although these media can be applied to many surfaces, avoid supports that contain wax or oil as the paint will peel right off. Cardboard, plywood, chipboard (sometimes found in junk piles at hardware or home improvement stores), as well as a strong paper for watercolors can be used. Synthetic brushes work well with these media, and they are the least expensive. However, choose those that have a good point. If you work on cardboard or canvas, you may want to invest in bristle brushes, as they are relatively sturdy and will last. There are four shapes of brushes: flat, bright, filbert and round. Choice of brushes will be personal, and you will know which brush works well for your paintings. Work with primary colors as well as black and white to create both shades and tints of these colors.

Paints come in all colors nowadays, so you should consider working with small tubes or bottles of paints just to see which ones you like, and which colors mix best to express your aesthetics and intentions. Right out of the tube, tempera has the consistency of liquid chocolate, whereas acrylics have a buttery texture. They both retain a good brushstroke, especially on good supports.

Practice Mixing Primary Colors

Paint allows for richness of color and, in my work with students, is one of their favorite mediums for expression. With your knowledge of color theory, start working with primary and secondary colors. Place dollops of the primary colors red, yellow, and blue on a Styrofoam plate or palette. Mix these colors with a toothpick or the end of a paintbrush by moving some of each color into the space between the three colors. Do you see the secondary colors emerge? What happens when you continue to mix colors? Which colors mix well and evoke strong emotions? Which colors are less desirable or clash? Now, using one primary color, add various amounts of white and black to change the intensity, or brightness or dullness, of a color. How does intensity change the meaning of the colors? When combined with white or black, red can produce a number of hues including chili pepper, coral cove, or rose petal. What ideas, emotions, or expressions might be associated with these hues? Explore other primary and secondary colors in this way. Come up with your own names for these colors. How does looking for shades of color also push you to consider the shades of meaning associated with them? Let the colors dry on this palette and keep it for future reference. ▪

Ken Nordine: Writing With Color

One of the most exciting connections among language, art, and music can be seen in Ken Nordine's personifications of color. In the late 1960s, Nordine was hired to create short radio commercials for the Fuller Paint Company for colors the company introduced that year. He wrote short texts, poems, dialogues, and narratives about paint colors, set them to music, and then narrated them. Nordine placed colors in dramatic and humorous situations and gave them life: "Lavender is an old, old, old, old lady, lavender is, aren't you? I thought you were. Lady Lavender in the indigo house by a purple wood, cobwebbed by spiders in magic magenta." These two lines offer students insight on how Nordine uses personification, repetition, color, metaphor, atmosphere, and dialogue in a single text. Furthermore, by using shades of same hue—indigo, magenta, purple, and lavender—he teaches readers about shades of meaning in both written and art texts.

Think about Nordine's description of lavender. What personality comes to mind, especially when he repeats "old" four times? How does he suggest setting and atmosphere with such imagery as "indigo house by a purple wood" or "cobwebbed by spiders"? As ELA teachers, we want our students to begin to think about how writers use shades of meaning in their writing, and how their words capture character and create mood. Nordine's playful use of language allows listeners and viewers feel chartreuse's frustration because it wants to "let green or yellow take over." He also challenges listeners to see color critically: "Flesh, as a color, is about as close to a problem/as a color can get," and that flesh hues "vary from complexion to complexion." Nordine's radio commercials are now available on a CD titled *Colors* (Nordine, 2000), and the picture book of the same name contains wild illustrations of his texts. Nordine's texts provide exciting connections among music, art, and language, and offer a gold mine of resources when working with art and language.

Practice Writing Colorful Texts

Listen to several of Nordine's texts at an online retailer like Amazon.com. Notice and study his use of written, musical, and visual language to create characters and stories. Create your own color by mixing various paints together, and give your color a name. Write a short narrative, dialogue, poem, or story about this color, and personify it. Also, draw and paint a portrait of a character that could be this color. Figure 3.16 shows Syretta's self-portrait, which contains an original color that she calls *Desert Yellow*. What follows is short text she created to describe this color:

The scrofulous sun, with scorching scrutiny,
coaxed Desert Yellow to crawl out from the
burnt orange cracks of the earth,
paled yellow from thirst....

Figure 3.16 *Syretta's self-portrait,*
Desert Yellow.

Creating character from colors can generate exceptionally original and carefully designed texts! ▪

Symmetrical Prints

Color is an important element in many writers' stories, and can support students as they learn narrative structure. *Symmetrical prints* are what they imply, mirror images on opposite sides of a paper. The process is simple. Fold a piece of paper in half, open it, and drop one dollop of a color onto one side of the paper. Then fold and smooth the paper, and reopen it to reveal a design. Add a different color dollop, fold the paper and smooth; reopen to reveal the new design. Repeat this process as many times as you wish to create a range of patterns. These prints can be as simple or rich with color as you or your students imagine. When you look at Figure 3.17, an example of a symmetrical print, what comes to your mind? What emotions are generated from the greens, blues, and whites in this print? Some viewers suggest that it looks like a flower, a butterfly, the hands of a gorilla, or a squirrel's tail. Do you see these objects or are there others that you see? Color within symmetrical prints can inspire an illustrated story, and can invite learners to study aspects of story structure including the who, what, when, where, why, and how. Symmetrical prints require little technical knowledge of art, and students often produce very complex semiotic texts.

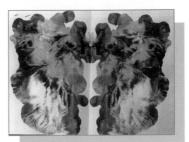

Figure 3.17 *Symmetrical print.*

Symmetrical Prints and Story Writing

As one of their first experiences with writing, Kay Cowan, a former K-6 instructor, teaches young writers how to think about narrative structure through symmetrical prints, and how color helps authors think of and shape ideas for stories. Kay begins by holding up a color wheel. She and her students talk about color theory, and how colors make us feel and experience the world in a range of ways. She asks, "If a character is red, what kind of character would she or he be? What emotions might she or he have? What activities would they participate in?" They continue this discussion across the colors.

Students then gather around a table filled with different color tempera paints and paper. Kay demonstrates the steps in creating a symmetrical print, described above. After the print is made, students engage in a discussion about the possible stories that can emerge from this print. *Who* might this character be? *Where* might this character live? *When* does this story take place? *How* does this character feel? How do we know? What character would be a "red" character? What facets of the character make her or him red? *What* is the conflict that this character faces? *How* does the character resolve the conflict? Students then create their own set of symmetrical prints and write their stories, as Chloe did in the example seen in Figure 3.18 (Cowan, 2001a).

Eisner (2003a, 2003b) argues that art enables learners to see and compose relationships among elements within a single text. Through this series of symmetrical prints, Chloe learns to see and compose relationships between her written and artistic texts. The story in Frame 1 presents Flow as a beautiful flower with two spots of yellow. In Frame 2, Chloe creates conflict linguistically—"the bugs came and ate her"—and shows how Flow battled the bugs. By Frame 3, Chloe resolves the problem—"the bugs went away"—and shows the bugs moving away from Flow. Chloe's visual text works well with her written text.

Symmetrical prints and use of color provide all writers with support to generate ideas about characters, storyline, conflict, and symbolism. Rather than

Wos thr was a flowr nemt Flow. Se had tow lefts. They wr yellow. Se had a log green stem.

Flow was so predy al uv the bugs cam and at hr. Flow ded nott like it. Flow wavt hr lefts and hi the bugs.

The bugs wet u way. Than ne vr wet tow bit hr a gen. Se was vayr happy.

Figure 3.18 *First grader Chloe's symmetrical print and story.*

merely ask students to create stories after they have read several, invite them to create their own characters and begin to think about how this character might respond in a particular setting. When students have such ownership in concrete characters, they can more easily construct stories, benefiting especially students with limited language skills or those who struggle with written language.

Practice Creating Symmetrical Print Stories

With a piece of paper that takes paint well, create your own symmetrical print using two or three colors. Think about color theory, which colors work well together, which ones express more energy or passion, or choose your favorite colors. Once your print is finished and is drying, begin to generate ideas for your story in your sketchbook. Who is this character? Based upon the colors you have chosen and the print design, what will the character be like? Where might this character be? What will its struggle be? How will the character resolve its conflict? In your sketchbook, write a story in which this character becomes your protagonist. To create a multipage book, work with the same colors and create different prints, working with placement of the dollops of color. ■

Compositions Using Complementary Colors

Like Ken Nordine, we often associate people's personalities and actions with colors: feeling blue, green with envy, yellow-belly, or red with rage. If you were to be a color, which one or ones would you be? We are not merely one color, but a composite of many. The colors we wear often depend on our mood or events in our lives.

As you learned earlier, complementary colors are pairs of pure color that reside across from each other on the color wheel: red and green, purple and yellow, blue and orange. These colors contrast the most and, when placed side by side, are visually appealing and harmonious. Beth Strong a teacher from Winnipeg, Manitoba, Canada, invites her students to study complementary colors, create self-portraits, and write autobiographical stories that work with these images.

Beth's literacy instruction includes not only reading and writing workshop, but an art workshop to support students' thinking and learning in both sign systems. Beth wants students to communicate across art and language to create the kind of texts they truly desire. Figure 3.19 presents a self-portrait by one of Beth's students. She integrates her knowledge of facial proportion with her love of purple and yellow. She blends these two colors to show where the light hits her face through highlights and lowlights. She changes value by adding white to the left cheek and the right lower jaw. She blends in black to show depth on the right side of

Figure 3.19 *Elisa's self-portrait, complementary colors.*

her nose. Simultaneous to drawing and painting their portraits, students work on written texts, like poems, narratives, personal essays, that work in synchronicity with their portrait. They learn that just as choosing the right shade or tint is important to their art, choosing the right word to express the feeling they wish to convey is important to their writing. Such careful attention to writing is what students learn with careful attention to color.

Practice Creating a Complementary Color Self-Portrait

Choose two complementary colors that you believe best fit who you are. To begin, draw only the shape of your head in black permanent marker on a large piece of paper (good for taking paint). Use thick lines as they will become your outline. On another piece of sketch paper, draw your eyes, eyebrows, nose, mouth, and ears in black permanent marker. Cut these parts out and paste them onto the head you drew in your sketchbook. The cut-outs add depth to the portrait, allow you to move the features around to position them proportionally before pasting them down, and also serve as guides when looking for highlights and lowlights in the facial features. Attention to these details will give your self-portrait qualities of 3-D (see example in Figure 3.20). Now, on one half of the face shape, paint one complementary

Figure 3.20 *Preliminary self-portrait with 3-D elements, before applying complementary colors*

color, and on the other half, paint the other complementary color. Try to blend the colors in the middle. Lighten the value of the hue by adding white to areas of the face that catch light. Darken the value by adding black to those areas that do not catch as much light.

Figure 3.21 shows Billie's self-portrait in complementary colors. What mood does she capture with the purples and yellows? How do her facial features help

 viewers interpret that which is on her mind? How does the dark background set the mood of the portrait? Consider her use of purple and yellow as contrasting colors. How does the color affect your reading of her portrait? If Billie had used orange and green, how would this affect our reading? After you complete your own portrait, reflect on what you learned about yourself through this art experience. How does color shape the details of your personality and features? How do others read you? Such analysis is precisely what we want our

Figure 3.21 Billie's self-portrait, complementary colors.

students to engage in when they read literature. Illustrating characters or themselves using complementary colors can invite students to study the complexity of human nature. Authors often write characters with a great deal of complexity, and often with contrasting personalities or characteristics. Consider Dr. Jekyll and Mr. Hyde, one character with two very distinct personalities. Or think about Francisco Jiménez's (1997) autobiographical story *The Circuit: Stories of a Migrant Child*. His life is rich with contrasts and complexities, from his difficult life in the Fresno, California, area as a migrant youth, to his success in high school. Studying contrast through complementary colors helps students understand distinctions within their own and characters' lives. ■

Working in Watercolor

Students enjoy working in watercolor. Its translucent quality generates feelings of impressionism and magic. Edward Hopper, one of America's foremost painters of the Depression era, used watercolor as a medium in many of his paintings during this time. Unlike regional painters, like Grant Wood or Thomas Hart, Hopper chose to depict not local culture, but the very soul of the country. The melancholy expressed in some of his paintings, often represented in cool colors, is similar to themes expressed in several of the writings of Sinclair Lewis, Langston Hughes, or John Steinbeck. Just as these authors depict melancholy through their words, artists paint emotions through color. Hopper's compositions are almost always about silence, deserted landscapes, lighthouses, against an immense blue sky or houses closed up after a summer's season. In Figure 3.22, *House by the Sea*

(Whitney Museum of American Art, New York City), notice how Hopper's use of cool values of blues and whites elicit a feeling of isolation. If this painting had been done in warm colors, or yellows, oranges, reds, and whites, how might the overall feeling change? Ed Young (1989), Allen Say (1993), and Stephen Gammell (Ackerman, 1992), illustrators of award-winning picture books, work in watercolor to create dream-like and imaginative story worlds. Say writes, "A Chinese painting is often accompanied by words; they are complimentary [sic]. There are things that words do that

Figure 3.22 House by the Sea; *watercolor and graphite on paper (Edward Hopper 1923-1924), Whitney Museum of Art, New York; Josephine N. Hopper Bequest. Reprinted with permission.*

pictures never can, and likewise, there are images that words can never describe" (www.vickiblackwell.com/lit/lonpopo.html). Combining watercolor images and writing offer opportunities to create stories that are rich in both color and character.

The unique properties of watercolor make it an exciting, spontaneous, and interesting medium. Watercolor, however, is not a medium to be mastered or conquered. Rather, think about how this medium, with its unpredictable and unexpected qualities, offers insights on painting a story you want to tell. You will enjoy working with watercolor because it will offer you unexpected effects. When these surprises occur, record them into your sketchbook so that you can reproduce these later, or show your students how you achieved these effects.

Materials for Working With Watercolor

There are two different sets of watercolor paints: *dry pans*, which is made up of dry pigment and is often used for outdoor work, and *semiliquid tubes*, which is wet pigment used for indoor work. Classroom teachers often work with dry pans, partly for economical reasons (less paint is used and it is easier to store), and for easier control of the medium. Begin with a small palette of colors, from five to seven, ranging from warm to cool colors. You can mix these to generate other colors as you need. You can buy watercolor paper in sheets, blocks, or pads, in varying thicknesses. Choose a paper that is designed for working with a wet medium like watercolor; 140-lb. weight paper or thicker is best because water will cause lighter paper to wrinkle. Inexpensive synthetic brushes of various sizes and shapes will offer interesting options for designs. Other materials to have handy include paper towels, cotton swabs, tissue, small sponges (or large sponges cut up) for adding textural interest, and a water container for rinsing brushes. These materials will support both texture and design, as well as easy clean-up.

Gradated Washes

Figure 3.23
Basic wash in blue.

One of the first steps in creating a watercolor landscape is to do a *gradated wash*, or a wash of color that moves from dark to light or light to dark. Gradated washes help you consider the setting, or the time, place and atmosphere, of the composition, and establish the sky and the ground. Notice in Figure 3.23 how the top of the paper is darker than the bottom. What kind of landscape might this wash generate? A storm? Sky over snow-covered ground? It is a good idea to have some composition in mind before you start.

Practicing Gradated Washes

When creating a gradated wash, have ready your palette of colors, a piece of paper that will support wet media like watercolor, and several containers with water for rinsing your brushes. The first step is to make your paper ready to accept color and to let it flow more easily when applied. Dip a flat, wide brush into a jar of clean water. Holding the brush at arm's length, cover the entire paper with water using a series of vertical and horizontal brush strokes. Let the water soak in for a couple of minutes. Now, with the paper propped up on an easel if you have one, or even clipboard leaned against a stack of books, to allow the paint to flow smoothly down toward the center of the paper, use a slightly wet brush (with water pressed out), and place it into the blue color to paint the sky. With a downward stroke, move the blue down the page. Again, dip your brush in blue and brush downward until you have covered the entire paper. You should notice that the top part of the paper will be darker because the brush contained more pigment and lightened as the pigment was carried down the paper.

On another piece of paper, do another gradated wash, but this time with two colors—one for the sky and one for the ground. Again, dip a wide brush with blue, but put less pigment onto the brush. Move the brush downward and stop at the center. This means you will use less color than you did when you did a gradated wash across a full page. When you finished with the blue, turn the paper upside down, and with green, do a wash on what is the bottom of the painting. Play with the movement of color. For instance, with a wet brush, dip it into another color and layer it onto the blue or green. How do the colors change? With a pressed-out brush, add just the color blue or green to the painting. Notice how dark the color is when you use a drier brush. With knowledge of and experience with washes, you are ready to start your first watercolor composition. ■

Painting Watercolor Landscapes

Many times, artists choose to paint exterior or outdoor scenes like landscapes, waterscapes, or cityscapes. Such work involves *perspective*, or using space and line to show depth. To create the illusion of *depth*, or the distance from the front of the canvas to the back, artists use space and arrange objects on the canvas in particular places. Distance, in terms of size and space, can be shown in a few ways. Artists overlap objects in which one object appears closer to you than the other. They also draw or paint objects towards the front of the canvas much larger than those in the back. Perspective is also achieved through line. When parallel lines move away from you, they seem to meet at a point and then disappear.

Where they meet is called the *vanishing point*, and is located on a *horizon line*, or the place where the ground and sky meet. Study Kathy's landscape in Figure 3.24. How do the size and placement of the tree, and the pathway help to establish distance? Do you see the vanishing point on the horizon line? It is placed almost near the center. An artist allows us to notice perspective by dividing the canvas into three distinct areas: foreground, middle ground, and background. The wide

Figure 3.24 Kathy's watercolor landscape.

path and the tree are in the *foreground*, the part of the painting that appears to be in the front or closest to the viewer. The *middle ground* refers to the objects or area of the painting that are in the middle. In Kathy's painting, the rising hill and the vanishing path are in the middle. The objects in the far distance are said to be in the *background*, behind the foreground and middle ground, and appear to be much smaller. The clouds and the sun are in the background. All of these elements contribute to the mood Kathy expresses and help to establish distance. What time of day is it in this painting? What is the impression Kathy creates in this watercolor? How do the various elements of the painting contribute to its overall mood?

Watercolor paintings have the potential to inspire many genres of writing, from short stories, to poems, to autobiographical narratives, to storytelling. For

Figure 3.25 *Candice's desert landscape.*

instance, after a short workshop demonstration in watercolor, teachers created their own watercolors, which inspired haiku. Figure 3.25 shows Candice's watercolor painting of the desert, and the following is her haiku:

The sun is orange
sets at evening's end
A lovely display

What do you think Candice wants to communicate? How can you see the importance of the desert in her life?

Practice Painting a Watercolor Landscape

Think of an outdoor scene that you would like to paint. Consider the objects that might be in this painting, the time of day, and the kind of weather. Choose your color scheme accordingly; for instance, a sunny, warm day will require lighter hues while evenings, early mornings, or storms will require darker hues. Now, on your paper, draw in the horizon line, and your objects (keep them simple) in light pencil. First, do a gradated wash for the sky, remembering to stop at the horizon line. Turn your paper upside down and do a gradated wash in a second color to represent the land or sea, again stopping at the horizon line. Return to the background, or the sky, and add some clouds, lightning, or even a balloon or two. Clouds are not pure white so you may want to add a bit of blue, and add a darker hue on the bottom to give them definition. Or, add small amounts of red and white to create a pinkish hue to give them visual interest. If you add balloons or lightning, consider how close they are to the viewer or how far away. The smaller the lightning in the sky, the further away it will be, and vice versa. Blend the edges of the objects so that they have the appearance of distance. Add a path or a road, perhaps in brown or black, which vanishes into the horizon line. Start with a lighter hue, and then continue to layer more pigment on to intensify the color, and to achieve the hue you want. Notice how the road in Kathy's landscape (Figure 3.24) is larger in the foreground and gets smaller the closer it gets to the middle ground, and then vanishes into the horizon line.

With a thin bristle brush, lightly define your horizon line with a dark hue, a brown-black or brown-green. Now, paint in the objects that will appear in the middle ground. They should be slightly larger than those in the background. Keep the edges blended to give the appearance of some distance. Now, move to the objects in the foreground. Add other objects—such as a horse, a building, a lake, a tree—that you want in the foreground. Paint leaves, rocks, bushes, and so on using a nearly dry small brush. The edges of these objects should be sharp and clear. Try using textures like small sponges, your fingers, or small crumpled tissue to add depth to some of your objects, such as trees or bushes. Your landscape is ready to be displayed! ■

Reflection on Working With Color

Reexamine Figure 3.2 on page 51, a page from a larger illustrated story about a family vacation and based upon Munch's painting *The Scream*. Do you notice how line and space are used to create the illusion of depth? Notice how the main figure in this composition is much larger than the figure in the background. Now, consider the color choices. What colors do these students use in the foreground? The background? What other ways are color used to direct the viewer's eyes toward elements of the composition? What feeling is conveyed by the colors in the image?

Overall, this image is a bit frightening and conveys a feeling of some impending doom. The facial features of the figure in the foreground look almost skeletal without hair, small dots for the nose, wide eyes and mouth. The strong curved lines in the sky and the water, in the middle ground, serve to create a dream-like quality. The dark colors in the foreground grab our attention, while the reds and blues bring us into twilight. Notice the strong straight parallel lines. They lead our eyes directly to the almost indiscernible figure in the background. What is going to happen to the figure in the foreground? What does the figure in the background have in mind? How do blues and whites of the water in the middle ground, juxtaposed to the dark colors in the foreground and the reds in the background create a mood, an atmosphere? Can you almost envision a story here?

As noted earlier in this chapter, this composition was created in the classroom of Marc Patterson, a high school art teacher in the Fresno, California, area. In collaboration with a teacher in the English department, Marc created this engagement in which both art and language students worked together to generate an illustrated story. Both groups met to discuss the sequence of the story, the characters, and the climax. Together, these students wrote a story about a family vacation gone wrong. How well does this single image foreshadow events to come?

Teaching students to use color provides them with another tool with which to explore elements of literature and language we value—detail and description. When we see Marc's students using color and composition to tell a story through art, we can also imagine a written story. Providing students with strong arts-based experiences will engage them in thoughtful and careful writing.

Harste (2005) argues that when we integrate the arts, we feed four underlying processes of mind: observation, analogy, generalization, and critique.

In large part, he suggests, we tend to gloss over key concepts and move far too fast in favor of covering the curriculum. Learning must be slowed down. We must *observe* the world. Working with color makes us slow down; it makes us consider shades and tints of color and how these convey shades of meaning in the visual text, as well as a written text that might accompany it. Cutting and layering pieces of colored paper to create a self-portrait, painting contrasting colors, or creating a landscape makes us slow down and notice the details we put into place and what we intend by these details. We become observant of our worlds.

Analogy suggests that meaning is at the center of learning. This does not mean simply that one object is substituted for another, but it is "a pairing through meaning. We can make sense of something outside our experiences by pairing it with something known" (Harste, as cited in Albers & Cowan, 2006, p. 517). The collaborative illustrated book shown in Figure 3.2 demonstrates students' decision to pair what they know about Edvard Munch's work with their everyday world of family vacations. When we create such analogies and metaphors through art, Harste states that we *generalize* about our world, or we connect what we know in language and apply it to art. We make "abductions, or leaps in our thinking, that allow new ideas to continually reshape our theory of the world" (p. 517). Abductions lead to divergent thinking, or generating a range of solutions for a particular problem, rather than convergent thinking, or coming up with a single solution. The net result is often a more creative perspective on the world (Harste, 2005). Marc's art students and the students in the ELA class collectively generated a range of solutions to how they might write and illustrate their book. When Billie contrasts her personal life and recasts it in complementary colors, or creates a stylized image of herself, she becomes divergent in her thinking; she generates a range of choices from which she selects details or ideas through which to present herself. *Critique*, or a constructive reflection on our work, enables us to look back against what we currently know, and work with others to outgrow ourselves and consider future work (Harste, 2005). This process of critique allows us to ask questions of our work: What did we like? What didn't we like? What did we learn from this experience that we want to integrate in future work? Observation, analogy, generalization, and critique, when viewed through color and other aspects of art-making, provide learners with important tools for future learning.

CHAPTER 4

Inquiry Into Three Dimension

- *What is three-dimensional (3-D) art?*
- *What media can be used in 3-D?*
- *What thinking is involved in additive or subtractive techniques?*
- *How does 3-D encourage complex thinking and problem solving?*
- *What engagements can I introduce to support literacy learning?*

How the Arts Are a Part of My Life: A Teacher's Story
by Kay Cowan

I received no formal art instruction in my schooling in the rural north Alabama, USA, of my childhood. However, I've been intrigued with forms of expression or communication since my earliest childhood. After school and during summers, my friends and I entertained ourselves by writing and producing plays, by drawing and holding neighborhood art exhibitions, and by creating three dimensional (3-D) pieces by sculpting with clay and creating models of structures. One, then another, and another of these art forms have garnered my attention. As I recall these experiences, I realize that through play, I learned basic visual and performing art concepts, partly because of my curiosity, but largely because of the generative nature of the arts. In school, I began using these different forms to communicate my learning. As my classmates memorized algorithms, I used diagrams to reason my way to the same math solutions. Similarly, while my classmates relied on verbal explanations to address science concepts, I built 3-D models so I could see solutions from different perspectives. The arts encouraged me to see more closely and to problem-solve by looking at objects and concepts from all sides. Further, I had to attend to the different details of my subject. These early experiences informed the future work I would do as a teacher.

Some 30 years ago I began teaching, and although no one around me was integrating the arts into reading, writing, math, science, or social studies, I quickly found myself adapting content lessons to integrate the arts. Initially, there was some resistance to my approach; however, when my students of all ability levels began to show significant gains in performance on achievement tests, I was allowed—even encouraged—to continue with my approach. Beyond gains in performance, integrating the arts into instruction encouraged a whole range of communication from students and also encouraged community. Once students created a drawing, a sculpture, or a play, they wanted to share it. They drew models and then created a variety of 3-D sculptures, puppets, and masks. In a series of arts-based minilessons that middle school students work through to strengthen their vocabulary (Cowan & Albers, 2006), they build papier-mâché masks (see Figure 4.1) and work with selected words in terms of their color and texture. At the same time they construct these 3-D masks, they study vocabulary and the importance of choosing just the right word. Within this art-language context, they get extremely excited, and often talk about being "on fire" (Cowan, 2001b, p. 122). The understanding that they gain through this process of working in 3-D makes a major difference in the quality of their writing!

When I consider the progress of my students using an arts-integrated approach to literacy instruction, I am convinced that as the arts become an integral part of our schools the performance of students from across ability levels will improve. Connecting content to the arts energizes the learning process; it makes the learning process concrete and increases retention. If we are serious about academic performance, our answers are to be found in the arts.

Figure 4.1 *Students' papier-mâché masks, unfinished.*

*K*ay's story reminds us that the arts are generative, not only in what they have the potential to say, but in how the artist is compelled to share his or her meaning with others. Kay's visual texts encouraged talk, both about its content and its making, and became a second language through which she could communicate her interpretations and ideas about learning. She designed and built models, wrote and performed plays. The arts helped her closely observe phenomena across disciplines. In particular, 3-D art enabled her to problem-solve, and to see how the visual arts could support the literacy learning of her students. As a teacher, Kay drew from her own experiences and study with the arts to create a classroom environment in which the arts encourage students to pay close attention to details, to color, texture, and form, all of which impact students' achievement and success in ELA.

Eisner (2002a) argues that the arts involve sensory knowledge, and our senses are "our first avenues to consciousness" (p. 2). The arts help us refine our sensory system and encourage development of our imaginations. Within a curriculum that supports imaginative thinking, learners take pleasure in exploration of the senses and the materials they use. Working in *three dimension*

Figure 4.2 *Papier-mâché mask.*

(3-D), or with images that have height, width, and depth, supports learners' attention to the senses, which heightens their "ability to perceive things, not merely recognize them" (Eisner, p. 5). When working in 3-D, artists always want to share with their audience how they achieved their effects, and readers of their art want to know these secrets. Read Figure 4.2, a papier-mâché mask created by Mary Lou, a teacher of seventh-grade ELL students. What feeling do you think she is trying to communicate through color, shape, facial features, and other art elements? How were the 2-D face drawings in chapter 2 different from this 3-D mask? What questions are generated from your reading of this mask?

From the earliest recordings of man, humans were carving 3-D images like *bas-relief*, or images that project slightly from the canvas, and sculptures. The earliest sculptors used stone, ivory, bone, and wood as primary media. The Sphinx in Egypt, for instance, is one of the earliest 3-D sculptures crafted from limestone.

In the last two chapters, you have been working with drawing and painting, trying to create an illusion of 3-D or volume in objects. In this chapter, you will learn to work in 3-D, in which space becomes important. You will learn about and use the tools and techniques that sculptors and artists who work in 3-D use. You will work in paper, clay, and mixed media. Eisner (2002b) writes that art is about breaking from rules and developing somatic knowledge, or knowledge that tells you when something feels right, a sense of closure. When working in 3-D, you will begin to sense when something is complete, especially because you will be examining your work *in the round*, or as it exists in space.

Sculpting Techniques

Sculptors use four basic techniques in constructing their work: carving, casting, modeling, and assembling. There are two basic qualities of these techniques: (1) *additive*, or the artwork is produced by adding to or combining materials; and (2) *subtractive*, or produced by removing or taking away from the original material. We will work with three of the four techniques, but *casting*, a technique in which melted material is poured into a mold, is far beyond the scope of many classrooms and therefore beyond the scope of this book. *Carving* is a sculpting technique in which media is cut or chipped away. In carving, the subtractive quality is more apparent; artists are left with less media than they start with. *Modeling* is a technique in which a soft or malleable material is built up and shaped, like papier-mâché and clay, and the additive quality is more apparent. *Assembling* is a relatively new technique in which different kinds of materials are gathered and joined together. This technique is additive in nature and is often associated with wood, plastic, wire, string, and any number of objects. Assembled sculptures are often joined with glue, nails, and screws.

Reading 3-D Artworks

Reading art means that we understand a visual statement made by the text maker. Speaking art means creating a visual statement through our choice of materials and techniques. Goldonowicz (1985) suggests that when we have trouble reading art, it is because we have yet to understand it. Reading visual texts, like reading artworks, suggests that we understand not just what the artist or text maker says, but how the message is said.

Examine the two artworks in Figure 4.3. What message, concept, or idea do you understand when you read them? What statements are the artists making? Which technique is used in each artwork? What qualities do you notice? Are they additive or subtractive? Which artwork do you like the best? The first sculpture is primarily achieved through assembly. After I had thrown the base, cylinder, and the individual pots, I assembled and attached the small pots onto the base and cylinder. This artwork has additive properties; I added small pots on a long cylindrical shape. My intention was for the viewer to notice the collective nature of clay; potters make a range and variety of different pots.

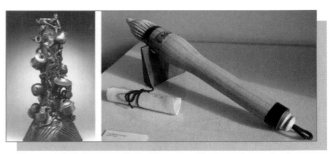

Figure 4.3 *Techniques of 3-D. Albers assembly, clay sculpture; Sandy Culp, modeling carving, assembling; clay sculpture, Atlanta.*

The piece is also subtractive, though. Notice the diagonal lines on the base. I carved away clay to create this texture. Adding and subtracting from a medium creates surprises for viewers; it gives them something else to consider in the whole piece.

Sandy Culp, a clay artist from Atlanta, Georgia, USA, uses three techniques: model, carving, and assembly. She models a clay slab to create the undulation in the handle of the paintbrush, carves the bristles, and assembles the two pieces that complete this artwork, a paintbrush and a rolled up piece of parchment. The style in which Sandy works is *trompe l'oeil*, a French term meaning to "trick the eye." The viewer sees a paintbrush and paper but, in actuality, Sandy has created a functional clay teapot. The water is poured into a small rectangular hole on the upper part of the handle, and the water pours out through the bristles. Again, Sandy uses these techniques to surprise the viewer. Artists want their work to intrigue the viewer and elicit questions not only about what the work means, but how it is made.

How art is made is all about problem solving. Sandy needed to consider the functionality of a teapot in order to determine the placement of the spout in relation to the teapot body. In 3-D art, an artist must ask herself or himself many questions: Which quality, additive or subtractive, is important to the expression? How will this be accomplished? How do the four techniques of sculpting add to the interest of the piece? As ELA instructors, we want our students to consider these same concepts. We want them to know when to add or revise a word, sentence, or idea. We also want them to know when to remove part of the piece and to understand how the writing becomes a more refined piece because of this revision. When you work in 3-D, you will learn the techniques and qualities to use as you build your own visual texts.

Working in Collage

One of the most common forms of 3-D work is *collage*, or a work created by gluing materials such as paper scraps, fabric, and photographs onto a flat surface. Writers actually create characters through the concept of collage: They give the reader snippets of information along the way, and readers construct a visualized image—a mental collage—of the character over the span of the story. For example, consider how Lee (1988), creates her descriptive collage of Boo Radley through the eyes of

Figure 4.4 *Eighth-grade boy's collage representing Scout Finch.*

6-year-old Scout Finch in *To Kill a Mockingbird*. Or think about Gaines's (1994) portrait of Grant Wiggins, the teacher in *A Lesson Before Dying*, who was sent to teach Jefferson, a convicted murderer, about being a man. Lee and Gaines layer details alongside or atop one another, and readers visualize characters as a collage of experiences, actions, and details. Figure 4.4 presents a collage that Charlie, an eighth-grader, created to show his interpretation of Scout Finch and where she lives.

Reading Collage

Although you might think that Charlie's collage is 2-D, the technique of assembling or adding images, one atop the other, defines it as 3-D. Unlike painting or drawing in which we see the student's original visual thinking, collage—by nature of using other people's photos, images, or everyday objects—encourages both the student and the viewer to suspend their disbelief and imagine that these images or photos could be something else. When magazine images are pasted onto paper, the student interprets the cut-out image, then pairs it, or makes an analogy, with something he or she knows. As you read in chapter 3, making such visual analogies provides a way for students to explain their intended meaning. Charlie's collage, for example, helps us to understand his interpretation of Scout and her surroundings. As viewers, we know these are not actual photos from this novel. Charlie chose these images to stand for Scout's house, her father, the camellia bush outside their house, and the books as part of her family's home library. Charlie uses analogy and pairs what he knows in today's world to the world 60 years earlier.

Notable collage artists include Romare Bearden, Aminah Robinson, David Hockney, and Bryan Collier. Greenberg's (2003) picture book, *Romare Bearden: A Collage of Memories*, illustrates both the art and life of Bearden, who used a variety of papers including matte colored construction papers, glossy photos, colored sheets of paper, wallpaper, wrapping paper, bright foils, and patterned fabrics to create his collages. The cover clearly shows Bearden's use of a variety of solid and print papers to give both texture and color to such details as the guitars and the musicians' clothing and faces. These collage elements invite viewers to understand musicians and their multifaceted and colorful selves as Bearden may have interpreted them, and how we might also understand them. In addition, Bearden altered the surfaces of these papers and other collage elements in a variety of ways by painting, both spray paint and brushed on paints, or sandpapering to roughen surfaces.

Robinson's technique, discussed in *Symphonic Poem* (Robinson & Genshaft, 2002) is simply called African American vernacular art, or art that is done with a sense of "a language that differs from the official language of power and reflects complex intercultural relationships charged with issues of race, class, region, and education" (p. 11). Robinson's use of mixed media (such as fabric, paper, paint, and found objects including shells, twigs, and bark) enables her to tell complex stories, especially inspired by Poindexter Village, the community in which she grew up. Her work is diverse, ranging from woodcuts to drawings to sculptures, many of which are made from natural elements or synthetic materials. Yet her collage work is inspired, and common people such as the Vegetable Man, the Iceman, and the Chickenfoot woman, were part of her life and she has brought them immortality through paper, color, and fabric in her book *A Street Called Home* (1997).

Many other artists have used collage to express elements that reveal to the viewer different aspects of their lives not always represented in biographies. David Hockney, a British artist, used photographic collage in which he combined several different photographs to present himself in the style of the Cubists. Collier (2000) uses Bearden's technique of collage as well as watercolor in his picture book, *Uptown*, a wonderful memory walk through Harlem during Collier's boyhood days.

Collages are exciting because they can be made from any type of material from paper, to photos, to cloth, to wood, to found objects. When working in collage, try to think about breaking rules, and moving your 2-D paper into a 3-D

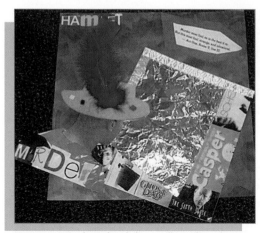

Figure 4.5 *Student's found objects collage of Hamlet.*

artwork. In the ELA classroom, creating collages can inspire students to synthesize information about characters, and reinvent them, through a range of materials. Greene (1995) calls such reinvention a release of imagination, essential in the development of creative minds. For instance, students can use objects to create a collage of a character, much like this student did for Hamlet (see Figure 4.5). She assembled feathers, felt, shiny objects, tin foil, magazine images, and written text onto a fabric square. Three-dimensional objects were added, attached, and moved both inside and outside the boundaries of the square. Her choice of representing Hamlet with a varied set of objects invites viewers to enter into and more fully experience his fictional world.

Practice Creating an Autobiographical Photographic Collage

You will work with digital or still photos of yourself to create an autobiographical collage in a Pablo Picasso–like style. Picasso's cubist work initiated new perspectives on how to represent objects and people. He is known for introducing art as an emotional medium, rather than as a need for representing a perfect ideal form (Penrose, 1998). His use of fragments of features and geometric planes encourages viewers to sense the freedom of expression in his work. Penrose (1998) suggests that Picasso "decomposes and destroys" the human form, but then reinvents "new anatomies" to synthesize a mundane reality with a world of dreams (p. 17). Like Picasso, you will also decompose and destroy various photos of yourself, preferably headshots, and reinvent yourself in photographic image.

Before you start, find digital photographs or have someone take photographs of your face from different angles, and print them onto photo or a thicker typing paper. Another option is to make duplicates of photographs that you have from different times in your life. Cut apart elements of these photos—an eye, an ear, one side of your face, different hairstyles—and arrange them onto a blank support (paper, wood, wallpaper, any support will do) into a composition that you like. This collage can express your physical features in a striking and energetic way and, at the same time, as you compose your collage with individual features, you will reinvent how you interpret yourself.

In the collage shown in Figure 4.6, Mary has reinvented her personality and disposition by layering various parts of her face onto other parts. Teachers, like

Mary, find such photographic collage exciting because "It leaves a lot of room for interpretation." Learners can work with this same technique to de-compose themselves, and re-compose themselves from a new perspective. Furthermore, this technique can be applied to character interpretations. Imagine how learners might interpret through photographic collage a complex character such as Edna Pontellier in Chopin's (1982) *The Awakening*, Holden Caulfield in *Catcher in the Rye* (Salinger, 1951), or Morrison's

Figure 4.6 Mary's photographic collage.

(1970) character Pecola Breedlove from *The Bluest Eye*. What angles or features would they include? What might their arrangement be like? This engagement may also be expanded to include everyday objects that represent the collage maker or the characters studied in narratives. ∎

Andy Goldsworthy: Nature, Inquiry, and Collage Making

Andy Goldsworthy, a British environmental artist, is well known for his exploration of, experimentation with, and assembly of various natural materials to create his artworks (see, for example, www.sheepfolds.org/html/info/info00.htm). Some of his art is dependent on the seasons of the year and weather. For example, one of his artworks may arise from melting snow at different times of the day, or he may rearrange stones found in nature to create his own artworks.

Winnipeg, Manitoba, teacher Beth Jones invites her first- and second-grade students to inquire into Andy Goldsworthy both as an artist and a naturalist. They discuss how he creates his art with his hands and found tools like sharp stones, quills of a feather, or thorns. They discuss the temporal nature of his art, especially with artworks that are built around melting snows and in natural settings. Ms. Jones's students tour their school site, and seek out natural objects that will become their found art. Like Goldsworthy, her students collect sticks, stones, shells, and flowers to create their own natural collages generated by found objects. While studying their collages, students write poems. Both the visual and the language texts are created simultaneously, both carrying the whole meaning. Nichola, a first grader, describes her art using lovely imagery and alliteration through her poem: "sticks squished beside pinecones with sand glued to it, circles everywhere switching stones in shells" (see Figure 4.7).

sticks squished beside pinecones with sand glued to it circles everywhere switching stones in shells

Figure 4.7 First-grade student's environmentally inspired collage.

Think like Andy Goldsworthy and venture outside to see how objects are situated in their natural environment. Photograph some of the natural compositions that you see. Study the relationship between and among the objects, and write words and phrases that describe these relationships and compositions. Now, pick up some of these objects (leaves, branches, bark, grass, etc.) and arrange them into a collage using any kind of support you like (the ground, cardboard, paper, metal, wood, bark, stone, etc.). What did you choose? What colors in nature did you choose? How many different arrangements or compositions did you make before you were satisfied with your image? Write a short piece, either autobiographical or narrative, or a poem. Such thinking is the somatic knowledge of which Eisner (2002b) speaks, the sense of knowing when you are done. Reflect upon the differences between a found-objects collage and a photographic collage. ■

Eric Carle: Collage, Color, and Creativity

Figure 4.8 *Teachers create their own colored paper with tempera paints.*

Eric Carle is a favorite storyteller and collage artist who has written or illustrated a number of books, including *The Very Hungry Caterpillar* (1981), *Brown Bear, Brown Bear, What Do You See?* (Martin, 1996), and *Draw Me a Star* (1992). His artwork is distinctive, and uses original hand-painted papers, which he cuts and layers to create warm and assuring images. In a video titled *Eric Carle: Picture Writer* (Searchlight Films, 1993), Carle describes the process through which he creates his picture book collages: He paints with tempera on white tissue paper, using a range of brush sizes, and small textured objects. To create texture, he scribbles onto the wet paint with the tip of the brush, presses small textured objects (like sponges) onto the wet surface, or uses his fingers to move paint around. He also uses a spattering technique in which he taps the wooden end of the brush against a straight edge toward the paper. This action sprays small flecks of color onto the paper.

Figure 4.9 *Emma cuts out, designs, and creates a page for the class-generated book on the Harlem Renaissance.*

Teachers in Figure 4.8 use Carle's technique, and design and create their own colored papers. They choose the colors and the movement of the lines that they want to make up their composition. The process frees up their minds to consider the variety of shades and tints within colors, and how such subtleties open the range of interpretive possibilities. In Figure 4.9, Emma cuts out the sun and its rays from the colored paper the class generated. She then glues individual parts onto her canvas, and ultimately creates a page for the class-generated picture book on the Harlem Renaissance.

Practice Eric Carle's Collage Technique

Using white tissue papers, you will now create your own hand-painted colored papers. Like Eric Carle, use tempera paints with lots of water handy. You will want to paint a number of different colored papers so you have choices in hues and patterns to use in your collage. Using the same technique that you did for a watercolor wash, dip your brush into water, and then into color, and paint brush strokes—wide and thin, straight and wavy—across the tissue. The tissue tears easily so you will want to brush carefully and use water quite sparingly. Add color spatters to create texture, or dip stamps or other textures (sponges, fingers, fabrics, lace, etc.) into the paint and press onto the tissue to create different patterns.

Once you have painted a number of sheets of paper, consider the composition you want to create. Perhaps you want to replicate one of Carle's animals, or return to your lion sketch or your pencil drawing of your cartoon character (from chapter 2), or create a landscape (like you did in chapter 3). Draw a light pencil sketch of your composition on a large piece of your selected support. Look carefully at your colored papers and decide which colors and patterns best suit this character or this landscape. Cut out the basic shapes of the composition from the colored papers, and glue the shapes onto your paper canvas. Fill up the pages with color, as Emma does in Figure 4.9. Reflect upon this process of creating collage. How does it differ from the photographic collage? The found objects collage? What did you think of making and designing your own paper? How did knowledge of drawing and color inform your compositional choices? Did you like exploring this technique? ■

Working in Papier-Mâché and Construction Paper

Like collage, *papier-mâché* is a favorite medium of all aged learners. Papier-mâché is a French term meaning "chewed paper," and it also identifies several sculpting techniques using newspaper and liquid glue. Working in papier-mâché encourages learners to develop their sense of touch, and think multidimensionally (Patterson, 2003). Papier-mâché encourages learners to problem-solve from a 3-D perspective in which the piece and the space around it are important aesthetic considerations. Learners must consider the additive quality of this medium, and make decisions about how elements of the representation are attached, how elements look in relation to each other, how to shape elements, and so on. Work in 3-D encourages in-depth and below surface analysis, the type of analysis we expect when studying characterization, or time and place settings in literature.

Techniques in Papier-Mâché

There are three papier-mâché methods—strip, drape, and pulp—and these methods can inspire one to create the smallest of objects to life-size figures. The *strip method*, perhaps the most common method used in classroom settings, involves tearing strips of newspaper, dipping these strips into a liquid glue and then applying them to a support such as a balloon, plastic or metal bowl. (Figure

4.10 shows examples of masks made using the strip method.) Wide strips are used for faster coverage and large shapes, and smaller, thin strips for smaller objects or details. The *drape method* is used to swathe a figure in clothing or create undulations in landscapes. The draping method is common in Mexican paper artwork (see Figure 4.11). The blouse and skirt on this sculpture of a female worker is draped over pieces of criss-crossed wood and shaped to create the effect of clothing. The third technique, and my favorite, is the *pulp method*.

Figure 4.10 Second graders' papier-mâché animal masks.

Shredded newspaper or multipurpose paper is soaked in a liquid glue, preferably overnight, until it reaches a pulp state. (Adding a couple drops of oil of cloves will prevent the paper from spoiling.) The paper can then be used to model into a variety of forms (see Figure 4.1 on page 79).

When working with papier-mâché, students must focus on detail, look at and understand the joining of elements, think about color and emotions, and think about line and shape (Cowan & Albers, 2006).

Papier-Mâché Mask Making and Descriptive Writing

Mask-making to generate strong writing is inspired by Kay Cowan and her work with students (Cowan & Albers, 2006) and is an approach I use when working with teachers to help them consider art–language connections. While studying strong figurative language, teachers create a papier-mâché mask and a personification poem. I use Brown's (1982)

Figure 4.11 Mexican papier-mâché figurine.

Caldecott-winning poem *Shadow* to demonstrate a personification poem, complete with beautiful similes, metaphors, and symbols. To start, all learners know is that they will create a mask and a personification poem. Together we prepare the papier-mâché mixture. While that sets up, we read and study Brown's writing style, and note where her use of figurative language is most powerful

> But Shadow does not sleep.
> It is always watching.
> If you open your eyes in your sleep,
> Shadow is there.
> It has already stolen back like a thief,
> and now it is spying on you.
> The eye has no shadow,
> but it sees Shadow stirring the embers until the log on the hearth crumbles without a sound and falls to ash.
> Ash has no shadow either.
> That's why Shadow is blind, for its eyes are two small heaps of ash. (n.p.)

We talk about this text as a personification poem, and note where Shadow, the main character, takes on human traits. To begin their poem, learners are asked to visually imagine a memory that elicits a strong emotion. They generate a list of words that they associate with this memory, and choose one with which they wish to work. Many choose descriptive words like *despair* or *confusion*, but others choose simply *happy* or *sad*. At this point, they may not have other words to describe the emotion. I invite them to consult a thesaurus to help them generate a list of synonyms, and then choose a stronger word that most closely represents the emotion in their mind. These words will jumpstart their own personification poems, in Brown's style, and also lay the foundation for their mask-making experience.

Three-dimensional artworks offer a different kind of insight on how meaning is represented. For the first time, teachers who work with papier-mâché are so encouraged and energized by their work that they share their masks with their students and they, in turn, want to create their own masks. Heather, a high school English teacher, invites her students to generate personification poems along with their mask. Nancy invites her third-grade students to create their own masks (Figure 4.12) and write their own poems. Timothy writes, "Agony is a broken bone beneath your skin/It moves around/Up and down/All around." These young children like Timothy can write strong imagery when mask-making is a part of the experience.

Figure 4.12 *Third grader Timothy's mask.*

Practice Sculpting a Papier-Mâché Mask

Before you begin building your 3-D mask, have the following materials ready: papier-mâché (pulp), a small mirror, the corner of a sturdy cardboard box (about 12" high), tempera paints, colored markers, paper for sketching and painting, and Brown's book *Shadow*. Read *Shadow* before you begin building your mask, and note in your sketchbook any examples of descriptive language that you really like. Get a feel for how Brown writes and expresses Shadow's range of emotions. To contextualize this experience, think of an event that generated an intense emotion in you, one that you want to convey. Using a thesaurus to generate your own list of synonyms encourages you to consider the nuanced differences between such words as *enthusiastic* from *eager, excited, keen, cheerful,* or *fervor*. Or consider the difference between *shocked* and *surprised, stunned, upset, shaken,* or *dazed*. How do these choices in words change meaning? Such an exercise helps students consider the importance of choosing just the right word to convey the shade of meaning that they want to present. Now, from your list, choose the word that best fits the emotion you wish to convey.

Now, make a face that expresses this emotion, and study this face in a mirror. How does your mouth look? Your eyes? Your cheeks? Note the highlights and lowlights in your face. Feel the undulations in your face. How far out from your face does your nose extend in relation to your mouth? Your eyes? Your cheekbone? Draw a sketch of your face in this emotion over the corner of a cardboard box, keeping in mind whether you want to create a stylized or a realistic image (see example in Figure 4.13). With a hobby knife or sharp knife, cut out the eyes and mouth. Depending on the emotion, your mouth may have an opening that curves upward or downward, or perhaps a small slit is enough, or perhaps the mouth will remain closed. Once this part of the project is complete, you are ready to apply a papier-mâché pulp.

Figure 4.13 *Sketching facial features on cardboard corner.*

Cover your cardboard with a thin layer of papier-mâché (as demonstrated in Figure 4.14). Build the skin up until you feel it is right (using your somatic knowledge of skin texture). Now, think about the shapes of facial features in relation to the emotion you wish to convey. To build the nose, for example,

Figure 4.14 *Layering papier-mâché for skin and building up facial features.*

begin with a hefty amount of pulp, mold it into a triangle, and then place above the mouth. Shape and smooth it into the bridge area of the face. Build in eyebrows, cheeks, chin, and other features that you would like, and which will help you convey your emotion.

Because papier-mâché is a thick medium, it can take several days for your mask to dry in the open air, but it can be more quickly dried with fans, in the sun, or in a warm oven (no more than 200 degrees, and not more than 30 minutes). While your mask is drying, think about what you now know about color, shades, and tints (from chapter 3), and which one(s) will best fit the emotion that you are illustrating. Consider how, for example, depicting an emotion with lavender will be different from depicting an emotion in purple. Understanding the concept of shades of meaning is essential in generating art and language texts that more closely represent your intended meaning.

Once your mask is dry, mix tempera colors to achieve the closest color you can to represent the emotion of your mask. Decide on the exact hues or shades and paint them on your mask. You may even choose to decorate your mask with glitter, feathers, jewelry, and other materials that will enable you to create a precise and imaginative text.

Part of learning a craft is to mimic it. Return to *Shadow*, and try to capture the structure and beauty of language that Brown does in her extended metaphor and personification. Study Brown's style of writing—her use of metaphor, simile, and symbol—and mimic it as you write your own personified poem about your emotion to accompany your own mask. What follows is a snippet from *Shadow*:

> But Shadow does not sleep.
> It is always watching.
> If you open your eyes in your sleep,
> Shadow is there.
> It has already stolen back like a thief,
> and now it is spying on you. (n.p.)

Figure 4.15 is a mask made by a teacher named Nancy. The following is an excerpt of the semiotic text she has titled *Panic*:

> Panic is a thief creeping through the night
> Silently, but ravenously searching for control
> Guard your minds
> For he has no boundaries
> He will find you
> Even in the most private places
> He feels no remorse
> Just Victory
> When he steals control...

Figure 4.15 *Nancy's semiotic mask*, Panic.

Notice Nancy's use of extended metaphor and vivid figurative language. Her language is alliterative, and she integrates metaphor and similes to personify panic. Nancy used pinks, lavenders, and creams to accent her facial expressions, and stylized these features to illustrate panic. She also integrated streams of lime green raffia for hair to give her mask a sense of disorganization. Notice how Nancy has integrated Brown's writing style and made it her own. Reflect on the process of making the mask, in relation to the emotion and colors you chose, and the poem that you wrote. How do visual and written language operate together to help you generate a complex text such as this? How did you respond to making a mask that is so engaging?

Upon completion of these semiotic texts, you could perform your written piece, and engage in literature and process discussions about the texts, as well as pedagogical talk about classroom applications with your colleagues. Kandace, a teacher in one of my workshops, talks about her mask, pictured in Figure 4.16:

Figure 4.16
Kandace's semiotic mask, Exuberance.

My emotion was "exuberance." I wanted the smile to be the biggest part of my mask. I thought about shadowing and where facial features should be. I wanted to define my cheekbones and nose and eyebrows, and tried to make my eyes have normal eyelids. When I painted it, I tried to shade it a little bit, where the light would hit. I then put hair on it. I loved the way it turned out, except I didn't like how empty the eyes looked. For such a happy face there should be bright eyes. This is such a wonderful idea for my 7th graders who study Africa. I'd like to have them make 3-D masks like these, and then create texts based on their inquiry and perform them. ■

Techniques in Construction Paper

You may not have considered construction paper as having the potential for 3-D, but many interesting faces and objects can be made from this medium using some simple techniques like cutting and pasting. David Wisniewski, illustrator of *Golem* (1996) and *The Wave of the Sea-Wolf* (2005), cuts his characters from a range of construction papers. To attempt this, students can design their own characters for a story, sketch them out, and paste them onto a magazine exterior scene, or they can paint their own backdrop. When studying literary texts, especially those with abstract concepts of love, envy, or greed, students can examine the range of works by Frank Stella (see www.artnet.com/artist/ 16079/frank-stella.html). Invite them to study his forms, and replicate them in paper. Another project might be to invite students to create a paper mobile, based upon events in a narrative, an art form that many students enjoy. Students generate symbol or objects that stand for events, and using wire, a freestanding base, or other support, they problem-solve how to present these objects in a way that tells the story.

One project that I especially enjoy is generating a 3-D mask based upon a favorite literary character, create stylized masks to teach exaggeration, satire, parody, or to create an original text. Figure 4.17 shows the basic cuts you can use to craft a construction paper mask. In general, you will make three distinct area cuts: the cheekbones and chin, nose, and the eyes. The cuts for the cheekbones and chin are made approximately 1/3 of the way from the top and from the bottom. For the nose, there are two cuts, both about at a 45-degree angle in the bottom corners of the piece of paper. To create 3-D, fold the top part of the paper twice on each side, with the flat side of one fold taped or pasted to the face of the mask. The eyes have two cuts on either side of a horizontal oval. These cuts may need to be adjusted based upon the emotion you want your mask to convey. As with papier-mâché, working with construction paper invites us to consider how visualizing, writing, performing, listening, reading, revision, and so on, must operate together and be made available to students as they construct various types of texts.

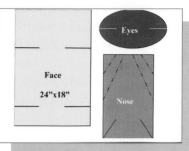

Figure 4.17 *Various cuts and folds for construction paper masks.*

Practice Making a Construction Paper Mask

For this project, you will need several large sheets of colored construction paper—one at least 24" x 18" (for the head), and several smaller scraps (for the nose, eyes, hair, eyelashes, etc.)—plus scissors, glue, and tape. Before you begin your mask, get a feel for this technique by trying the cuts shown in Figure 4.17. Use typing paper so that you will not waste any of your construction paper.

Rather than create a personal mask, you'll create a mask for a character in a literary text. Choose a character, and as you did in the papier-mâché experience, think about words you might associate with this character; use a thesaurus, if necessary, to find strong descriptive words. Now, consider the key character trait you want to capture, whether you want the mask stylized or realistic, how this decision informs where features will fall on the face, and how color choice will reflect this character at a particular time in the written text.

On a 24" x 18" sheet of construction paper (which will become the face of your mask) move your scissors just over 1/3 the way down from the top of the paper. (Refer again to Figure 4.17 as needed.) Cut a straight line toward the center about 1/3 of the way in on both sides. Now make two similar cuts for the chin area, 1/4 of the way up from the bottom on both sides. Fold over the edges of the cheekbone cuts and see how you like the shape of your mask. You may have to trim the edges a bit at a time to get the shape you want. Once you are satisfied, you can glue one fold over the other. You should have cheekbones that are now 3-D. Do the same for the chin, keeping in mind that deeper cuts make more severe angles. (To make a severe and very pointed chin, move your scissors to bottom center of the paper, and make a cut 1/3 the way up toward center. Trim around your mask to make the head more rounded, if this is the effect you want.)

To cut your 3-D facial features, use scrap pieces of construction paper. To make the eyes, cut the shape of the eye that you want—an oval, circle, rectangle, etc. Cut a slit on each side of the eye, about 1/3 the way across. Fold the slits and trim if necessary, and glue the two folds together. Notice how the eyes now have depth. Do the same with the pupil and iris, choosing colors that you want, and glue together. Cut the mouth into the shape you want, and then cut slits on opposite sides. Create depth with a black pen to separate lips or create an opening. With the nose, cut a rectangular shape of the size that you want. On the bottom edge and in both corners, cut a slit about one inch toward the center (see Figure 4.17). Fold over the two edges, glue together, and trim if necessary. Fold the sides of the rectangle toward the center to make a triangle. Fold each of these two folds again so that you can glue this nose onto the face. Any kind of hair can be added—paper ribbons that are curled with a scissors' edge, curled holiday ribbon, yarn, or Easter basket grass. Your imagination offers many choices (see Figure 4.18 for examples of teachers construction paper masks).

Figure 4.18 *Teachers' construction paper masks.*

Reflect on your process in making this mask. What problems needed to be solved to make this mask work? How did you have to rethink dimension for the facial features? How was your cutting technique? How did your knowledge of shape, form, color, line, and facial proportions help you solve problems of proportion in working in 3-D? Jot your notes in your sketchbook.

Once you are satisfied with your mask, write a descriptive piece, narrative, or poem about the character and trait you represented. For instance, teachers created a variety of masks (shown in Figure 4.18), and performed their written poems as Readers Theatre.

Vickie, an English teacher participating in one of my workshops, considered the characteristics of Ophelia in Shakespeare's *Hamlet*. An immediate word that came to mind was *crazy*. Consulting the thesaurus, she came up with alternate words, *wild*, *passionate*, *fanatical*, and *mad*. She chose *mad*. She then chose colors she thought represented Ophelia and madness, and created a 3-D construction paper mask based upon her interpretation of this character (see the middle mask pictured in Figure 4.18). As part of the representation, she wrote a short dramatic text (excerpted) in a Shakespearean's style: "Oh, Hamlet, my love doth/make you mad! How soest?/But will it not also make thee sane?" ■

Working in Clay

Warren McKenzie, a renowned potter from Minneapolis, Minnesota, USA, writes, "Let the pots speak" (Lewis, 1991, p. 23). He is right. Pots *do* speak. With a quick turn of the wheel or a pressed texture onto the surface of clay, potters convey multiple meanings through the vessels they make. The language of pottery is as old as human history. Shards excavated by archeologists are older than writing and tell many stories of their use. In my ELA classes, I often use potters' clay, instead of modeling clay or play dough, to support learners as they conceptualize holistic meanings of texts, as visual metaphors for interpretation of texts, and as a way to express concepts about text. Clay is one of the most generative and sensuous of media with which to work; it is malleable and offers the learners multiple opportunities to revise their representations. Further, clay offers interesting problem-solving situations, especially in terms of how to attach elements, how to create texture, and how to keep the object from collapsing. Because the artist's hands are the most important tools, meaning must be both visualized and *felt*; a clay artist must feel when the object is right—in texture, weight, and balance.

Clay and Transmediation

In my work with teachers and students of all ages, I often use clay to demonstrate transmediation, a semiotic strategy in which learners retranslate their interpretation of a text or a theme being studied from one media to another. For example, transmediation occurs when a learner reads a literature text and retranslates his or her interpretation through clay, paints, pencil, markers, or found objects. Transmediation encourages symbolic and metaphoric thinking, and clay as a medium allows the learner to rework ideas easily.

In an arts-based workshop in Toronto, Ontario, I invited teachers in Jerry Harste's graduate course in multimodality to express their interpretation of Bradby's *More Than Anything Else* (1995). Figure 4.19 shows Jerry's clay sculpture that represented his critical interpretation of Bradby's book, especially in light of African Americans' ongoing efforts to escape the impenetrability of racism and inequality. Although written language can communicate some aspect of his interpretation, the physical weight of this sculpture (nearly 10 pounds) was oppressive—perfect for expressing the weight of

Figure 4.19 Jerry Harste's clay sculpture.

oppression that Jerry wanted to communicate. As a medium, clay offered Jerry a way to express meaning that was not easily expressed through written language. As you read his sculpture, what sculpting techniques (carving, modeling, assembling) do you think he used? Does it have additive or subtractive qualities or both? How did he form the hat? The face? The arms?

A lump of clay, as benign as this may sound, has the potential to offer choices in how it is worked, and supports a large range of responses because of its malleability. Such choices and opportunities encourage learners to move beyond the simple techniques of working in clay, and into areas of imagination that might not be tapped with other resources or media.

Materials and Techniques in Clay

Materials that you will need to work in clay include potter's clay, which can be purchased at art or hobby stores; common tools like toothpicks and plastic forks and spoons; textured objects such as the bottoms of your shoes, discarded kitchen tools, rocks, various types of lace, plastic doilies, newspaper, and water. I recommend using potter's clay because it is firm and holds together well; other molding materials, like play dough, do not have the same malleable properties as clay, are less easy to work with, and are somewhat oily. There are many different *clay bodies*, or types of clay, including porcelain, stoneware, raku, and lizella. You can ask for the *end run*, or the clay that has a mix of two types of clay, and costs about half as much as a single clay body. Clay is commonly sold in 25-pound or 50-pound bags, and this amount is enough for your class. However, to experiment with this medium on your own, ask your school's art teacher if she or he can give you a few pounds. Furthermore, the art teacher may have a *kiln* in which your piece or pieces can be *fired*, or baked, once completed.

Take some clay and get a sense of how it feels, how it moves, and the spontaneous shapes that can be made from this play. In your sketchbook, draw several sketches of objects you may want to make with clay. Let your imagination and your problem-solving sense guide you, and look at some clay books that demonstrate how to sculpt a variety of different objects. I look for inspiration in trade journals like *The Clay Times*, *Ceramics Monthly*, or *Pottery Illustrated*. These journals are full of beautiful photos of the many types of pottery that can be thrown or sculpted from clay.

Hand-building, or shaping clay by hand, is the most ancient method of making pottery. When the potter's wheel was invented, the making of symmetrical forms was made easier and faster, yet all forms that can be made on the wheel can be made by hand. Hand-building, however, allows a clay artist to make many more forms than those than can be made on the wheel. Those who work in clay and primarily do sculpture are called hand-builders. Hand-building is often talked about in contrast to *throwing*, or creating pottery on a wheel. Potters are clay artists who do their work on an electric wheel or kickwheel. Throwing on a wheel really demands outside instruction and access to a wheel, so we will focus solely on hand-building, a process easily used in the classroom and extraordinarily versatile.

In hand-building, no one technique is exclusively used; potters integrate knowledge of the pinch, coil, and slab techniques to create their art. However, you will work with each of these to give you experience with the techniques. Have about one to two pounds of clay available to work with each of these techniques.

Practice the Pinch Technique

The *pinch* technique is just as it sounds: you pinch the clay into shapes. One of the first and most basic forms that hand-builders learn is the pinch pot. Earl Baum, a clay artist from Atlanta, Georgia, has become known for his pinch pots, which he calls "beggars bowls" (see Figure 4.20). These are bowls made by using your hands to pinch the clay to create thin sidewalls and a thin rim. Hand-builders always have in mind the function of a piece when they create (but also allow for the clay to inspire new elements while the sculpture is made). For Earl, beggars bowls can be used to hold liquids or solids, or can be displayed as art. These bowls are functional, and with some texture, become beautiful forms.

Figure 4.20 *Earl Baum's pinch pots, or "beggars bowls."*

To make a pinch pot, examine Figure 4.21, a series of three photographs taken of Ingrid Weishofer demonstrating how pinch pots are made from a ball of clay. Pinch pots can be shallow, in which the clay is pushed out to a nearly flattened shape, or tall and thin, and any depth in between. The type of pinch pot you choose to make depends on its use.

Figure 4.21 *Ingrid Weishofer sculpting a pinch pot.*

To create your pinch pot, first roll clay around in your hands until you have a ball about the size of a large plum. Hold the ball of clay in the palm of one hand and press your thumb into the center of the clay. Rotate the clay ball, pressing your thumb against the inside wall of the clay. Continue to rotate the clay while you gently press the wall between your thumb on the inside and the first two fingers on the outside. Notice how the wall of the clay is getting thinner and the walls higher. Also, notice how you begin to "see" with your fingers; your fingers will tell you when the wall of the clay is too thin or too thick. The top of the pinch pot will be somewhat uneven. To make the rim more even, turn the pot upside down and gently press it onto a flat surface covered with soft material, like a dish towel or newspaper. You can create larger more rounded, oval shaped bowls if you wish by using larger chunks of clay. As you finish your first pinch pot, consider its function. How could it be used? Position it upside down, on its side, square the rounded edges. How does this change the aesthetic of the pot? How does it change its function? ■

Practice the Coil Technique

Like the pinch technique, the *coil* technique is an ancient method of making pottery but allowed for the making of large containers. Coiling is the process of building a pot by adding separate coil rings atop one another. Examine the photographs of Ingrid Weishofer creating coil pots in Figure 4.22 to get a sense of this technique. To start, take a piece of clay and roll a sausage shape between your hands, or roll it out onto a hard surface covered with newspaper. Start rolling the clay from the center of the coil. Gently but firmly with the palm and the lower flat part of the fingers, roll the clay in a continuous outward movement. With each

pass of your hands over the coil, the coil should become thinner and longer. Make several coils at once; this will allow you to work continuously on your pot. The thickness of the coils depends on the purpose that you have in mind for them. For example, if you want a

Figure 4.22 *Ingrid Wieshofer sculpting a coil pot.*

delicate pot, thin coils may be better than thick; for larger pots, such as flower pots, you will want to use thicker coils.

To make a base for your pot, cut out a flat, circular piece of clay, about 1/4-inch thick. Take your first coil, place it on top of and just inside the rim of the base, and wrap it around until the ends of the coils meet. If the ends overlap, pinch off the excess. The first coil should be the largest because it is a foundation for the rest, linking the base and the evolving sidewalls of the pot. Think about the shape of the pot you want to make. If the pot has an outward movement, each subsequent coil should have a slightly larger circumference than the previous one. Conversely, for a pot that moves inward each subsequent coil should have a slightly smaller circumference than the previous one. It is important that each coil, when wound around, should be well lubricated with water (but not too much water; clay becomes very slippery with water). This will glue the coils together. To smooth out the inside and outside sidewalls, you can use the backside of a plastic or metal spoon. Support the inside of the coil sculpture with your fingers while you smooth the outside walls of the coils with the spoon; conversely, support the outside walls while you smooth the inside. With the coil technique, you can create decorative plates, small teapots, jars with lids, or sculptures such as busts and figures. Notice how in Figure 4.23, a sixth-grade student, in her clay representation of Daphne from the Greek myth "Apollo and Daphne," uses the coil technique to sculpt the arms and staff, while she uses the pinch technique to form the skirt. She has figured out how to keep her figure upright by using thicker coils for the legs and thinner coils for the arms. ■

Figure 4.23 *Sixth-grade student's use of clay techniques.*

Practice the Slab Technique

The *slab* technique offers a great deal of versatility, and can allow you to build large pieces quite quickly. A slab is a slice or sheet of clay. Creating sculptures from slabs works well especially when you want to build objects with straight sides and objects with texture. Slabs can be cut into any shape or size, and can be used to make cylinders. In the sculpture pictures in Figure 4.24, the artist, Earl, has drawn much of his inspiration from the environment of the Southwest region of the United States, particularly New Mexico. Notice how the slabs function as the floor, walls, table, and door. Earl uses the pinch technique to make his chimenea and the small bowl on the table. Notice how he carves into the sidewalls so that individual bricks are visible.

Figure 4.24 *Earl's work with slabs.*

To work with slabs you will need to have a few tools: a straight edge or ruler; a hobby knife; textured tools such as a fork, a meat tenderizer, strainer, or anything that raises or indents the smooth surface of the clay; and a rolling pin. Take a ball of clay, place it on some newspaper, and flatten it slightly. With a rolling pin, roll it into various thicknesses, alternating directions, and starting from the center. Notice how strong thicker slabs are and how weak thinner slabs are. Occasionally lift the slab from the newspaper so the paper doesn't stick to the clay. When the slabs are at your desired thickness, place them on flat surfaces like cardboard, or tables lined with plastic or newspaper. ■

Practice Animal Shapes in Clay: Sculpting Frogs

Students enjoy making, drawing, or painting animals, and in this section, you will learn to sculpt a frog, drawing upon all three sculpting techniques. Joe Bova, a clay artist from Santa Fe, New Mexico, USA, has made a name for himself making animals from clay slabs, amphibians and reptiles, in particular. Before he sculpts, he studies the physical features, nature, and behavior of animals. He considers how they respond in the wild–if they are under attack by a predator, or if they are

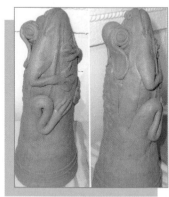

Figure 4.25 *Clay frog, Joe Bova.*

the predator. He wants the reader to know his animals' purpose: Are they hunting? Resting? Fleeing? Study Bova's frog in Figure 4.25, and consider the physical elements he includes. Notice that the frog's body blends into a cylinder on which it sits. Notice the lines of the frog's arms and legs, the eyes, and the textured belly. Now think about the elements you want to include in your sculpture. You may want to gather a few images of frogs to get an overall sense of what they look like, their shapes, their features.

To sculpt a frog, roll out two small slabs of clay, around 8 inches, and cut them so that they take a rounded teardrop shape. Put one slab aside. With the other slab, create several ridges with the edge of the rolling pin. This will be the frog's back. Any alteration of the smooth surface is called *texturing*, which adds life to what can otherwise be a boring surface. Textures can be created from shoe bottoms, kitchen tools, wooden/plastic stamps, or lace fabric. Notice the texture of the ridges in Figure 4.26 that bring life to the frog's back. To create the bumpy

Figure 4.26 *Adding texture to frog's skin with blunt tip.*

surface of a frog's skin, hold the slab that will become the frog's back gently in your hands, and with the wooden end of a paint brush, poke into, but not through, the underside of the clay to raise small round bumps. To give volume to the frog, hold the slab upright and gently push out the slab with your fingers, as shown in Figure 4.27. With this done, set this slab aside onto a soft surface such as a towel. Take the other slab into your hands, and to create the frog's belly, add volume to this slab and set it aside on the soft surface. You should now have two slabs that have shallow bowl shapes which, together,

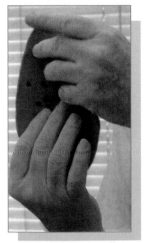

Figure 4.27 *Giving frog volume.*

form the body of your frog. Let these slabs set up in the open air for about an hour, after which the slabs should feel stiff but not brittle.

Now you are ready to join these two slabs. To make slab walls stay together, you will need to score and slip the surfaces of the clay you want to join. Take the belly of the frog and place it curved side down, into your cupped hand. With a plastic fork, *score*, or make small cross-hatched scratches, on the edges of the slab. Do the same with the edges of the frog's back. Now, wet your index finger, and move water across the scored edges. The water and clay together create a glue or *slip*. Place the frog's back gently onto the frog's belly, edge to edge, and seal the edges by running a wet index finger around the seams. With the slabs joined, you will now add eyes, nostrils, mouth and legs.

To sculpt the eyes, take a small ball of clay and flatten it slightly. With a smaller wooden tool with flat end (such as a pencil whose eraser is worn away), press into this small clay ball. The eye now has a rim. With the end of a small paintbrush, push into the center—you have now made the iris. Make the second eye in the same fashion. Score the bottom of each eye, wet it, and attach it to the part of the slab that is the frog's head (see Figure 4.28 for an example of what these eyes will look like).

Take a bit more clay and make four coils that taper at one end, two somewhat larger than the others; these will become the frog's legs. Think about the physical nature of arms and legs: The shoulders are bigger than the wrists, and the thighs are larger than the ankles. Take the two smaller coils, and gently press the untapered side to flatten it slightly. Score the back side of this coil, wet it, and attach to the frog's body, just slightly behind and below one of the eyes (see Figure 4.29). Let the frog's forearm and the hand rest near center of the underbelly. Affix the coil to the body with water. Using a dry finger, smooth the frog's shoulder into the body until it looks like a shoulder to you. With the rounded end of a popsicle stick, press the edge into the frog's hand to give it fingers. Repeat this process for attaching the other arm and the two legs (refer again to Figure 4.29). Bova has attached the body of his frog to a thrown cylinder. You can do the same with your frog by attaching it to a pinch pot. In this way, your frog functions as a drinking vessel.

Figure 4.28 *Sculpting and attaching frog's eyes.*

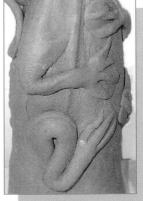

Figure 4.29 *Attaching and texturing coils for frog's arms and legs.*

You can use the pinch, coil, and slab techniques to develop any animal. Bova's work has intrigued me for years. I study animals and their behaviors, and I make rhytons, or ancient-style drinking

Figure 4.30
Elephant's head, ears, and eyelids sculpted using slabs; tusks and trunk sculpted using coil technique; and eyes sculpted using pinch technique.

vessels such as the elephant shown in Figure 4.30. I continue to find a range of ways to work with these three sculpting techniques and teach them to students of all ages and teachers. ■

Learning From Clay Sculptures

When teaching and conducting workshops, I bring clay into my university and public school classrooms, teach the three techniques of hand-building. I also bring a variety of different types of textures so that learners can explore the possibilities when the surface of the clay is textured. I invite students and teachers alike to explore the potential of this medium in the same way. Students and teachers read and study a range of texts and represent their interpretation of the text through clay. After making their pieces, the group engages in "Save the Last Word for the Artist," a literacy strategy developed by Short, Harste, and Burke (1996) in which the group interprets the artist's representation individually and collectively. Following this, the artist has the last word and shares her or his original intent, but which is extended by the group's interpretation. Figure 4.31 demonstrates a collaborative clay interpretation of the Greek myth of Narcissus by two sixth-grade students. Notice how these students use prefabricated face molds to represent Narcissus's

Figure 4.31 *Sixth-grade students' work with texture on clay surface.*

reflection in the pond. Also notice their use of texture to indicate the rippling water and the integration of leaves to create a *mixed media* representation.

After a 20-minute demonstration in hand-building techniques, preservice teachers respond to their study of the Harlem Renaissance. Teachers are given about 20 minutes to complete their sculptures. Once they are finished, we gather around the artwork and discuss it. What follows is an excerpted conversation about Bobbie's clay sculpture of a hammer, shown in Figure 4.32:

Shakiel: I see that the hammer represents strength. This is a striking image; it is forceful and active. It seems to represent a change of African American people from being confined, forced to be passive to a symbol of strength.

Sonda: This seems to suggest that African American people were beaten down, and were not able to show themselves as they are.

Glenda: The hammer—the symbol of strength—seems to have always been there. It is now just coming up to the surface.

Bobbie: I like what all of you saw in my piece. It could be all of those things. This is a hammer. I really liked Jacob Lawrence's images. He painted collections of tools. He saw these tools as symbolizing building, building of a culture, a people. He saw this as a positive thing. African Americans were building their identity, their lives, and their creativity. They were building spirit. Your comments and ideas helped me consider aspects of my sculpture I hadn't thought of before.

Figure 4.32 *Bobbie's clay sculpture in response to Harlem Renaissance study.*

Conversations such as these that emerge from arts-based engagements suggest that learners recognize that particular art techniques are successfully used and that meaning is generative. Learners respond to the art informed by their reading, interpretation, and synthesis of all the texts studied in a theme or topic.

Reflection on Working in Three Dimension

Linda Arbuckle (2003), a Southern potter who teaches ceramics at the University of Florida, Gainesville, USA, writes, "There's only one way to grow while making art: Take risks and allow yourself to make a lot of bad work, then look at it" (p. 96). As learners, we may not want to look at bad work; rather, we want to move it to the side and create better work. Three-dimensional work offers learners the opportunity to study, in the round, their conceptualized and actualized work.

Inscribing, editing, and communicating are cognitive processes developed when representing meaning in 3-D. How often have students said that they have difficulty sharing their interpretation or articulating their thoughts? Inscribing their thoughts through 3-D (and art, in general) stabilizes and preserves the thoughts that they have, and makes it possible to have a dialogue about these thoughts. For example, when sixth graders create a collaborative sculpture of Narcissus or teachers create sculptures centered on the Harlem Renaissance, they inscribe their thoughts, make them concrete, and encourage a dialogue with others about their thoughts. When teachers create 3-D construction paper masks, they learn how the volume of their masks transforms their initial interpretation of themselves or a character in a literary text.

In addition, in their making of the objects, learners understand how the editing process cuts across media. Although editing is almost exclusively associated with writing in ELA classes, it occurs in all art forms: pencil drawings, mask-building, clay sculptures, painting, and others. Editing their representations encourages learners to consider not just how they want to revise in the medium, but also what they want their representation to say. They learn that the decisions they make about their representations matter. Learners notice the small details that make their representation either strong or less appealing. They learn that the shades of difference in colors they choose (e.g., lavender, magenta, indigo, purple) for their masks matter and can change meaning. The size of the opening of their mask's eyes or mouth, or the objects that they add to their masks matter. The thickness of the coils or the thinness of their slabs matters. In the process of editing, they also reconsider the message they wish to send. Furthermore, representation becomes a recursive, rather than linear, process. Students may start with an idea, but the idea changes as they build and edit their representations. They erase the smallest of marks or add the slightest of details. Their interpretation of the character, the story, or the idea becomes clearer as they build, edit, and represent their thoughts.

As they encounter and study various techniques associated with 2-D and 3-D techniques and media, students learn to make decisions about which media best suits the message they want to convey. Pencils, markers, or paper may not have the same potential as clay or thick papier-mâché to communicate concepts like oppression or melancholy. Conversely, clay or papier-mâché may not be the best media to communicate such concepts as *delicate* or *frail*. Students learn to build an essential knowledge—somatic knowledge, or the knowledge that tells them the representation is just right (Eisner, 2000a).

Communicating across media and languages encourages learners to inquire into media that intrigues them, supports their interests, or best helps them represent their thoughts. ELA classes should be spaces in which students explore, discover, and experiment with the various types of media, techniques, and processes that sign systems invite. With support from teachers who have basic knowledge of techniques associated with 2-D and 3-D art, students learn to *read* the world of art (found in advertisements, colors, websites, billboards, galleries) with informed eyes, as well as *write* in a range of languages with informed purpose and meaning. Techniques used to communicate are starting points for embarking on more complex ways of making meaning. Learners will no longer be satisfied to represent meaning through one language system, but will want to continue their inquiry into multiple avenues of communication, and how systems work with and against each other.

Inquiry Into Technology and Media-Rich Experiences in the Teaching of English Language Arts

- *What role does technology play in ELA instruction?*
- *What are good software programs to support my inquiry into technology?*
- *What can I do with limited technology?*

Photography as Socio-Semiotic: A Teacher's Story
by Kathy Egawa

My involvement with photography began early in my teaching career. A close friend with a long-standing interest in photography invited me into his darkroom and gave me a chance to develop my own photographs. During one of those first darkroom sessions, I played around with what was an ordinary family shot and cropped out the extraneous details to highlight my niece standing in front of a backlit apple tree. I was pleased with the results and gave the photograph to my sister-in-law as a gift. The following summer I entered the same photo into the Kodak national photo contest. Imagine my excitement, several weeks later, when that photograph was featured in the newspaper as the first week's winner in the local contest and then again, seven weeks later, as one of several finalists to go on to the national Kodak contest.

The experience was an important one, as the skilled "eye" I brought to the cropping of this photo had been acknowledged. I continued taking photos with renewed enthusiasm and confidence. People shots were a favorite. Close-up photographs of my students served as Mother's and Father's Day gifts each spring. I regularly photographed students and their learning, as well as my travels, and exhibited several more photographs in local art shows. This time period, with its emphasis on photographs as products, could be called phase one of my involvement with a camera.

This experience transported me from that phase to the next. In graduate school, my colleague Beth Berghoff and I invited prospective teachers to sort a collection of photos into two piles: those that represented the kinds of classrooms they would like to create, and those that did not. I built on that new knowledge and created similar "learning beliefs in practice" documents. In my own elementary classrooms, I invited students to create similar documents about how our room worked. The documents served several purposes: as curriculum manuals, as classroom visitor guides, and most important, as a tool for me to assess if the student comments meshed with my purpose and intentions for creating different routines and engagements. Now, with advancements in technology such as digital photography and software programs such as Photoshop, we can create photographic documents that can be altered, colorized, cropped, flipped—the effects are endless—which offers us and our students a range of ways in which to work and represent. Original and altered photographs can be integrated into PowerPoint presentations to create mood, suspense, and atmosphere, or to support writing in newsletters and flyers. Each time I use these two semiotic systems in tandem—photography and writing—and consider them in light of technology, I learn more about their potential to support reflective thinking and better understand the different strengths that each offers.

Kathy Egawa's story about the role of photography, visual texts, and technology signify the changing nature of ELA instruction and learning. For Kathy, photography enabled her to document personal experiences, but also supported her research and teaching in which students found photography a way to capture and reflect upon their learning. Further, she now recognizes the role that technology plays into representing and re-creating photographs. Like Kathy, middle school teacher Katya believes that technology in the classroom is indispensable. She states,

> I think [technology] might be the answer to many of the problems we are having in education today. We are experiencing a decline in not only test scores, but in enthusiasm for learning in general, it seems. Part of the reason we are losing the kids is that they are qualitatively different from previous generations. Computers and other electronic media are the ideal tools for educating these kids in a way that keeps up with their interests and experiences. Technology is a huge part of the solution to keeping kids engaged with learning.

Katya's thoughts about the important role of technology in the teaching of ELA also support the need for ELA educators to understand how technology is very much a part of the learning that many students bring into the classroom. In a recent presentation, Jerry Harste (2005) stated, "To be literate, you have to see yourself in literacy." To support students' literacy, then, means that ELA educators must talk about and teach the new literacies, the technology-rich literacies, that value and honor the experiences our students bring to our classrooms daily.

Why Technology?

In 1985, Dennis Stevens, a colleague who taught high school chemistry, came into my classroom as I was typing. He said, "Why are you still typing on a typewriter? You are going to learn how to use a computer." That afternoon, in a couple of hours, I learned how to word-process on a computer, and I created my first digital document. Twenty years and hundreds of questions later, I now work with a range of software programs—including Microsoft PowerPoint, Publisher, and Excel and Adobe Photoshop—that enable me to think, work, and create in ways I never thought possible. Most recently, I have learned to design and develop documentaries with Microsoft Windows Movie Maker and Adobe Premiere Pro, and I am now learning the details of podcasting. Instead of fearing technology as I did over 20 years ago, I now embrace its potential to change the way I teach and think about ELA instruction. I am challenged and am energized by its possibilities. To this day, I thank Dennis for forcing me to work with computer technology. If you are skeptical or hesitant to use technology tools, as I was, I hope this chapter will inspire you to work with technology that enables you to teach ELA in ways you may have not yet imagined.

Students and teachers must know how to work effectively with technology, including software programs and hardware (such as flash drives, CD burners, digital cameras). IRA/NCTE standards (1996) state that students (and teachers) need to display an understanding of the role of technology in communication, and incorporate technology and print and nonprint media into instruction. ELA teachers in Georgia, my home state, must meet minimum standards in technology as described by the International Society for Technology in Education (ISTE) and the Interstate New Teacher Assessment and Support Consortium (INTASC). Explicitly, new teachers must be able to "use knowledge of effective verbal, nonverbal, and media communication techniques to foster active inquiry, collaboration, and supportive interaction in the classroom" (www.ccsso.org/content/pdfs/corestrd.pdf, p. 25). In other words, both pre- and inservice teachers must work with and integrate technology whenever possible in planning, instruction and assessment.

Advancements in technology enable educators to work with print, visual, musical, and electronic texts of all types in single presentations, and encourage educators to work with multiple media. Furthermore, technology tools in presentation software (special effects, transitions, background format, slide layout) offer educators a way to present information and design instruction in ways that bring content to life. English language arts and technology standards, through innovations in software, can be integrated in substantive ways.

However, the availability of technology in any one school is not uniform. For instance, some schools in the metropolitan Atlanta, Georgia, area have wonderful technology resources, such as laptops for all teachers, desktop computers in all classrooms, available LCD (liquid crystal display) projectors, and both PC (personal computer) and Apple technology labs. On the other hand, some schools have limited resources, and teachers must reserve LCD projectors one month in advance or work with TV monitors that are far too small to project text or images well. If you are in the former group and in a technology-rich environment, integration of technology will be less complicated. If you are part of the latter group and access to technology is limited in your school, I suggest you remind your principals or those in charge of budget of the IRA /NCTE, INTASC, and ISTE standards, and the importance that technology plays in your teaching. I agree with Kajder (2004) who argues that students must learn to become effective rich communicators, and knowledge of the tools of technology will support and develop their ability to communicate. But always keep in mind, technology should not drive learning; technology should support and encourage thoughtful, innovative, and creative communication.

This chapter will describe the various aspects of three presentation software programs: Microsoft PowerPoint, Publisher, and Windows Movie Maker. These programs will enable you to design and create media-rich presentations that are engaging, and interactive, and integrate a range of media. The first section will address basic functions in PowerPoint, and explain, through two projects, how to build content presentations. The first project will introduce you to such commands as inserting images, call out buttons, and music. The second project illustrates how to create a self-running PowerPoint presentation focused on the Great Dust Bowl. Following this, I describe how to work with Publisher, a software program that allows you to generate a range of texts including posters, newsletters, cards, and programs. After this, you will learn the basics of how to create short movies by using Windows Movie Maker. Hopefully, you will have a basic working knowledge of these software programs, enough for you to develop your own projects.

PCs are the computer of choice where I teach, and this chapter will address how to work with technology associated with a PC platform. If you work on an Apple computer, you may be able to translate these ideas based upon your own software programs. If you have difficulty, I encourage you to talk with your instructional technology specialists; they will be able to help you. This chapter is not meant to be the final authority of what you may need to know, but it will offer you a start in designing and developing media-rich and engaging ELA projects.

What Is Technology? Starting With What You Know and Building From There

In the past few years, the word *technology* is often used synonymously with the word *computers*. Yet, what is technology, really? For me, technology is a set of tools, both hardware and software, that support our thinking and engagement with learning. Technology, especially computers, the internet, and a range of software programs, help us interpret, compose, and share information and knowledge quickly and efficiently.

Literacy has evolved from reading and writing one's name to the ability to invent, design, and create complex texts in social settings that draw from a number of different resources (Lankshear & Knobel, 2003). In recent years *new literacies* has emerged as a field of study to explain how the influence of media, technology, the economy, and access to international information, affects the social and literacy practices in everyday life (Kist, 2005). For example, once considered revolutionary and still widely used today, the overhead projector as technology, or a tool, affected how information was shared with large groups and in large places. Now, new textual practices, or actions that involve different types of texts, are becoming as commonplace as the overhead (OVH) projector (Lankshear & Knobel, 2003). PowerPoint has replaced the OVH projector for many, and content presentations are now jazzed up with special effects, images, sound, and hyperlinks. In some U.S. states, educational standards require teachers' and students' use of technology (ISTE, INTASC), especially presentation software programs like PowerPoint and Publisher.

Working With PowerPoint

PowerPoint is a tool that I use every time I teach or present at a conference because of its flexible and generative nature. I also require my teachers to use it in their presentations. At first, they are reluctant because they believe it will be too hard to learn, but after they become familiar with PowerPoint, they find it a very useful teaching tool. In this section, I will talk about the toolbars, and basic functions associated with this presentation software program for Windows XP. (If you have Windows 97, you should be able to work with the ideas presented in this section.) The scope of this chapter does not allow me to talk through each of the effects, but I hope you will explore some of the other features on your own.

Becoming Familiar With the Menus, Commands, and Tools

Basic to PowerPoint is the concept of slides. A slide is like an individual transparency on which you can type text, insert images, sounds and video, and integrate special effects. When you first open PowerPoint, you will notice that many of the commands look familiar, especially if you use word-processing programs like Microsoft Word or AppleWorks. We will go through each of the commands, look more specifically at the drop-down menus, and how you can explore the many tools of PowerPoint. Although there are many different commands within the basic menus, we will work with only a few just to get you started. When creating a PowerPoint presentation, save your work every few minutes so you do not lose any work.

The *File menu* allows you to create a new file, open an existing one, save a file that you are working on, change the name of a file, and preview your presentation before you print. In the *Edit menu*, you can paste text or images into a slide, select all the slides and make them all look alike or add the same text or image onto it, or delete a slide. In the *View menu*, most common is the "normal" view, in which you see the toolbars at the top, the slides that you have already created on the left side, and the slide on which you are currently working is largest and located in the center.

When working with PowerPoint, I find the Insert, Format, and Tools menus particularly useful in creating interesting presentations. It is in the *Insert menu* that you can insert all sorts of interesting texts, such as images, sounds, movies, music, or a chart or table. The *Format menu* allows you to change the size and type of font, the slide design, layout, and the background of the slide. In the *Tools* menu, you can check your spelling (the most commonly used feature) and explore other commands.

Within the Format menu, three commands are most useful: Slide Design, Slide Layout, and Background. Each of these will offer you innumerable options for your presentation's appearance. PowerPoint offers a number of different slide templates, which you can find under *Slide Designs*; these templates provide popular backgrounds and colors for presentations. Look across the number of designs in PowerPoint and imagine how each of these could enhance your presentation, create a mood, set a tone, or provide atmosphere as you present ELA ideas to your students.

Slide Layout, also under the Format menu, enables you to choose how each element of your slides can be placed within each slide. When you first open PowerPoint, the default title slide will appear because the program assumes you will need some sort of title for your presentation. After that, the default slide is a subtitle slide with bullets because PowerPoint assumes you are going to make particular points in your presentation, and bulleted items function well for this purpose. In Slide Layout, you can choose any one of the many layouts from title page, to bulleted text, to side-by-side bullets, a blank slide, or a slide that combines images and text. Explore the various types of slide layouts. These may inspire you to present your information to students in a creative way.

Background, also found within the Format menu, allows you to choose the texture (designs that are not solid colors) or background design of your slide and gradations of color; you can even use an image as the background. Click the Background command in the Format menu, then place your cursor onto the upside-down arrow at the right side of the color bar and a menu appears (see

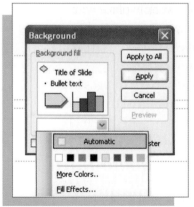

Figure 5.1 Background.

Figure 5.1). If you want a solid color for your slide background, you can choose any color shown in the window, or click on "More Colors" to choose another color. Or, you can choose a gradated color design when you move your cursor and click "Fill Effects." In this window, you have several options: Gradient, Texture, Pattern, and Picture. Explore each of these options to see if any are interesting or will support the concepts you want to present. My favorite command is "Picture" because here I can create my own backgrounds using photographs. I take lots of photos of my students in my classes, talking, writing, reading, and working with each other. These photos then become part of my presentations.

To create a picture background, place your cursor on "Picture" then click the command, "Select Picture." Another window labeled "My Pictures" may appear. From your computer's directory, select the photo that you want to become your background. (For instance, I have a folder on my computer's hard drive called "Photo Album" where I store all of my photos. I select my file from there.) Once

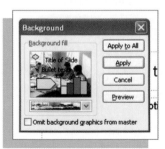

Figure 5.2 Photo as background fill.

you have selected your photo, click "OK" or "Apply" to view the slide. Another window will appear in which PowerPoint asks you to "Apply to All" slides, "Apply" to the current slide on which you are working, "Cancel" the photo background, or "Preview" the photo background before you apply (see Figure 5.2). If you want this photo to appear on this slide only, click "Apply." The photo becomes your background fill. If you want this photo to be the background for all your slides, click "Apply to All." If you have chosen a Slide Design for most of the other slides in your presentation and want only your photo to appear, click "Omit background graphics from master." This will omit all graphics from the background and only your photo will appear. Now that you are familiar with these commands, play around with each option so that you are familiar with their functions.

Within the View menu, the *Slide Show* command allows you to customize your own presentation with animation and slide transitions (these options are discussed further in the next section of this chapter). At any time while constructing your presentation, you can click "View Show" and preview the show you have created. In this view, you see what your viewers will see. Within the View menu, you can also click the icon with the four squares, called the *Slide Sorter*. This provides a type of story board and shows you the entire show at a glance. In the Slide Sorter view you can move around any of the slides that you have created. For instance, if you think one slide should appear before another, simply place your cursor on the slide that you want to move, left click and hold, and drag the slide to the position that you want it to appear. To return to Normal view, or the view in which you are working, simply double-click on the slide on which you want to continue to work. Play with some of these commands to see how they operate.

Practice Building a Slide Show

My first PowerPoint presentation, created in 1997, was basic but provided an insightful learning adventure. I used the Slide Design named "Father's Tie." I liked the simplicity of the design and thought that it would enhance my text and images. Because I did not know about animation or special effects, my text and images were static and did not move. I could have easily produced this presentation on transparencies, but I wanted to try my hand at PowerPoint. From this experience, I pushed myself to inquire more deeply into technology, in a simple and comfortable way.

When I develop a PowerPoint presentation for any of my classes or conferences, I always consider the focus of the presentation. Will it be a demonstration of ELA concepts? Will it be a presentation that is just for viewing? Is it going to be interactive? I also consider the design of the presentation: layout of text, when I want text to appear, texts that I want to include. Before you start your presentation, determine the context in which you might present an idea or topic using PowerPoint. What content do you teach? Elizabethan theater? Life cycles of animals? Oceans? Now consider the media you might need to teach this content. What images will support the content? Which texts, poems, quotations, diagrams, and so forth would be important for students to know? What sounds or music might add interest? You'll explore these concepts and the many possibilities PowerPoint offers—in this practice section.

Saving and Inserting Images. To make PowerPoint presentations or any document interesting, I always include pictures or images of the texts or concepts with which I want to work. Be warned, however, of two potential pitfalls of using images found on the Internet: image quality and copyright issues. Many of the images I use in my presentations are photographs of my students, personal photographs, or photographs that I have scanned from materials that I own. Nearly all images saved onto the Internet are *thumbnails,* or smaller versions of larger pictures. Although thumbnails save space and take less time to download, they are often low resolution, which means if you insert one into your PowerPoint slide and enlarge it, it will probably be blurred. Double-click onto the thumbnail itself to see if there is a larger version of it. If so, save the larger image because it has a higher resolution (an image that has more pixels).

To save images from the Internet (always check to see if they are public domain or copyrighted), right click on the image. A window will appear displaying many options. If I think that I might use this photo again, I will click on "Save Picture As..." and save it into a folder where I can access it now or at a later time. I have a folder on my computer called "Images" in which I keep images of all kinds (book covers, artists, animals, etc.) so that I can work with them in later documents.

To insert an image into your PowerPoint presentation, go to the Insert menu, click and hold *Picture* and another window will open displaying several options. You can choose to insert Clip Art or, if you have saved an image to your computer that you want to insert, click on "From File" and follow the directory to the folder where you saved the image you want to insert. Click on the file or photo that you want to insert, and click the button that says "Insert." The photo should now appear in the slide on which you are working in. You can resize the image as needed by clicking once on the photo. Six small, white circles will appear around the photo. To keep the photo's proportion and to make it larger or smaller, place your cursor near one of the four corner circles until you see a double arrow (an arrow point at each end), then click and hold to drag the edges of the photo to resize it. To move the photo within the slide, move the cursor on the photo and two perpendicular double arrows appear. Click and hold to grab the photo and move it where you want onto the slide.

Writing and Inserting Text. Examine Figure 5.3a and Figure 5.3b. Which slide is more appealing? If a slide has too much text, as in Figure 5.3a, viewers will find reading it difficult and time-consuming, especially if they are expected to write

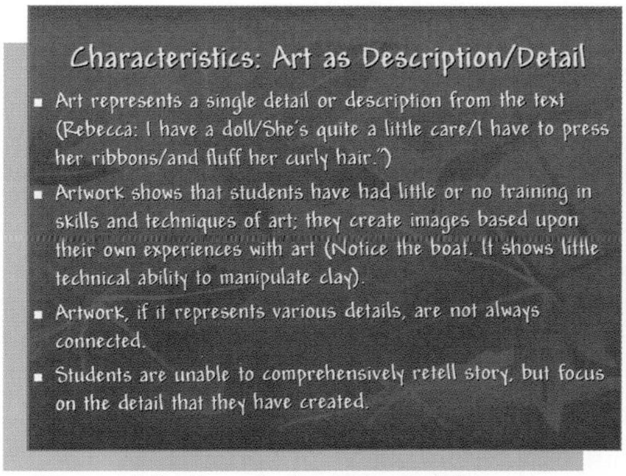

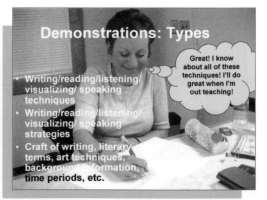

Figures 5.3a *Example of a text-heavy slide.*

Figure 5.3b *Example of a visually appealing, user-friendly slide.*

down these notes. Students often focus only on one task—writing or listening—so, if they write down all the notes in Figure 5.3a, they may not fully understand any explanation that goes along with these concepts. Over the years, I have learned to economize the written text I use, and always include visual and audio texts to support the content, as in Figure 5.3b. Viewers can more easily read the written information because the font is plain and the font size large. Furthermore, when I teach, I value interaction, and often integrate photos of my students with callout buttons, also called speech bubbles.

When you design slides, always use simple, large, clear fonts so that everyone can read it from wherever they sit. In typed text, there are two types of fonts, serif and sans-serif. *Serifs* are any short lines that extend or are at an angle to the upper or lower ends of a letter, the "feet" of the letter. Some fonts that contain serifs are more difficult to read. For example, the font called Gothic has sweeping serifs, which, while attractive, challenges the best of readers, so students will focus more on deciphering the written text and less on reading the content. However, a font without serifs, or *sans-serif*, like Arial, may be much easier to read in a presentation. Attention to the serifs and font size can make or break a presentation. Also, a text without images often is less interesting. Furthermore, as students read written and visual text presented concisely, they learn to recognize and record important information from both texts.

As an added design concept, consider the background colors of your presentation slides. Black print against a light or pastel background is easiest to read. And reds, although intriguing, seem to vibrate when viewed on screens and are hard to see. In my recent presentations, I have used white letters on a black background; I like this color combination because the viewer focuses on the sharp contrast of the bright print text against the dark background. Further, visual images also seem to be sharper and easier to read. Be careful when choosing backgrounds and colored fonts. The resolution on your computer screen is far greater than that on a school audio-visual (AV) screen in your classroom. What may appear sharp and clear on a computer does not translate as clearly on an AV screen.

You can insert text in several ways. First, you can use one of PowerPoint's templates in Slide Layouts in the Format menu. Then you simply click inside each text box and type. To create the slide shown in Figure 5.4, I used the compare/contrast slide layout. I typed in a title for the slide ("Text Sets"), and then typed in information in the two boxes, both containing bullets in which I type in information that I want

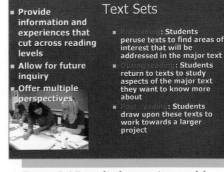

Figure 5.4 *Example of compare/contrast slide layout to insert text.*

to present. These slide layout templates force you to think through important and unimportant information because PowerPoint automatically resizes the text as you add more. You will find that you can write only so many words before the text moves off the slide or becomes too small to read from a distance.

A second way to insert written text is to use the blank slide layout and create a text box. Click on the Insert command to get the drop down menu. Click on Text Box, and a text box appears with a blinking cursor inside. You can then begin to type your text. To create the slide shown in Figure 5.5, I used a text box to type in the title of David Robinson's artwork. As with images, you can move text boxes around by clicking on the text box you want to move, and when you see the crossed double-arrows, you can move the text box. You can also resize a text box as you did with images.

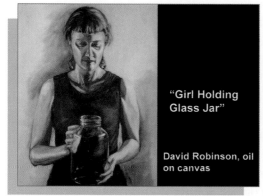

"Girl Holding Glass Jar"

David Robinson, oil on canvas

Figure 5.5 Example of blank slide and text box to insert text.

Background and Font Colors. There are several commands to help you change font color, to fill the background of a text box or shape (circles, rectangles, squares), or to draw lines around text boxes or shapes. Figure 5.6 shows a screen shot of the icons you can click to manipulate these elements; you can also do these things by going into the Format menu and clicking "Font." To change the color of a font, click on the written text that you want to change. Drag your cursor across the text so that it is highlighted. Go to the bottom of the screen and move your cursor to the icon that is a capital "A" with a line of color underneath. Left click on the arrow just to the right of the "A" and a window with various colors will appear. You can choose one of the colors that appears or you can choose "More colors." To change the background fill of a text box or shape, click on the icon that looks like a little pail with paint pouring out. A palette of

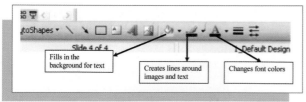

Fills in the background for text

Creates lines around images and text

Changes font colors

Figure 5.6 Commands for changing font colors, background fill color, and line colors.

colors appears and you can choose the background fill. The paint brush icon allows you to create any color line you want around text boxes, images or shapes. Practice some of these effects on your slides now to get a feeling for these tools.

Inserting Callout Texts. To engage students in my presentations, I often use callout text boxes, commonly referred to as speech bubbles, that act as dialogue texts (for an example, see Figure 5.7). Callout text boxes can serve several purposes:

(1) Students are personally and actively involved in the presentation because they read the text in the callout text box that points directly to their picture, (2) callout boxes demonstrate the literacy element of dialogue, (3) students practice reading, and (4) callout text boxes can generate humor in the classroom. Students love to see their photos on the AV screen and to read the text inside these speech bubbles. Callout text boxes also provide more space for student talk; I often leave speech bubbles blank, which encourages students to create their own dialogue and keeps them focused. I also use photos of authors, singers, poets, researchers, or theorists that we study, and insert callout text boxes with their quotations inside. When I do this, students see and "hear" Langston Hughes, Maya Angelou, Nikki Giovanni, Louise Rosenblatt, Elliot Eisner, or Jerry Harste. I find that students like to see photographs of authors, artists, and scholars, and combining photographs and callout text boxes provides visual context for specific ideas or statements.

Figure 5.7 *Callout text boxes engage students in presentations.*

To add a callout text box, first place your cursor on the arrow next to "AutoShapes," near the Start button. Then slide the cursor over "Callouts" and click to open a box that shows a number of different shapes available for your callout text box. Click on the callout box shape you want, then click and drop it in the slide to insert it. Once you see the callout shape in your slide, type in the text you want to appear in the callout. You can adjust the size, shape, and position of the callout box by clicking on an edge or corner of the callout box itself and dragging the cursor.

Inserting Sounds and/or Music. PowerPoint slides that have sound bytes or music often surprise and delight students. Inserting sounds into your presentation eliminates your need to operate other pieces of audio equipment like a CD or tape player and facilitates the integration of music or sound bytes. You merely click on the sound icon to play the sound byte, or program the sound to play automatically. (To get an overview of how to work with sounds, consult Microsoft training on the Internet, http://office.Microsoft.com/training/, and enter "PowerPoint sounds" in the search bar.)

To insert sounds into your presentation, follow a similar procedure as when you inserted images. Go to the Insert menu, and then go to "Movies or Sounds." Another window will appear and ask if you want to insert a sound file from your computer, from a CD, or from "Clip Organizer." Let's first work with a music CD. If you have favorite music that you want to include into your PowerPoint presentation, insert the CD into your computer's CD drive. A window will appear asking you if you want to "Copy music from CD," "Play audio CD" (using a program such as Real Player, Windows Media Player or MusicMatch), or "Take No Action." I usually copy my music files into a file on my computer so that I can access them more easily later.

When you click "Copy music from CD," another screen will appear letting you know that your computer is automatically copying the music from your CD. The software that controls this (such as MusicMatch, Windows Media Player, iTunes, etc.) automatically checks all songs and begins to copy them to your hard drive. You can uncheck the boxes of the songs that you do not want to have copied. At the bottom of the screen, you will see a directory that tells you where the songs are being copied to; usually, the songs go into the default music folder— C:\Documents and Setting\[Your Name]\My Documents\My Music—unless you have changed that setting.

Once you have songs in your music folder, you can insert them into your presentation. You can use music in PowerPoint presentations for several purposes. First, music can act as a timer and encourages different forms of thinking. For instance, if I ask students to complete some work (discussion, artwork, writing responses, etc.) and give them five minutes, I choose a song that is approximately five minutes long. When the music stops, so do the students. Second, music influences the texts we create. In a recent class, I invited students to write a short autobiographical piece. After about two minutes and while they were still writing, I started a PowerPoint presentation on which I had inserted the song "Black Magic Woman" by Santana (1998) on one slide along with a photograph of the band. After the song finished, the class talked about how music had an effect on their thinking and writing. One of my students remarked that the

Figure 5.8 *Working with sound, image, and written text.*

autobiographical story she had started writing changed when the music played; the song had inspired a very different story.

The third way is to use music and sound bytes is to accompany written and visual texts studied in the classroom. For example, to teach a poetry analysis tool called TPCASTT (title, paraphrase, connotation, attitude, shift in tone, title revisited, theme) used by teachers in the metro-Atlanta area, I use rap musician and poet Tupac Shakur's (1999) poem "The Rose That Grew From Concrete," the title poem in his collection of the same name. In 2000, this poem was set to music. Figure 5.8 shows a slide of a ninth-grade student artwork completed after studying both the poem and the song version of "The Rose That Grew From Concrete." As another example, in my PowerPoint focused on the Harlem Renaissance, I also insert sound bytes of poets reading their work, including Langston Hughes reading his "Dream Deferred," and Gwendolyn Brooks reading "We Real Cool. " Both of these sound bytes are a part of a wonderful resource called *Poetry Speaks* (Paschen & Mosby, 2001), a collection of a wide range of authors and poets reading their work.

The fourth way to work with music is to contextualize it within particular time periods or thematic units studied in English language arts class. Music also has accompanied presentations I have created to give an overall sense of the Great Dust Bowl when I teach *Out of the Dust* (Hesse, 1999), immigration when I teach *A Step From Heaven* (Na, 2003), or the Harlem Renaissance when I teach *Their Eyes Were Watching God* (Hurston, 1998).

You can include songs in your PowerPoint presentation in any of three ways: (1) to accompany one slide; (2) to play across several slides; and (3) to play continuously throughout a presentation. To simply insert a sound or sound byte on a single slide, go to the Insert menu, and select "Movies or Sound." From there select "Sound from file" Make sure that you are on the slide in your presentation in which you want to play the music. You will need to find the file on your hard drive where your sound or music is located—as you did when inserting your photos. Once you have located the folder on your hard drive, select the song or music that you want to insert by double-clicking on the song file and the song will be inserted into your PowerPoint. A small icon that looks like a speaker will appear in the middle of the PowerPoint slide. (I always move this icon to a less conspicuous part of the slide. To do this, I left click on the icon and drag the icon to the bottom right hand corner.) Another window will immediately appear and ask you if you want the music to play "Automatically" when the slide appears or if you want to play the music "When Clicked." If you want a song, or a portion of one song, to play on one slide, click "Automatically"; however, if you want to control when the song is played, you can choose "When Clicked." The speaker icon will appear on the slide, and can then click the icon to start and stop the song.

I also like to insert sound bytes on individual slides. *Poetry Speaks* (Paschen & Mosby, 2001), mentioned previously, is invaluable. Sourcebooks Mediafusion, the publisher of this resource, also produces CDs with sound bytes of historical figures presenting speeches from such events as the Civil Rights movement, the Hindenburg, and the September 11 terrorist attack on the World Trade Center. To insert a sound byte of a poet reading or a famous historical figure speaking, follow the same procedure as you did with music.

To create presentations in which music plays over several slides or runs continuously, as in a movie, you need to know about Custom Animation and Slide Transition. These two commands allow you to control how much of a sound byte you want to play and how long you want a slide to play in the slide show. Often I want to play only an excerpt of a long poem, to just play the poem that a poet performs, or to play just a portion of a song. On the main toolbar at the top, click on Slide Show, and click on "Custom Animation" in the drop-down menu. The audio file that you inserted will automatically appear in the small window. Now, right click and another window will open; right click again on "Effect Options"– this command allows you control when and how much of the audio file you want to play. For instance, the Langston Hughes's audio file begins with Hughes talking about how he wrote the poem "The Negro Speaks of Rivers." In my presentation, I want to hear him read only the poem. In the "Start playing" section of this window (see screen shot in Figure 5.9), I click in the circle "From time" and type in the start time of this audio file. After listening to the entire audio file, I know that Hughes begins reading his poem 1 minute and 39 seconds into the audio file, so that is the time I type in. The audio will begin playing at this point. I also have the option of playing this audio byte over several slides. In the section "Stop playing," I can tell PowerPoint how many slides I want this audio to play over. In this instance, I have chosen three slides because I want to show three images of Hughes as he reads his poem.

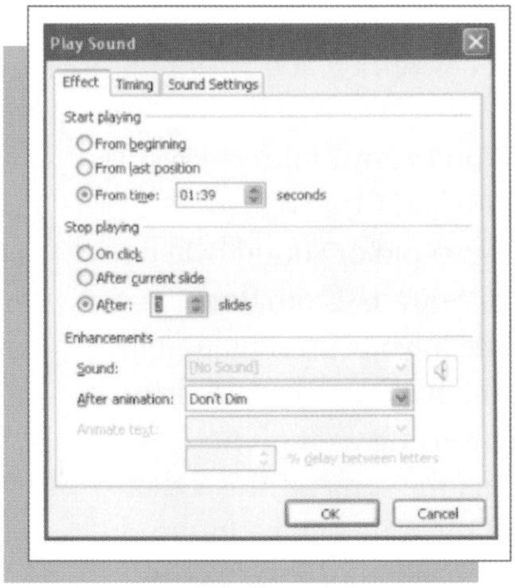

Figure 5.9 *Sound effect options.*

Custom Animation. Custom Animation allows you to control how and when written and visual texts enter and exit on a slide. For example, Figure 5.10 shows two sets of visual images and three written texts that I want to animate. When the slide appears, the Elements of Shape appear. I then click to have the first written text and the cover image of *When Clay Sings* (Baylor, 1987) appear. Once the group and I have discussed that written text, I click again and we talk through the second written text. After that discussion, I click and the third text appears.

To animate written, visual, or musical texts with Custom Animation, highlight the text box or the image that you want to

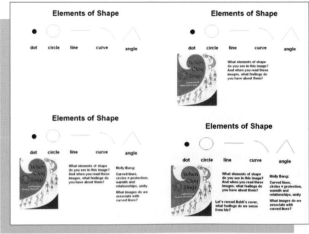

Figure 5.10 *Animating visual and written texts on slides.*

animate by clicking on it. Notice the toolbox that appears on the right side of the screen. When you highlight a text box or image, anther command will darken, "Add Effect," at the top of the toolbar. The drop-down menu will ask if you want the text/image to enter, exit, show emphasis, and motion path. Left click on "Entrance" and you will see a large number of entrance choices, and you'll see the same for the exit, emphasis, and motion paths. Choose an animation and see what the effect will look like in the presentation by clicking on the command "Play" at the bottom of the toolbar. Experiment with the variety of choices to see which one you like best for your presentation.

Defining Transition Effects and Times. An important final feature of PowerPoint is defining transition effects and times between slides. If you want a self-running presentation, you will need to tell PowerPoint how long each slide should play before moving to the next slide. Find this Slide Transition command under the Slide Show menu. Click on "Slide Transition" and the toolbar on the right-hand side will switch to the commands within Slide Transition. Now you can tell PowerPoint how you want each slide to transition to the next. Or, you can tell PowerPoint that you want to control the transitions between slides with a click of your mouse, or that you want PowerPoint to transition for you automatically. If you choose the automatic transition, you must tell PowerPoint how long you want the slides to remain on the screen. To manually assign time to each slide, go to the Slide Sorter view, highlight a slide and assign a time in the "Automatically after." If you want all slides to have equally timed transitions, click on the "Apply to all Slides." You can preview the slide by clicking "Play."

Creating Hyperlinks. Another important feature of PowerPoint is its ability to *hyperlink* to other documents in your computer, which allows you to show another document or presentation, image, or website without having to minimize or close out of PowerPoint. (Think of this as switching between transparencies on your traditional overhead projector presentation.) If you have two or more documents that you want to present or websites that you would like to access during your PowerPoint presentation, it's useful to create a hyperlink to the documents or websites.

On the slide where you want to hyperlink, create a text box. Go to the Insert command and click on "Hyperlink," which will take you to your files on your hard drive. Select the file you want to hyperlink to, and PowerPoint will create a link to this file on the slide. When you click on this link, your document will come up on the screen . Note that creating hyperlinks can only be done while in the Slide Show mode, not in the screen where you are composing this presentation. Hyperlinking will enable you to access so many different types of documents with just the click of a mouse! ■

Although there are many more interesting and inviting features of PowerPoint, it is my hope that you have become familiar with some of its basic commands in this practice exercise. With this knowledge of PowerPoint, you can create media-rich, engaging, and interactive presentations. One of my former students, a middle school teacher, sent me an e-mail recently to say that she really found PowerPoint to be extraordinarily important. She now takes photographs of her students, uses callout text boxes, music, and special effects when teaching content. Her students enjoy this type of presentation, as will yours, especially when you integrate the various media suggested. Further, your students will be inspired to create their own media-rich projects.

Flexibility of PowerPoint

One of the most important features of PowerPoint is that you can use virtually the same PowerPoint every time you teach the same class, although it's a good idea to periodically update information and customize presentations with images of your current students and their work. Once the original PowerPoint is created, updating and customizing takes little time; if you want to include more special effects, different backgrounds, music, or videos, you can do that without having to redo the entire presentation. Now that many schools have their own websites and servers, you can even upload PowerPoint presentations to the server so that students, who miss class or need to revisit the information presented, can access this presentation at home or at school in their spare time. This can save you an enormous amount of time explaining material or trying to show transparencies or notes to students who were absent from class. Personally, the more I learn about PowerPoint, the more it becomes a tool to enhance my teaching. In fact, I cannot teach without this program anymore, nor can I teach without using images or music; these communications systems have become integral to how I teach ELA concepts. When I first started working with PowerPoint, I let it guide my instruction. Now, I let PowerPoint know what I need to do to teach ELA. In time you may have this different perspective, as well.

Working With Microsoft Publisher

I work with Publisher to create newsletters for a number of reasons: (1) to present concepts, literary periods, or themes that students will study; (2) to serve as an assessment tool for students' learning; and (3) to share information learned within and outside the class (parents, other teachers, etc.). There are so many other ways to integrate newsletters into instruction and my purposes for including them into ELA instruction and learning is to teach elements of design, layout, visual appeal, and concise writing.

To introduce students to a unit of study, theme, or literary period, I often create a newsletter to give them an overall sense of the authors, historians, and literary works of the period; sometimes, I include an Internet search that invites students to do preliminary research. For example, when studying the Harlem Renaissance, I created a newsletter that highlighted Hurston's (1998) work, *Their Eyes Were Watching God*. I wrote a brief biography of Hurston and integrated critical comments on her work. I also gestured toward our future study of painters of the Harlem Renaissance by inserting an artwork by Lois Mailou Jones. I also placed four photographs of famous Harlem Renaissance figures at the bottom of the newsletter to encourage students to research their lives and works. Newsletters provide introductory engagements that encourage students to see how information can be presented in an interesting, concise and visually appealing way.

Figure 5.11 shows a newsletter that one teacher created on immigration, focusing on the novel *A Step From Heaven* (Na, 2003). When writing newsletters, both teachers and students show not only what they have learned, but how they organize and share this learning. They also demonstrate evolving knowledge about design, layout, and concise writing and clear text. Furthermore, unlike book reports that often are mere summaries written with the purpose to inform, newsletters encourage students to integrate a range of texts including photographs, drawings, and cartoons. When creating newsletters, teachers and students can explore writing in different genres, such as lyrics, journalistic writing, poetry, exposition, and persuasion.

Figure 5.11 *Teacher-generated newsletter.*

When you have worked with one Microsoft presentation software program, working with others becomes easier. The toolbars in Publisher also will be recognizable, and their commands are similar to PowerPoint and Microsoft Word. The icons and their functions are similar across programs. The Standard Toolbar allows you to change font, bold, italicize, underline, etc. You can also insert images, clip art, and if your newsletter is online, you can insert music files and video in the same way that you did when working in PowerPoint. For this reason, the instructions in this section are not as detailed as in other sections of this chapter, but I encourage you to play with as many icons and menus as possible to familiarize yourself with Publisher's capabilities.

When you first open Publisher, a window appears that enables you to choose the type of document you want to create. Click on "File," then choose "New Document"; the New Publication toolbar will appear. Select "Publications for Print," and within this menu you'll see numerous types of documents (such as signs, newsletters, business cards, certificates, special occasion cards) that you can create. Once you have selected a document type, let's say "Flyers," a variety of flyer templates will appear in the window. Once you choose a layout, a larger image of the layout appears in the right-hand window. From the left-hand menu, you can choose color and font schemes. When you select those, Publisher automatically makes these changes for you.

You are now ready to begin writing your flyer. Place your cursor inside a text box and type your heading, your details, and your story. Where there is an image on the flyer, click on the box, delete the Publisher image and insert your own photo from your file, using the same procedure as you did with PowerPoint. Create your first flyer and then play with the other designs and layouts. ■

Flexibility of Publisher

Publisher enables you to consider a number of different ELA inquiry-based projects. Students can write a brochure about research projects they have done, such as investigation into Shakespeare's Globe Theatre, animals, favorite books and students' critical analysis of them. Or brochures can serve as documents that relate the overall work that students have done over a nine-week period. Students can publicize flyers for any presentations that they will do in the classroom or as a school project. Students can hold the responsibility of creating birthday or special occasion cards for their classmates during a particular month by generating and presenting the cards to their classmate on the date of their birthday. The ELA teacher or students can generate a program layout text that highlights the various presentations that students will make on a topic, and provide a summary of what that presentation will contain. Like PowerPoint, Publisher pushes students to think about design, concision in their writing, images to enhance content, and overall aesthetic appeal. These are standards integral to all ELA learning.

Working With Windows Movie Maker

Windows Movie Maker is a user-friendly yet powerful program you can use to create your own movies, or invite students to create original movies, or video adaptations of short stories. Movie Maker is not just for videos, but supports the integration of photos, sounds, music, and special effects. Best of all, Movie Maker is a software program that you can download free from Microsoft.com. Since you learned to insert and drag photos and texts in the earlier sections, you can quickly create professional looking movies. I find videotaping my graduate students in literature studies, or in presentations, or collaborative work and creating movies, inspires these teachers to do the same with their own classes.

You will need the following materials to create your movies: a computer that has a FireWire port, a basic digital camera, a digital camcorder, a FireWire, and a USB cable (that connects your camera to the computer). A FireWire (also known as i.Link or IEEE 1394) is a digital audio/digital video cable that streams large files(such as video) from your camcorder or digital camera quickly to your computer. The FireWire is connected directly from your camcorder to your computer. Without a FireWire port on your computer, you may not be able to create movies.

Getting to Know Movie Maker

The main Movie Maker window contains all the tools and commands you will need to know to create your first movie, and further, all these tools and commands are clean, precise, and simply integrate the various media into your presentation. Look at the menu and get to know it before you start building your movie. The top menu bar is similar to others that you have seen in Microsoft Windows applications: File, Edit, View, Tools, Clip, Play, and Help. Use the File menu to import files, save and reopen project files, and to save finished movies. The Edit menu houses common editing tools like Cut, Copy, and Paste. The View, Tools, and Clip menus are specific to Movie Maker, and you will learn how to use these in the practice exercise that follows, when making your first movie. If you hold your cursor over the icon, a ToolTip will appear and describes the function of the button. (See Figure 5.12 for a screen shot of the menu and toolbar icons.)

The left side of the main window, Movie Tasks, is where you will do most of your work. The first set of commands, under the heading Capture Video, helps you build your movie. *Capture from video device* is the command that

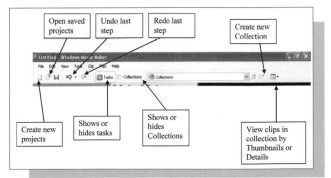

Figure 5.12 *Menu and toolbar, and their functions.*

streams the video from your camcorder to your computer. The *Import video* command allows you to import video clips, or segments of raw, unedited moving image footage, that you have saved on your hard drive or have used in other projects.

Import pictures enables you to bring into your movie any photos you have saved on your computer. *Import audio or music* allows you to integrate sound bytes or songs. The second set of commands can help you edit your movie. *View video transitions* shows effects that you insert between clips or photos to move between one image to another. Transitions can create a mood or surprise a viewer and make the movie more real. *View video effects* contains special effects you apply to your clips to make them appear different from the raw footage or to enhance them. They are different from video transitions because they are used directly on the clips, rather than between clips. You can also use up to six different effects on a video clip, while you can use only one video transition between clips. *Make titles or credits* allows you to add titles, credits, and put in text anywhere in your movie.

Practice Creating Your Own Movie

When you complete this practice exercise, you will be familiar with many of the tools in the Movie Maker program. Keep in mind that this movie may not be perfect, but it is a starting place, and will allow you to discover all the features that Movie Maker offers.

Before creating your first movie, brainstorm a topic or a person you would like to video. If you have video footage from a family event, you can use this. My first movies were about potters and how they soda fire or raku fire pottery pieces. Keep the movie short, perhaps less than two minutes, but be sure to have much more video footage than you think you'll need. A two-minute video sounds extremely short, but I have found that it takes about one hour to edit every minute of video. For instance, before creating my pottery video, I took many photographs and about three hours of raw video footage of potter Bill Buckner doing a soda firing. These three hours of video footage I eventually edited to a 27-minute movie. Next, consider the other media you would like to include in your movie: favorite song, still photos, or audio files. These files should be on your computer rather than on a flash drive or on a digital camera storage disk to make importing these files easier.

Importing or Capturing Video Clips. Now you are ready to import some of your video. Video files must be captured from a camcorder or imported from existing video footage on your computer. If you have video footage on your computer that you want to use, click the "Import video" command and select the file you wish to import. The footage will import into this project (unless it is a file that cannot be read by Movie Maker). If, however, you have to retrieve footage from your camcorder directly, you must capture video by following these steps.

First, make sure that your video tape is rewound and ready to go. Next, attach your FireWire from your video camcorder to your computer. Turn your video camcorder on to "VCR" setting, and the computer should recognize your camcorder. Click on the command, "Capture video from device" in the Movie Tasks Bar on the left. A screen will pop up and identify your video camcorder and download any drivers it needs to stream the video. Once it identifies the camera, click "Next." A window will then appear and ask you to name the video clip and place it in a folder. Click "Next." Now you'll be asked to select a video quality for your video file. This setting determines how large the file will be, and the quality of its playback on a large screen. Although you may be tempted to go with the recommendation offered by Movie Maker, I suggest you select "Other" and highlight "High Quality Video (large)." The resolution quality of this clip will be higher and therefore clearer on larger screens. Click "Next."

Finally, you will select the video capture method. The Capture dialog box appears and offers you the choice of letting the video stream automatically or you can capture the video manually. For this project, select "Capture parts of the tape manually," and check the box at the bottom that allows you to preview the video while it is streaming. Click the "Next" button to get to the next screen. The "Start Capture" screen will appear (see screen shot in Figure 5.13) which allows you capture video from your camera.

Click the "Start Capture" button. Your video should appear in the Monitor screen as it is being streamed. Allow at least two or three minutes of video to stream. When the video clip is over or you want to stop the video stream, click "Stop Capture." Movie Maker then translates the video tape into a digitized video clip. Notice the commands underneath the preview window. They look much like any recording device with which you may be familiar, such as play, stop, rewind, and so forth. These controls allow you to start and stop the movie, once you begin building it, or start and stop the video capture.

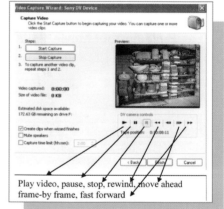

Play video, pause, stop, rewind, move ahead frame-by frame, fast forward ►

Figure 5.13 Functions under Monitor.

Once the video has been streamed, the video clip(s) appear(s) under the Collection pane, or the middle part of the Main Menu (see screen shot in Figure 5.14). Sometimes, if the video clip is large, Movie Maker will automatically make smaller clips for easier handling in the movie building part.

Importing Photo Images. Once you have your video captured or imported, consider including

Collections pane: Images, video and audio/music.

Figure 5.14 Collections pane: Images, video, and audio/music.

photos into your movie. You can import photos from your hard drive or your "My Pictures" folder that you think will fit well into your movie. Under the Capture Video menu on the left side of your screen, click on the command, "Import pictures." The dialogue boxes will ask for the files you wish to import. Follow the directions for importing pictures as you did with PowerPoint. The photos that you choose will appear under the Collections, or the middle part of the window. Once you have imported your photo images and captured your video clips, you are nearly ready to build your movie.

Importing Music. Consider adding a soundtrack to your movie, or music that sets the mood or atmosphere of your movie. You will import music using a similar procedure as you did with importing photos. Click on the "Import audio and music" link in the Capture Video menu. Browse for the folder where your favorite music is, click on the file you wish to import, and click the "Import" button. The song(s) that you import will now also appear under the Collections pane. You will recognize the file because of its musical note icon and file name. Now, with your songs, photos, and video clips imported, you are ready to build your movie!

Building Your Movie. Building your movie is as simple as dragging and dropping images, music, and video onto a timeline or a storyboard. A *timeline* uses time as the scale to measure the length of clips (visual, musical, special effects), and replays in real time when the movie is played back (see Figure 5.15). A *storyboard* is a series of graphics, or small thumbnails, sequentially organized in terms of how the scene will play (see Figure 5.16). You can easily shift between these two views by clicking on "Show Timeline" or "Show Storyboard." Working in the timeline view allows you to add music, audio, and edit clips. It also maximizes your overall work time. The storyboard view is really meant only to work with video clips. The timeline has several places on which particular media is placed. Let me familiarize you with the various functions in this area. These functions will enable you to fine-tune your movie, and to review it from any place on the timeline.

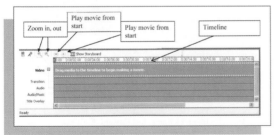

Figure 5.15 Movie Maker storyboard.

Figure 5.16 Adding images to the storyboard.

128

It's important to know the five lines within the timeline before you drag and drop your media. The first line, *Video*, is for still photos or video clips. (If you try to place this media into another line, Movie Maker will stop you). You must click the plus sign next to Video on the timeline to see the Transitions and Audio lines. To increase or decrease the size of the thumbnails on the timeline, check the plus or minus signs in the magnifying glasses. The *Transitions* line is where you will drag video transition effects. When you want to add audio to your movie, there are two basic commands. The *Audio* line is for audio bytes (voice-overs, narrations) and the audio from one of your video clips. When the video clip is used in this way, only the audio is heard. The *Audio/Music* line is where songs and sound effect clips are added. These clips can be shifted underneath the video and audio clips and are meant to act as background music or sound effects. On the *Title Overlays* line you can create titles, subtitles, and credits and add them to your movie.

Adding Photo Images. Scroll through your collections until you find the photo image that you want. Click and drag the image to the Video bar of your timeline. It will go into the first large square on the left (see screen shot in Figure 5.17 for an example), and appears as a thumbnail with the image name along the right side. The photo is now a part of your movie! To get more practice, drag a number of photos to your movie, click on the first photo in the timeline, and then click the play button under the Monitor screen. Your movie will play in real time.

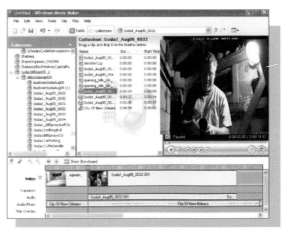

Adding Video Clips. As you did with your photo images, click and drag a video clip to the storyboard. You can drag it between photos, after the photos, or before the photos. The movie

Figure 5.17 *Adding video and music clips to storyboard.*

clip can be *trimmed* to remove any footage you do not want in the movie. To trim a clip, select the clip on the timeline. Move the cursor to the beginning or the end of the clip. A double-headed arrow appears. Click on the arrow, and move it to the right or left. The clip is now trimmed. To do fine-tuned trimming, click on the magnifying glass with a + and the clip is enlarged. You can trim full seconds, minutes, or fractions of a second from a clip as well as a photograph or music.

Now that you have added photos and trimmed your video clips, play your movie to see if you like it. It is easy to shift around some of the media. You can move photos and clips around by simply clicking on the thumbnail on the timeline, and dragging it to the position you want it to be placed.

Adding Transitions and Video Effects. Film directors transition from one scene to another using a number of different effects; using Movie Maker, you can use transitions, sepia tones, or aging effects to add interest. To add transitions, click on *View Video Transitions* on the Tasks menu on the left side of your screen. A number of different transitions appear. To preview the transition, click on it and then the play button under the Monitor. If you like this transition, drag it to the timeline and place it before or after the photo. Click on the photo in the timeline to see how it looks in your movie. If you do not like it, you can delete it by clicking on it on the Transitions area, and pressing the delete key.

To add different video effects, click on *View Video Effects* to see the choices you have. Like with Transitions, click on an effect, and then click the play button under the Monitor to see if you like it. Then drag the effect onto the media file on your timeline.

Adding Music. The mood or atmosphere of your movie can be greatly enhanced by adding music. Usually, I add the music to the movie toward the end of the editing process. My choice of music is driven by the way the movie flows, and it is not until the final edit that I know what soundtrack to add. Because you are making a two-minute movie, you will need to trim the music in the same way that you trimmed video clips. As you did with photos and video clips, click and drag your song to the Audio/Music line. Now that you have music, play your movie and see what you have created! ■

Reflection on Working With Technology

Learning the tools of various software programs provides flexibility in expression, encourages interaction between teachers and students, and supports students as they generate meaning across design, intention, interest, and content in ELA learning. The possibilities are endless when you consider how PowerPoint, Publisher, and Movie Maker can be useful tools to teach the English language arts. For instance, just recently, I have asked my students to create Public Service Announcements (PSAs) in Movie Maker. They choose an issue that is raised in a Young Adult novel, and create a 30- to 60-second PSA on this issue.

Although there are many other exciting features to PowerPoint, Publisher, and Movie Maker, it is beyond the scope of this chapter to describe them all. I hope you will continue to explore in the ways multimedia presentations can enhance your teaching and learning experiences.

Reading Artworks: The Grammar of Visual Texts

- *How are pictures designed?*
- *What relationships exist within elements in an artwork and the artist?*
- *What relationships exist between the viewer and the artwork?*
- *What aspects of an artwork reveal something about the art maker?*

Reading Artworks: Learning About Students' Literacy and Lives
by Mark Fishburn

Last year, I took a class in which the reading of my own artworks and those of students' enlightened me to the way in which I now integrate the arts into my high school English classes. As a teacher in an alternative high school, I look forward to assigning an art project based on what we have been reading in my class because my students surprise me with their art projects. I have heard many times from other teachers that high school students' responding to literature through art is not something English teachers should be doing: Students need to learn to read and write. However, when I read their artworks in response to literature, I learn about them in ways that I hadn't realized. Just recently, we finished reading *Monster* by Walter Dean Myers (2001). The protagonist in the novel, a 16-year-old boy named Steve, goes through a traumatic experience and is forced to question his identity. My students enjoyed this character's search for self and his ambivalence and confusion about his identity. In the art project, my students had to think about the character they were going to visually represent and how they were going to portray him or her. I wanted my students to think about what Steve had done and in turn look at their own identities. Some of them brought in experiences from the outside, and I found that they engaged both cognitive and critical thinking.

One student in particular, Kiara, intrigued me while she was doing this project. She was a leader in this class, always positively engaged in the activities,

Figure 6.1 *Kiara's art project, response to Monster.*

and liked to lead classroom discussions. Her smile and her energy brightened up the class. Yet, as I watched her work on her art project (see Figure 6.1), I learned that there was more to Kiara than I had thought. She chose to use poster board instead of drawing paper and painted a very large self-portrait in shades of gray. Then she painted the margins with bright colors. At the top of the poster she wrote, "In a world of color I'm..." Then, as a final touch, she put a logo on her shirt that said, "I can only be me," suggesting that she had accepted who she was. Her choice of materials and her logo

132

signified that she was not quite as confident as I had suspected, an aspect that eluded me from her classroom persona. I learned about Kiara that day through her art. Reading students' artwork enables me to consider just how important the visual arts become when learning about the literacy of my students.

In ELA classes, learners speak to teachers visually all the time. Their messages are humorous, satirical, serious, and sad, and have clear and distinct forms and structures that can be read and analyzed, much in the same way teachers analyze and respond to their written work. Yet, rarely do teachers respond critically to these visual texts, in large part because they are unsure of how to read visual texts. Whether students create visual texts in response to literature, to decorate the walls of the classroom, as notebook decoration, as book cover projects, or to doodle because they have finished homework, or are disinterested in learning for whatever reason, the important thing to remember is that their visual texts send messages from the student-artist to other student-viewers to the teacher-viewer.

Reading and studying students' visual texts support three important aspects of learning. First, visual texts show a distinct link between cognition and affect. Students share what they understand about ELA concepts through their visual communication, so effectively reading students' visual texts offers insight on the relationships students see across a range of texts. Second, as you learn to read visual texts, you can share this tool with students so they, too, better understand and are conscious of the marks they make on canvas (or paper, or walls, or computer screens). And, third, an ability to read visual texts allows you and your students to understand messages in more complex ways.

This chapter will demonstrate how to read student-generated visual texts, and what these texts can tell you about the literacy practices of students over time. That is, like written work, the visual texts that students create over the space of a marking period, semester, or year, tell a story about their literacy practices. When learning to read images, keep in mind what you have learned about the language of art in the first chapters, and apply this learning to your readings. By the end of the chapter, you will be able to read your students' visual texts with a more critical and informed eye.

Reading Visual Representations

Students represent meaning in ELA classes all the time, but what does the word *represent* mean? *Representation* is a process in which humans seek to interpret some object or entity, whether physical or intangible. In any semiotic system, representations are only partial, and can never convey a person's entire meaning. Representations are driven by our *interest* in the idea or object, and informed by our cultural, social, and psychological history and the specific context in which the representation is produced. That is, we make *intentional* decisions about what physical and intangible ideas we want to include or not include in representations, which are always based within past and present experiences. Furthermore, as in written communication, the visual textmaker's representation is as much about her or him as it is about the viewer's reading.

As an example, let us return to José's representation of Alice from the novel *Go Ask Alice* (Anonymous, 1998), which we first viewed in chapter 2 (see Figure 2.3 on page 23). José created this representation in the context of a class assignment. Thus, this representation was created with the intention of expressing his learning from a book he was reading to someone, usually the teacher or classmates. Study the physical characteristics José chooses to include in his interpretation of Alice. These physical marks on the page are what Kress and van Leeuwen (1996) call its *criterial aspects*. What are some of the criterial aspects that José includes? José draws Alice from the waist up, and she takes up nearly the entire canvas. Artistically speaking, Alice has *volume* in this representation. She holds a cigarette of sorts, and from the smoke coming from her mouth, she has just taken a puff. Her straight hair, parted in the center, is cropped unevenly, and her bangs lay in the middle of her forehead. José's Alice looks directly at the viewers with her diamond-shaped eyes, and her eyebrows are angular. When you look at the criterial aspects in this image of Alice, what impression do you have of her?

The criterial aspects that José intentionally draws tell a story about him as a learner in his transaction with Alice, as well as himself as a person. As a learner, José uses angular shaped eyebrows and diamond-shaped eyes, which forces viewers into a relationship with Alice. Her eyes lock onto those of the viewers', and almost challenge us to look away. José's broad-shouldered Alice, with her right hand up holding a cigarette, smoking, and an open body position all indicate his intention to depict Alice's confident defiance. Alice looks straight at the viewer, not flinching or asking for sympathy. Rather, she expects that viewers have no right to question her choices and decisions. Why does José represent Alice in the way that he does? As a person, José himself is a tough wannabe gang member. So the criterial aspects that interest him may be those with which he associates—or wants to associate—and which carry messages of defiance. The elements that he presents in Alice emerge from his own experiences and interests as a 15-year-old, at this moment in his life.

This example reinforces that when students construct meaning visually, they do so based upon their interests in particular events, characters, or themes in a story. They also represent their personal perceptions of these events or characters. José renders a defiant Alice, one that he finds interesting and compelling because of his own personality.

For the past 15 years, I have studied the artworks of many students and teachers across the United States in whose classrooms I have done research, or who have participated in my workshops or presentations. Over time, I have discovered that nearly all students, through their general and everyday interaction with art in the world, have internalized particular visual structures and use these structures to convey their interpretation of literary or original texts. In this section, you will learn about types of visual texts through which students structure their interpretations, how visual information is organized on canvases, how and why viewers interact with images, and how to read angles and perspectives in photographs. This knowledge can help you respond differently and constructively to the visual texts your students create.

Types of Visual Text Structures

In ELA classes, there are three basic visual text structures: aesthetic, narrative, and metaphoric texts. I have come to recognize these structures by studying the relationships among elements in the visual text, and engaging in conversations with students about their intentions and the purpose behind their artworks. Knowledge of these structures offers insight into how students perceive and work with art.

Aesthetic Texts

Aesthetic texts are those that are structured around perception, sensation, and imagination, and how they relate to knowing, understanding, and feeling about the world (Greene, 2001). When students create visual texts that are intended to be aesthetic, they perceive art as a way to show harmony, and a way to decorate their written pieces, much like they would decorate their rooms. The intention or purpose behind aesthetic visual texts is to make them pretty, creative, or decorative. Students often integrate art elements to make their visual texts pleasing to the viewer, and these elements may have limited connections to the literary text. Figure 6.2 shows two artworks that represent aesthetic texts. High school sophomores were invited to select from several options and respond to *Lord of the Flies* (Golding, 1959). Taje and Jill chose to write poetry accompanied by

Figure 6.2 *Taje's and Jill's aesthetic responses to* Lord of the Flies.

illustrations. Taje's intention is to decorate her poem with colorful and pleasant clip art images of bright pink pigs and bugs, sky blue birds, and the bright greens and yellows of nature. Her image is vertically oriented (read from top to bottom; seen on left side of Figure 6.2). Taje's use of bright and cheery colors contrasts starkly to the actual brutality and aggression in the novel, and these images invite viewers to read this text as aesthetically pleasing. Jill's text is a collection of poetry that she wrote about the characters and has a horizontal orientation (read from left to right). For her, art elements help her create a decorative project. Jill frames her poetry onto dark blue and green construction paper and adds curled strips of dark blue construction paper between the poems to add interest to the overall appearance of her project. Jill uses graphite and colored pencils to illustrate elements of the novel. Taje's and Jill's texts are pleasing to the viewer, and the art elements serve as decorative features within their poetry projects.

Narrative Texts

A second visual text structure commonly found in ELA classrooms is the *narrative* text, or artwork organized in the manner of a story. Much of the reading that students do in ELA classes is narrative literature, and students see art as a way to tell their stories or to interpret stories. Within narrative visual texts, visual stories can be organized in three different ways: schematic texts, descriptive texts, and multiphasic texts.

Schematic Texts. *Schematic* texts contain elements that are visually descriptive, but their relationships are not always easily understood (Gombrich, 1994) and will be either explicit or implicit.

Explicit relationships are those that can be identified, at least in part, by the

Figure 6.3 *Aaron's schematic text, response to* A Lesson Before Dying.

objects in a visual text. Often, explicit relationships contain arrows or lines that connect one visual object to another. Students organize, or *schematize*, visual information in a way that shows their understanding—as they do when reading. Schematic texts with explicit relationships often show objects in visual connection to a more central object. Consider Figure 6.3, a picture created by

Aaron, a high school junior, after reading *A Lesson Before Dying* (Gaines, 1994). In brief, this novel relates the events leading up to the execution of Jefferson, an African American man convicted of murder. Grant Wiggins, an African American teacher, is pressured to visit the jail and talk with Jefferson, who sees himself as no better than a hog. Over time, Grant's conversations with Jefferson reestablish Jefferson's sense of dignity and, as is his aunt's wish, he walks to the electric chair as a man. Aaron visually and explicitly organizes events that he considers important in the novel through his use of the long thick line that moves from the center of the visual text to the upper right corner, and the smaller tributaries that lead off the main line. Central to Aaron's interest is Jefferson and his incarceration. Jefferson stands behind thick black vertical lines that literally cage him in. Aaron draws a strong thick red line that explicitly connects the jail cell directly to the electric chair, which moves toward the upper right-hand side of the canvas. He explicitly connects other visual elements (hogs, radio, and teacher) to this path to the electric chair with smaller thick red, blue, and green lines. As viewers, if we are familiar with Gaines's novel, this schematic text makes sense and we can see Aaron's explicit connections to various events in the novel. However, if we are unfamiliar with Gaines's novel, we can infer that objects within this text—hogs around a table, a man holding up a pointer to a blackboard, and a radio—are connected somehow, by nature of Aaron's use of thick lines, to the overall final result, the electric chair. In essence, Aaron visually creates an explicit schematic roadmap of key events in this novel.

Sometimes schematically organized visual texts have implicit relationships, or connections that are not visually shown. That is, the objects on the visual text do not have lines or arrows that let us know how these objects relate to one another. After reading *Animal Farm* (Orwell, 1946), seventh-grade student Damek creates a schematically organized text that shows implied relationships (see Figure 6.4). Each of these animals is descriptively rendered (we recognize a horse, two cats, bird, and pig), but Damek visually implies their relationship in two ways: They are drawn on the same canvas, and all stare directly at the viewer. These animals could generate a range of meanings, but in connection to Orwell's novel, viewers can infer that these animals, together, are determined to fight against the farmer's tyranny.

Figure 6.4 *Damek's implied schematic representation of* Animal Farm.

Descriptive Texts. A second type of narrative visual text, *descriptive* text, visually represents a single recognizable captured moment or action in a literary text. Sarita's image in Figure 6.5 represents a particular scene

Figure 6.5 *Sarita's descriptive text, response to* To Kill a Mockingbird.

in *To Kill a Mockingbird* (Lee, 1988) in which Scout and Calpurnia visit a cemetery. Often, in such visual texts, there is a one-to-one correspondence between the details in the story and the details in the picture. Sarita's picture closely renders the book's description of tombstones that were disintegrating, the yellows and browns that shine like bottles of soda, and Calpurnia's ever watchful eye over Scout. In descriptive visual texts like Sarita's, the elements are dynamic and dramatic, and unlike schematic representations, they relate clearly to each other. In descriptive texts, viewers can interpret a story that may or may not relate to the literary text being depicted. That is, Sarita's text stands alone as a complete image and narrative, and does not depend on knowledge of Lee's novel. In my study of visual texts, students seem to create descriptive texts more often than any other visual text structure when they respond to literary texts.

Multiphasic Texts. A third type of narrative text is the *multiphasic* text (Sonesson, 1988), or a single static text that is constructed in phases. Collages are the most common multiphasic text found in ELA classes, and they contain many individual elements (pictures, text) that overlap, collide, or merge together to tell a story. Collages are built in phases; students layer images atop one another, many without any white space showing. Multiphasic texts are popular constructions in ELA classes for several reasons. Students are barraged daily with thousands of images

Figure 6.6 *Soje's multiphasic narrative text, response to* Lord of the Flies.

through music videos, complex advertisements, and special effects that crowd, cram, and alter images in ways before unseen. Collages also offer students a way to express meaning without having to show their ability to draw, which helps them get past any insecurity they may have about doing visual arts projects.

Figure 6.6 represents Soje's multiphasic text, or collage, produced after her reading of *Lord of the Flies* (Golding, 1959). Soje arranges images, language texts, size, and colors to tell the story of the destruction of civilization depicted in the novel. Soje initially chose natural images to indicate the setting, a remote and untamed island where the boys are stranded. Layered atop of this natural background are visual elements (conch, letters, words) that represent key issues and symbols in the novel. These images take on interpretive significance for Soje. At once they submerge the simplicity of nature and also emerge as the forces that destroy any aspect of civilization the boys once knew. The relationships among the art elements are clearly connected and convey a strong interpretation of the novel. Soje's visual text is multiphasic both in terms of its construction as well as her intended meaning.

Metaphoric Texts

The third visual text structure is *metaphoric*. As the word implies, metaphoric texts present metaphors in which physical elements in the visual text represent action, events, or situations in a literary text. Unlike schematic texts where implicit connections are not always clear, elements in metaphoric texts are often *prototypical*; that is, they are dense, intimately relate to each other, and seemingly have equal value (Sonesson, 2004). Unlike narrative texts, metaphoric texts expect that viewers know something about the metaphor's origin and why it was made. After reading *A Lesson Before Dying* (Gaines, 1994), Lakina creates a picture of Jefferson that is both prototypical and metaphorical, shown in Figure 6.7. All elements in the visual text are dense and closely related; there are no loose objects in the picture, and viewers see a unified image. Lakina chooses to illustrate Jefferson's mental transformation from hog to human through the anthropomorphic figure, which is both hog and human. For Lakina, Jefferson's mental state is like a hog, an animal that responds only to instinct. Yet by giving the hog human feet and hands, Lakina creates the transformation from hog to man metaphorically—and slowly. She wants the viewer to notice that she understands this transformation, a key theme in the novel.

Figure 6.7 *Lakina's metaphoric text, response to* A Lesson Before Dying.

Practice Reading Visual Text Structures

Look at student-generated artworks in Figures 6.8 a, b, and c, all visual texts in response to *A Lesson Before Dying* (Gaines, 1994). Are they schematic? Narrative? Metaphoric? Or a combination? What aspects of each text help you understand the distinctions? What criterial aspects do these students include? How do these details point to their interests? What do you learn about students' reading of the novel?

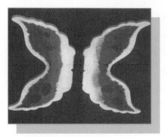

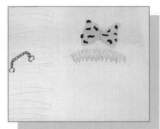

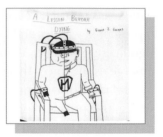

Figure 6.8a *Example of metaphoric text, 11th-grade student's visual representations of* A Lesson Before Dying.

Figure 6.8b *Example of symbolic and/or narrative text, Kelly's visual representations of* A Lesson Before Dying.

Figure 6.8c *Example of schematic text, 11th-grade student's visual representations of* A Lesson Before Dying.

Figure 6.8a is a metaphoric text; the butterfly represents Jefferson's freedom through death. Figure 6.8b could be both symbolic and narrative depending on your familiarity with Gaines's novel. By looking at this image, you can narrate a simple story of a human incarcerated and freed at the end of the story. However, the chains and butterfly can also be symbols of struggle and freedom, especially as viewed through the themes that run through this novel. Figure 6.8c is more schematic in nature. The objects within the image are identifiable; the figure in the electric chair is both hog and man. If we know the story, we can see that this part of the story, the transformation from hog to man, was complete when Jefferson went to the electric chair.

Notice how two of the images bring in the symbol of the butterfly as freedom, both images created by females. They seem to respond to an overall theme in the story of freedom. The third image, created by a male, is more concrete and presents a troubling scene, yet it still relates to the theme of freedom through the electric chair. These visual texts can help us better understand how some students respond to the novel's theme in a gentler, more abstract way, while the other in a more direct and literal way.

Knowledge of aesthetic, narrative, and metaphoric structures that appear in students' visual texts can help you understand that artworks are not just pretty pictures. Visual texts contain information (along with art elements) that help to explain how students read, the details they find significant, and how they interpret the literary texts they read. Close and analytical readings of visual texts demonstrate that students tell visual stories in a range of ways. By paying attention to the structures that underpin their visual texts, where elements are in a visual text, the colors that are used, the lines and their shapes, you can generate important discussions with your students about the relationships they see between their visual texts and literary texts. ■

How Visual Texts Are Organized

Have you ever studied advertisements and thought about why they are designed as they are? Look at several ads in any magazine or journal. Cut out one of these ads and paste it into your sketchbook. Use lines to identify the areas of this advertisement that you think are significant. Ask yourself these questions: What elements or objects do you immediately notice? Why? What elements are more prominent than others? Take a closer look. Where are the most significant details located? What appears at the top of the advertisement? The bottom? The left? The right? What does the designer of this ad want us to relate to? How does she or he accomplish this? Decisions about placement of art elements in advertisements are not haphazard; they are intentional and deliberate. In this section, you will study how elements on a canvas are generally organized, how various elements relate to the others, and how such organizations become visible in students' and teachers' visual texts.

Pictures are generally oriented *horizontally*, left to right, or *vertically*, top to bottom. They are also generally organized into four quadrants with an effective center of attention (Figure 6.9a). An image that has a *vertical orientation* will display information in the upper and lower two quadrants, and the image is read from top to bottom (see Figure 6.9b). The upper half of the picture often suggests freedom, happiness, and triumph (Bang, 2000), as well as the ideal (Kress & van Leeuwen, 1996). In advertisements with a vertical orientation, beauty (actresses, models, the ideal look) is often located in this area. The bottom half of the page, according to Bang, feels more threatened, heavier, sadder,

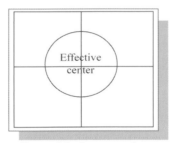

Figure 6.9a *Basic areas of a canvas.*

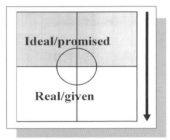

Figure 6.9b *Vertical orientation.*

and constrained, and grounds the image. In Kress and van Leeuwen's perspective, the bottom half is where the "real" (p. 186) of the image is located; this is where information is located, and where product is often shown. Images that have a *horizontal orientation* (illustrated in Figure 6.9c) are read from left to right, and the left side (left top and bottom quadrants) often presents information that is already known or given, while information on the right (top and bottom right quadrants) is new information. Because of our own understanding of Western language

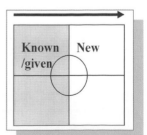

Figure 6.9c *Horizontal orientation.*

conventions, such organization makes sense, because written text is read left to right and top to bottom.

Students' visual texts are often oriented either vertically or horizontally. Let's read and examine Aaron's visual representation of Gaines's novel in light of what you now know about basic areas of the canvas (review Figure 6.3). Aaron's canvas has a vertical orientation and is read from top to bottom. Jefferson occupies the effective center of attention, and it is here that Aaron places Jefferson, around which all other events occur. The top two quadrants represent the ideal while the bottom two represent the real. Aaron creates an interesting visual paradox. Although the images in the upper quadrants are very real events in the novel, they take on ideal qualities. Each of the images—the hogs eating corn at the table, Grant's teaching, Jefferson's radio, and the electric chair—must happen before Jefferson can get to the ideal, the promise of transformation from hog to man, when he walks to the electric chair. The bottom quadrant is where the information is located, or title of the book. The viewer knows that this picture is literally grounded in Gaines's novel, and signifies a threatening, heavy, and sad situation: a lesson before dying.

Now read and examine Figure 6.8b, Kelly's image from *A Lesson Before Dying*. Place imaginary quadrant lines on this image. What is the orientation of this image? Kelly clearly uses a horizontal orientation, or a left to right, reading. The left side is the given information, while the information on the right is new. On the left side, Kelly draws loose, horizontal black lines as a backdrop on which she draw handcuffs. Both elements visually stabilize Jefferson's incarceration and inevitable ending. Jefferson's plight is known; it is the given. Paradoxically, Kelly draws open handcuffs, a visual hint that Jefferson is released from this incarceration. On the right, Kelly visually inscribes a butterfly flying above the

green grass to metaphorically represent Jefferson's transformation. Unlike the black lines, these green lines have an upward diagonal directionality, a move toward the top. Kelly visually represents Jefferson's emotional release from the confines of prison. For Jefferson, his transformation leads him to a new place, one above the earth's surface, and one that is free.

Read Figure 6.10, an image created by 5-year-old Tony titled *Starry Night* and based upon Vincent van Gogh's work of the same name. What is the orientation of this image? What emotion do you think Tony is trying to capture? What does he want the viewer to see? For me, this image is all about the ideal, the space where good things happen. The bright yellow colored stars are strongly accented against the marine blue sky.

Figure 6.10 Tony's
representation of Starry Night.

The dark purple, red, and greens of the ground are shadowed by the night, and only upon close observation do we see the small rectangular buildings at the bottom of the picture. Tony wants viewers to read the stars before the ground and cityscape; it is here in the top of his visual text that he has placed the ideal, the promise, of good things.

Students, even the very young like Tony, internalize how art is structured and oriented through their own reading of visual texts and the world. They learn where the effective centers of attention are, how the positive and ideal are located at the top while the real and grounded are located on the bottom. They learn to present information that is already known on the left and display new information on the right. These conventions, informed by their understanding of Western language conventions of left to right, top to bottom, appear in students' visual texts, and as such, can be part of the discussions surrounding why students design their texts in the way that they do. Why does Aaron place all the images above the center line? Why does Kelly place the open handcuffs to the left of the butterfly? How do they come to these decisions? Conscious attention to such orientations can lead students to consider how authors and artists alike engage readers, and how such decisions become visible in readers' interpretations.

Interaction Between Viewers and Images

Images convey messages to and establish relationships with us all the time. Sometimes the message and relationship is clear and sometimes it is not. When you look at Figure 6.11a, a self-portrait, and Figure 6.11b, a portrait of the artist's friend, both created by Atlanta, Georgia, artist David Robinson, what relationships do you think he wants to establish with the viewer? How does David establish this relationship? What aspects of each image suggest this relationship? What is your response to David's self-portrait? The portrait of his friend? What differences do you note?

Figure 6.11a David Robinson, self-portrait, charcoal and pencil.

Figure 6.11b David Robinson, portrait of friend, charcoal and pencil.

Understanding the Gaze in Images

Like authors, artists intend to establish a particular relationship with the audience, whether it be informational, persuasive, humorous, and so on. The way a character or person in an image looks, or gazes, at the viewer, establishes one of two types of relationships, a *demand* or an *offer* (Kress & van Leeuwen, 1996).

Understanding these two relationships will enable you and your students to read characters in a variety of visual texts.

Demand. Designers of images, especially photographs, portraits, and advertisements, seek to bring about an imaginary relationship between the people in the image and the viewer. When people or objects in an image establish direct eye-to-eye contact with a viewer, Kress and van Leeuwen (1996) call this a "demand." In such a gaze, there is a visually implied "you." People or objects in the image attempt to have the viewer think a particular way, seduce the viewer into a concept or idea, or indicate superiority over the viewer. Images of demand often define who the viewer is (male/female, teen/adult) and may exclude some viewers. For example, photographs of rappers like Eminem and Tupac Shakur appeal to certain viewers, while other viewers are uninterested or disturbed by their gazes. In images of demand, people, characters, or even objects (shoes, watches, lipstick) look directly at viewers and almost dare them to look away or defy them. Consider the World War I poster of Uncle Sam (Figure 6.12). Read the canvas orientation and quadrants of information. Where is the ideal? The real? Now, notice how Uncle Sam's eyes lock onto those of the viewers. He demands that viewers pay attention to him and his message. His foreshortened finger points directly at the viewer, and the written text demands viewers to strongly consider joining the navy. Whom do you think he is addressing? Who is excluded? What message is he sending to the viewer through his eyes and his arm position?

Figure 6.12 *WWI poster of Uncle Sam, example of demand gaze.*

Look again at Figure 6.11a, David Robinson's self-portrait. What relationship does he establish with the viewer? How do you feel when you look at this portrait? In essence, David wants viewers to see him, to look at him. The look is a demand, and viewers should not look away. Images of demand stop viewers and order them to participate in their world.

In visual texts generated in ELA settings, students often represent characters who demand viewers' attention. Look again at the line drawing of militant (Figure 2.8, chapter 2), José's portrait of Alice (Figure 2.3, chapter 2) and Damek's drawings of animals (Figure 6.4). Most noticeable is that all the characters stare directly at the viewer, and demand an imaginary relationship. Militant and Alice look directly at us, and demand that we, as viewers, identify with them. The animals also demand that viewers engage in an imaginary relationship; they stare strongly and directly at the viewer, and demand help from the tyranny they face.

Offer. In a second type of relationship, the viewer is *offered* a relationship with the image. As viewers, we are not the object of gaze, but are subject of the gaze (Kress & van Leeuwen, 1996). Minimal or no contact is made between the viewer and the people/objects in the image. Rather, the viewer's role is that of onlooker—we participate vicariously in the lives represented in the image—almost as if they were museum objects. People/objects in an image are often shown in moments of contemplation. Let us return to Figure 6.12a and 6.12b. Examine the differences between David's self-portrait and the portrait of his friend. The portrait of the friend is an offer; that is, David invites viewers to look at his friend. The slight turn of the head and the eyes not quite in line with the viewer encourage viewers to contemplate what David's friend is thinking. What type of relationship does David's friend want with the viewer? Which viewers does David want to address? In Figure 6.13, the viewer is invited into the world of the woman holding the jar. We wonder why she is looking down and what may be inside this jar. She looks contemplatively downward, and we are curious.

Figure 6.13 *David Robinson, portrait of a woman holding jar, oil.*

Students also create images with the intention to offer or invite viewers into a relationship. After reading *Bridge to Terabithia* (Patterson, 1987), Selena, a sixth-grade student, sculpts Jess, the book's main character, mourning the loss of his best friend Leslie (see Figure 6.14). There is no direct eye contact with the viewer; instead, the viewer is invited to look into the contemplative world of this character. Recall the drawing of Romeo from Figure 2.11 (see page 28) in which ninth-grader Omar positions the viewer as an onlooker, as Romeo grieves over his perceived dead Juliet. In both images, the viewer can only imagine the feelings that reside in the subjects. Yet elements of each visual text enable viewers to sense the grief—the slumped over body position, the hand or arm over the face, and the legs folded under the chest. Selena and Omar intentionally produce images that are not confrontational. Rather, they want viewers to observe the interpretations they have made regarding characters in these texts.

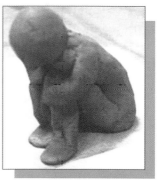

Figure 6.14 *Selena's image, example of offer gaze, clay sculpture.*

Readings of the interaction between the image and the viewer are important to consider when analyzing professional and student-generated visual texts. All literature anthologies contain paintings, sculptures, and various types of artwork, often connected to some assignment or engagement. When students know how to read the relationship between the character and the viewer, they cognitively connect the literary text with the visual text. They can better understand the reasons why an image does or does not fit a particular literary text. They also understand how commercial images, like advertisements, have their objects, people, or characters gaze at viewers for a particular purpose: to demand that they buy or participate in particular ways or interact vicariously in the commercial world. By learning about these relationships, students are encouraged to think more critically about the images they view, and to make decisions about how they interpret and represent a character like Alice or Jess or Romeo.

Reading Photographs: Basic Camera Shots and Angles

Photographs document many important events in our lives, from the work we do in schools, to family events. We encounter photographs in a number of texts including nonfiction books, newspapers, historical documents, subways, billboards, magazines, slide shows, and photo albums. Further, photographs appear in all textbooks and in many supplementary teaching materials in schools, yet many teachers and students know little about how to read photographic images. What can be learned from photos? What does the photograph reveal about its subject? Whose story is being told and whose is left untold? What is the intention behind the photographs taken by the photographer? In this section, you will learn some basic information about photographs and how to read them.

In my own university literacy and language arts courses, I continually take photographs of my pre- and inservice teachers at work, at pottery workshops and classes that I attend, family events, vacations, and things that I find interesting. Study the three photographs in Figures 6.15, 6.16, and 6.17 in the following sections and think about what makes each of these photographs different. In your sketchbook, jot down information you see, where you as the viewer are located, and the feeling you get from each of these photographs. Also, consider the intention of photographer in each of these photographs.

Figure 6.15 *Bill Buckner defining rim of platter, close-up photograph.*

Figure 6.16 *Preservice teachers reading and writing, medium shot photograph.*

Figure 6.17 *Princess Diana talks with friend, long shot photograph.*

Like wet and dry media artists, photographers must consider composition, or the content of the picture. Photographers use several basic shots to compose their images: *close-ups*, *medium shots*, and *long shots*. There are also several basic angles from which photographers shoot: *high*, *frontal*, and *low-camera*. According to Kress and van Leeuwen (1996), the position of the photographer and the angle at which the photograph is taken determine the difference between involvement and detachment.

Close-Ups

The close-up shot (CU) fills a frame with the most important information in a composition. A close-up should include only the action of primary interest. In Figure 6.15, the CU is of a potter's hands defining the rim of a platter. The photographer's focus is on the potter's hands and their position to show this part of the process. Close-ups help build viewer's interest in the subject matter. Viewers want to know what is happening in the photograph. In Figure 6.15, the photographer is interested in how a rim on a platter is made, and takes a close-up.

Medium Shots

A medium shot (MS) is between a long shot and a close-up. The camera brings the image or the main part of the composition into focus and answers the question "what." In an MS, people are usually photographed from the waist up. An MS is normally sufficient to show clearly the facial expressions, gestures, or movements of a single person or a small group of people. Figure 6.16 is an MS of teachers reading picture books and writing responses.

Long Shots

A long shot (LS) shows the setting, the people, and other objects to acquaint viewers with their overall appearance and location of a scene. An LS is used to establish all elements within the scene so the audience knows who and what is involved and where the action is taking place. Figure 6.17 is an LS of Princess Diana talking with a friend before she headed over to the tennis courts around the corner. I took this photograph outside my sister's home in London, England, in 1988. This LS shows that I have extremely limited participation.

Locating Power in Image Through Angles

Like artists in other media, photographers shoot photographs with intention and interest. A photographer reveals his or her relationship with a person, group, or setting through the choice of angles and location of the shot. For instance, when you study the angle at which the photograph in Figure 6.15 has been taken, can you determine where the photographer is located? Even though you cannot see her or him, you know the angle is slightly to the left and above the action. Such *high* angles give power to the photographer, and indicate that the photographer understands the action, but is not an actual participant.

Now look again at Figure 6.16 and notice the photograph's angle is a side and slightly *frontal* angle. Frontal angles indicate that the photographer and the people in the image are on *equal terms*, that the photographer knows about the composition and what the people are doing, or may even be a participant in the action. If you look again at Figure 6.17, you'll notice that the photograph is taken from a frontal angle that shows the details of the street and the two people talking. Although the frontal angle would indicate equality among the photographer and the scene, when combined with a LS view, you can interpret that when I took the photograph, I did not see myself as equal in this scene.

Angles shot from above tend to diminish the people in the photograph, and makes them look small and insignificant (Kress & van Leeuwen, 1996). Capturing individuals in this way dehumanizes them and "flattens [them] morally to ground level" (Martin, 1968, cited in Kress & van Leeuwen, 1996, p. 146). When people are photographed from high angles, the power of the photographer is evident. She or he controls who and what is seen.

To further understand power relationships and angles in photographs, examine the Ellis Island immigration photographs from the Library of Congress Catalog shown in Figures 6.18–6.20. Write down in your sketchbook what you notice about these images in terms of content, overall impression, and angle. Where is the photographer located when he takes each photograph? What do you think was the intention of the photographers who captured these events?

Figure 6.18 displays perhaps one of the most recognizable Ellis Island photographs, depicting doctors screening immigrants for diseases. In this LS, the photographer takes the picture from a frontal angle in which the vanishing point ends in the upper left-hand side of the photograph. The wire fencing and the stained glass window in the back lead the eye toward the vanishing point. The angle of the photograph indicates that the photographer is off to the left and outside the space of the immigrants; he is detached from this experience. What is seen in this room is not a part of the photographer's world; it is the world of the

Figure 6.18 *Health examination at Ellis Island.*

immigrant. The photographer, although on the same plane as the immigrants, has power through the sharp and deep angle of the shot.

Figure 6.19 *Steerage children playing on deck of a ship headed toward Ellis Island.*

In Figure 6.19, the photographer is above and slightly left of the steerage children playing on the deck of a ship heading to Ellis Island. The photograph is an LS in which the whole of the action is captured, but the distance from the immigrants also indicates that the photographer is not of the immigrant world. Faces of the immigrants are not recognizable, none of them looks at the photographer, and no relationship is established. This particular angle shows, again, a sense of detachment, and presents the world of the immigrant outside of the world of the photographer.

Now study Figure 6.20, a photograph of a Polish emigrant boarding a ship to come to the U.S. The angle is frontal and the photographer seems to be on equal plane with the subject, yet, as in the other images, this immigrant does not look at the photographer and, thus, shares no relationship with the viewer or the photographer. What is captured front and center, however, is the poverty that is often associated with immigrants.

Figure 6.20 *Polish emigrant boarding ship with trunk on shoulders.*

Reading Across Images in a Text

An individual photograph, or any artwork on its own, perhaps does not carry the weight that several do when viewed at once. Collectively, photographs and artworks can present a part of history or an event in a particular way. Now, with your knowledge of composition and angles, when you read across Figures 6.18, 6.19, and 6.20, what do you notice? How are immigrants represented in these photographs? How does the photographer treat his subjects, especially considering the angles he uses? Although the intention behind these historic photographs may be to document U.S. immigration in a positive light, the photographs tell a different, and quite opposing, story. Photographers distance themselves from the scenes, capture hundreds of immigrants arriving daily, and often capture immigrants at their desperate moments. Although photographs are often thought to capture the reality of a situation, photographs, like artworks, are not benign. They speak of the interests and intentions of the photographer or the person who hires such photographs. Photographs, like artworks, in and of themselves in isolation, may not suggest the less than positive view of immigration. Yet when viewers learn to read angles, understand the three types of shots, and critically examine the composition of photographs, they become more thoughtful about the messages that are sent visually to the readers.

For instance, I read the photographs in an issue of the children's magazine *Kids Discover*, which was focused on immigration. Although the cover contains the words *illustrious*, *industrious*, *ingenious*, and *immigrants*, the photographs tell a different story. The images show immigrants in impoverished, overcrowded, and challenging settings. Such images can induce feelings of xenophobia rather than celebration of difference. As teachers, we want to be able to share insights on reading photographs with our students. Knowledge of angles, involvement and detachment, and types of shots will enable students to read photographs more thoughtfully and critically. Furthermore, they will be more cognizant of the photographs they take or select to convey their intended meanings. Reading photographs that appear in content textbooks then becomes an essential skill for readers to learn—especially if they are the people represented in the photographs.

Reflection on Reading Visual Texts and Photographs

Significant in reading artworks is the concept that artworks have recognizable structures, and that students learn them through their everyday reading of the world. Interestingly, many students are unaware that they are even creating such structures, but when they have the opportunity to explore and analyze these structures, they become more cognizant of how and what they wish to represent. In addition, an ability to read visual texts, including photographs, in light of their composition, structure, interaction with viewers, and angles will strengthen the relationship between literary text and accompanying visual texts that students create or view in their anthologies, textbooks, or picture books.

As teachers, we must be aware of how the texts, books, magazine photographs, posters, and visual texts we use in our classrooms represent covert ideas. How often do we pass by posters on the school walls that say "Eat right" near a cafeteria, only to see batter-fried fish sticks for lunch? How often do you notice the billboards that advertise alcohol with text that reads "Get back into your father's will" and a bottle of whiskey wrapped in velvet? Advertisers, like photographers, artists, and others who communicate visually, want us to read the images as well as the written text. They understand that we interpret and internalize messages sent both verbally and visually. To help our students become more critical in their reading of both written and visual texts, we must be more informed readers of images and how and what objects are placed within a visual text.

I am reminded of the many classrooms in which I have asked students if they ever discuss the illustrations in their literature anthologies or the photographs in their social studies texts. Nearly all of them say they do not. Part of this is because we have yet to introduce the reading of image into our curriculum as a vital part of reading the world (Freire & Macedo, 1987). Freire and Macedo argue that it is important not only to be able to read the words in a text, but more importantly to understand the beliefs and assumptions that underpin these words. I believe this is the same with visual texts: In order to read critically the underpinning messages sent visually through advertisements, textbook illustrations, photographs, and so on, we must be knowledgeable about how such texts are structured. To read images with an informed eye will help us to examine more closely the whole message, both the written text and the visual text.

Figure 6.21 is one of about 10 images, all focused on autobiography, that one teacher created across a semester in a literacy course. Over time, criterial aspects, or details, kept emerging in each of these images. Water, nature, and preservation were all part of this teacher's participation in outdoor activities and beliefs about the significance of nature. Over time, not only did this teacher continue to include outdoor images and details, but his colleagues were able to identify his visual texts immediately. These texts, over time, tell a tale about him as a learner and a person with specific interests. When placed side by side, like the immigrant photographs, visual texts can tell stories about your own students' literacy practices as well as who they are as learners and people. Visual texts become a part of our assessment of our students' learning and thinking. I suggest that we must keep learners' visual texts as part of a portfolio of their work, alongside language texts, to more thoroughly understand the cognitive connections they make to the texts they study.

Figure 6.21 Mark Fishburn, collage.

Reading Art, Reading Lives: Critically Interpreting Visual Texts

- *What tacit meanings underpin the representations that children create in ELA classes?*

- *How do I learn to ask good questions about these visual texts? How do I read students' visual texts, especially as it relates to color choices, composition, and layout?*

- *Once I read these images in this way, what can I do to support a more equitable and democratic classroom?*

Reading the Image to Read Their World:
A Teacher's Story
by Tammy Frederick

After learning about semiotics and multimodal paths to literacy in a graduate course, I created a culturally relevant autobiography unit in which my English-language learner (ELL) students explored artists and artwork from their native country, Mexico. One exploration was a viewing of Diego Rivera's artworks and a critical discussion of what the students could read from the artworks. Despite a language barrier, my students demonstrated complex thinking as they were able to read social, political, and cultural meanings from the artworks. After this initial exploration and discussion of the meanings and backgrounds of these artworks, students chose an artist with whom they identified and created an artwork in the style of that artist. They then discussed and wrote about how that artwork was a representation of their own lives. All of the students were completely engaged and committed to the experience of writing about their life through art.

Miguel, a quiet, shy fellow, evolved into a respected artist within the class. His artwork represented not only his own Mexican background and story but those of his classmates. I probably would not have heard or understood his message had I not known how to critically read his artwork because Miguel did not feel confident enough to put his words onto paper. Further, his timidity and lack of proficiency in English prevented him from speaking up and out about himself. To illustrate, Miguel's unfinished painting (see Figure 7.1) can be read as a narrative representation. Strong vectors move diagonally from the trees, which are leaning to the right with triangular tops, and point toward the right side of the picture. On the right side, the reader enters into a transaction with the truck, which signifies Miguel. The truck is above the corn fields, implying a dominant position to the crops or the agricultural work associated with tending the crops. In

Figure 7.1 *Miguel's unfinished painting.*

addition, there is movement within the artwork; the truck follows a left horizontal vector away from the fields to a distant place. When read as a horizontal elongation, the image presents the unknown or future on the right side. The picture shows Miguel's interest in his past in Mexico as signified by the cornfields and the brown and green colors used, which represent the Earth, agriculture, and fertility—all an important part of Miguel's heritage and culture. The image also signifies a cognitive understanding that the person driving the truck will earn a better living and, therefore, have a better life. Miguel had been reluctant to write or speak in his classes and was generally very shy. However, the semiotic reading of his artwork demonstrates that he has much to offer and has clear goals for his future. As a teacher of ELLs, I cannot always rely on the written or spoken words of my students to fully know them. Reading their images allows me to understand them.

To start this chapter, examine Figure 7.2 and think about what you have learned thus far in this book; read this visual text and, in your sketchbook, jot down your initial readings. Consider questions such as, What is this student trying to convey in this image? What immediately comes to mind? What shapes are used? Who do you think generated this image, a girl or boy?

At first glance, this image may look much like the visual texts created in your own classes; it is a lovely expression of one student's meaning. Yet what tacit meanings, or meanings not visible, do students bring to their texts? Figure 7.2 shows a visual text created by a third-grade boy he believed a girl would

Figure 7.2 Third grader's image.

draw. Within this image are his tacit assumptions about what girls like, the colors they like, and the types of experiences they like. This image sets into discussion aspects of students' lives and beliefs that reveal the values they bring to their learning and literacy. Like Macedo (1994), I believe that the explicit information that students bring to their texts (in this case visual)—use of color, line, shapes, composition—is important to consider, but also important is the tacit information that underpins each visual text, or the reasons why students choose to use the colors they do, the lines, shapes and compositions.

In chapter 6, you learned how to read visual texts based upon their visible markings, and this chapter will build upon this knowledge and encourage you to read visual texts critically, or to look at the visible markings to understand the invisible beliefs of a text maker.

This chapter attempts to achieve three things: (1) to describe critical literacy, schema, and building knowledge about the world, and application to the visual arts; (2) to describe and demonstrate a way of reading visual texts critically; and (3) to highlight the role that students' lived experiences play in the visual texts they create.

What Is Critical Literacy and Why Is It Important?

Critical literacy has its roots in the work of Paulo Freire, a literacy activist who taught illiterate fieldworkers in Brazil how to read common day texts that were written to deceive and exploit them. To read critically means to examine a text beyond its surface—beyond the mere words and images that comprise it—and to explore the tacit meanings that underpin this text. Words or images are not mere squiggles on paper, but are embedded with beliefs and thoughts about the world (Rosenblatt, 1995). While language and visual texts celebrate some people, that same language or text can position others as inferior. Reading critically, both verbally and visually, offers teachers and learners insight into texts generated in the classroom.

In my classes, I ask teachers to sketch their learning for the day before they leave class. Figure 7.3 is a cartoon that Tim, a former professional cartoonist, drew after the second day of class. At first glance, his caption seems to say it all: "My visceral reaction to the amount of work we students have to do." The information is explicit—students in our graduate program have a great deal of work to do. Visually apparent is Tim's head exploding from the amount of work; his eyes are fearful and his teeth are clenched. Yet what is left unsaid? What does Tim's cartoon suggest about entry into graduate school, or the work that teachers must do? On the surface is a humorous rendering of Tim's response to his studies in English education, but invisible to the eye is his statement that perhaps, as his teacher, I am giving too much homework, and that he is in danger of going crazy before he finishes. Readings that involve an interpretation of tacit information require that readers notice not only what is explicitly represented by authors or artists, but what is also implicitly suggested—made visible—through what they *do not* represent.

Figure 7.3 *Tim's cartoon of initial graduate studies.*

Political cartoonists are expert at engaging readers with both explicit and tacit knowledge. Look in any newspaper for the barrage of cartoons that satirize politicians' mistakes. In a focused study on immigration, students in my class created visual texts that represented their understanding of issues they believe concerned immigrants. The upper frame in Matt's cartoon in Figure 7.4 shows a modest house that is built without the labor of undocumented workers, and in the lower frame a huge house that can be built with the labor of undocumented

Figure 7.4 *Student's cartoon on issues related to immigrants.*

workers. Matt, who lives in the Atlanta, Georgia, region, has witnessed a number of immigrants who position themselves outside the large hardware stores looking for day work. Matt's message is clear—we depend on cheap labor of undocumented workers to build big.

Engaging learners in critical readings is essential if we are to encourage strong thinking in any language system. Tim and Matt's cartoons, respectively, tacitly critique their beliefs about issues regarding education and economy. These visual texts present multidimensional thinking, or thinking that cuts across and questions the location of political, social, and cultural systems. In a genre considered humorous, their cartoons make serious statements. Being able to read a range and variety of visual texts is critical if we are to address the tacit beliefs that underpin visual representations.

Learning, Unlearning, and Relearning: Moving Toward Critical Readings

Wink (1997) simply and clearly describes three dimensions of learning to read critically: learn, unlearn, and relearn. She argues that over the course of our lives, as short or long as some may be, we *learn* about the world, what is valued in our families, communities, and schools, and build a knowledge about the world from this learning. This knowledge is often unquestioned and taken for granted as being the "right way" to live and think. *Unlearning* happens when new perspectives and ideas are presented, and which make sense to us, if we are open to these ideas. We unlearn present or past assumptions about the world, and rethink their meaning within our new knowledge. *Relearning* then results from a shift in thinking based upon what we have learned, what we are working toward unlearning, and the new perspectives that enable us to rethink our thoughts differently. Relearning suggests that texts that show alternative viewpoints must be considered if we are to unlearn what we have learned, and forces us to shift from "passive to active learning" (Wink, 1997, p. 15).

According to Matt's cartoon (see Figure 7.4), what is the learned knowledge about immigrant labor? We depend on undocumented workers for construction work to keep costs down; undocumented workers are willing to work for low wages, and should not be paid the same as American citizens. What must we unlearn? Several ideas come to mind: (1) undocumented workers only serve the

U.S. economy through their field labor; (2) undocumented workers should be paid less; and (3) undocumented workers should be happy with the work that they can get (building stuff). To relearn demands a shift in perspective about immigrants. Immigrants offer valuable resources across and within the U.S. They may be construction workers, but they are also teachers, lawyers, artists, translators, librarians, taxi cab drivers, doctors, scientists, etc. Matt's text offers the readers a way of engaging in conversation about U.S. society's perspective on immigration and immigrants.

Critical readings of texts then

• allow learners to challenge and transform long-held assumptions;

• encourage new interpretations and new questions;

• enable learners to acknowledge their beliefs and reflect upon why they hold onto them; and

• help learners identify their assumptions, unlearn through multiple experiences, and relearn new ways of thinking.

Schema and Visual Representations: Learned Knowledge About the World

Students bring strong assumptions to their ELA classes, learned from families, communities, school, and media, and build knowledge about the world that is then organized by *schemata*, or "organized chunks of knowledge or experience" (Weaver, 2002, p. 17). For example, think about the category *dog*. What are the types of dogs you know—golden retrievers, poodles, shelties, dachshunds? Depending on our experience with dogs, we can also classify them as friendly or not friendly. If we know quite a bit about dogs, we may categorize them based upon how they function in our world: Police dogs? Service dogs? Show dogs? House pets? Figure 7.5 demonstrates but one way to organize this information, and others are certainly possible.

Knowledge about how information is organized is important because it identifies what information we have learned, how we learned it, and why it remains in our heads.

Gombrich (1994) and Berger (2000) talk about schema as it pertains to visual images, and why particular visual

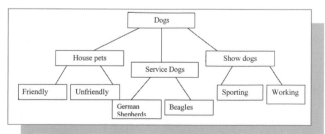

Figure 7.5 Schema, dogs.

representations are made. Artists, according to Berger, look at images or experiences, organize them in their heads, and objectify them—stop their flow—to preserve them or lock them in their memory. As artists encounter the same images over time, they develop what both Gombrich and Berger call a schema for particular images, or a way in which information is organized and interpreted. In other words, artists develop *schematic codes* for representation, details that nearly always appear in artworks that have a similar theme or composition. Understanding these recurring details in artworks allows readers to recognize the composition more immediately, and then to make their own meaning from these visual texts. In other words, artists develop "memory images" and continue to reproduce these images time and again. In so doing, they visually teach viewers how to look at particular aspects of culture, life, and experience.

To contextualize this concept of schematic codes, consider what you know about Native Americans. What elements come immediately to mind? What aspects of Native American life do you recall from your learning in schools or at home? Now think, why do these details come immediately to mind? Ever since

artists captured images of Native Americans, they have chosen to include particular aspects of their experience. Charles Russell (1907) in "The Scout" positions a single warrior atop a painted pony, alone and with spear in hand, ready for battle (see Figure 7.6). Olivia Schuster's (circa 1940) "Indian Canoeing" depicts a Native American in a canoe isolated in a natural world (see Figure 7.7). When you look at these images, how is knowledge about Native Americans represented? What details are noticeable and how are they organized? These images are but two among the many that present Native Americans in a historical and serene past. Notice that images of Native Americans are generally located in nature, with traditional clothing, and in harmony with the natural elements. What do these codes tell us about Native Americans? How do we perceive them—especially today's world?

Figure 7.6
Charles Russell,
The Scout, 1907.
Reprinted with
permission of the Sid
Richardson Musuem.

Consider the picture books that you may have read or are in your own library that portray Native American experience: *The Desert Is Theirs* (Baylor, 1987), *Raven: A Trickster Tale From the Pacific Northwest* (McDermott, 1993), *The Girl Who Loved Wild Horses* (Goble, 1978), *When Clay Sings* (Baylor, 1987), *The Rough-Face Girl* (Martin, 1998), *Knots on a Counting Rope* (Martin & Archambault, 1987). Individually, these books share some aspect of Native American experience, and yet collectively, the authors and illustrators build knowledge about how Native American experience is visually represented. Goble's illustrations from the late 1970s, Bahti's and Rand's

Figure 7.7 *Olivia Schuster,*
Indian Canoeing, *circa 1940.*

illustrations of the 1980s, and McDermott's illustrations from the 1990's reflect similar experiences as visually recorded by Charles Russell and Olivia Schuster portrayed 50 to 90 years earlier.

Informed by television, picture books, and school texts, children internalize and create their own memory images of culture. Figure 7.8 reveals one sixth grader's visual representation of a Native American. Notice how similar this image is to Russell's and Schuster's, or the illustrations in the aforementioned picture books. What has this sixth-grade student *learned* about Native American experience?

Artists are taught to read the language of art, and to represent images through schematic codes. Readers, then, are taught subsequently by artists to read this language and recognize these images represented across time. Even though schematic codes are interpreted and retranslated in slightly different ways, Gombrich (1994) argues "the way we 'see' the world leaves recognition unaffected" (p. 29). In other words, a reader may interpret an image in a particular way, but this interpretation does not alter the codes which make up the image. Images of Native American, Asian, Latino, and African cultures, in particular, will nearly always have similar elements so that readers immediately recognize these images. These established and recognizable codes then allow readers of art across ages and across cultures to recognize these codes and, thus, build their own memory images (Berger, 2000). These images become part of a reader's repertoire, become recognizable through time and medium, become learned information, and are often visually reinterpreted in similar ways, as Figure 7.8 indicates.

Figure 7.8 Sixth-grade student's visual representation of a Native American.

Critically Reading Visual Texts: Unlearning and Relearning

In our work as ELA teachers, we introduce books and texts that present explicit and tacit information that may go unnoticed unless we encourage critical conversations about both the written and the visual texts. Within images, like in written texts, artists convey both explicit details about their subjects (Native Americans, for example), and tacit beliefs. Let's consider the cover of the picture book *A Country Far Away* written by Nigel Gray (1989) and illustrated by Philipe Dupasquier to understand Wink's concepts of *unlearn* and *relearn*. When you look at Figure 7.9, what details, or codes, do you see? What is the explicit information? Do you immediately recognize the top frame as some place in Africa? Do you

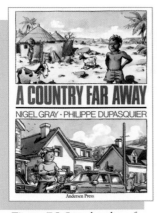

Figure 7.9 *Critical reading of picture book* A Country Far Away.

recognize the bottom frame as some place in the United States? If so, why is this information immediately known? Do these images confirm what you already knew about life in these two places? If so, in what way?

Gray's picture book presents similarities between children who live in the United States and those who live in a country in Africa. The illustration, as a whole, has a vertical orientation (top to bottom) and the images illustrate two very different life experiences, symbolically separated by the title, *A Country Far Away*, as well as the author and illustrator information. On first glance, the cover of the book seems pleasant enough, and many teachers with whom I have worked thoroughly enjoy this book, and believe that children will read it and learn about similarities that cut across both countries. Yet, upon closer reading—a critical reading, especially of the images— the book challenges readers/viewers into more thoughtful study. When critically viewing visual texts, we must acknowledge that many readings are possible. This reading is but one of many. Look at and read the elements in each frame more closely and more critically. Each frame presents a horizontal reading, in which the viewer's eye moves left to right. With this orientation, both are narratives about the lives of these two characters. On the left side of the top frame appear images of a thatched roof two-room hut, a female with a basket on her head, two goats, sparse vegetation, and rocky and dry ground. This is the given or the known information about this setting. Collectively, these elements encourage readings of an impoverished and primitive country in Africa. Elements on the right side of the image, or the new information, portray a smiling half-clothed boy, standing proudly with hands on hips in front of his home, isolated from any contact outside family and animal. The future for this boy seemingly will be the same as the present, or the left side, and he will live in this isolated wide-open space, struggling to survive on this parched soil. His position is static and immovable, and his smile tells viewers that he is content in this space.

In sharp contrast, the bottom frame, again a horizontal orientation read from left to right, visually places the young girl in the left side of the frame, the given or known space, and in an affluent setting. It is understood that her life is filled with excitement and energy. She lives in a large multilevel house, in a neighborhood filled with large multilevel houses and cars, and with a range of amenities including fireplaces, many rooms, and shingled roofs with birds flying overhead. Elements on the right side of the canvas portray more multilevel homes, cars, a telephone pole, and a professionally dressed woman getting into a car, perhaps going to work or shopping. The right side of the frame, the girl's future, is progressive and bright. Her future seems promising; she will be living in a middle-class neighborhood in which communication with others and the outside world is a given. She, like the professionally dressed woman, will live in such a neighborhood and have children who enjoy riding bicycles. Even the bicycle suggests a motion forward–progress–while the boy in the upper image is static.

Now let's look at these two frames as a whole picture. Both frames together have a vertical orientation; the viewer sees the African setting first before the U.S. setting. The visual details confirm what many perhaps assume is a life of hard work in Africa. In contrast, life in the United States is vibrant, affluent, and promising. The visual positioning of the African child on the right side of the frame and the U.S. girl on the left visually suggests their present and future positions. The boy will live his life in the village while the girl will have a range of possible living spaces. Both frames position African and U.S. readers in particular ways. African readers see the potential of one community (in the United States.) and the challenges of their own (in an African country). U.S. readers see the possibilities of their own lives, and the static nature of children in Africa. The illustrations set up a paradox: African readers might read these illustrations and build up knowledge that *all* U.S. children live with this excitement and opportunity, while U.S. children might build up or create memory images of impoverished Africa as a place that they may not want to go.

In critical visual readings, viewers must ask, "What is the tacit, or invisible, information being presented in these frames? What do illustrators say in their visual renderings of culture?" Readers/viewers are taught to understand Africa in particular ways. Gray's picture book is similar to other books that portray life in Africa. Often, little distinction is made among cultures within a single country, let alone the continent; life in Kenya is portrayed as similar to life in Nigeria which is like South Africa. Collectively, illustrated books on Africa often position culture as single, static, and primitive. Africans are often portrayed living their lives with farm animals in small, impoverished, and primitive spaces. See, for example, illustrators of picture books such as *Jambo Means Hello: A Swahili Alphabet Book* (Feelings, 1974), *Moja Means One: A Swahili Counting Book* (Feelings, 1971), and *Ashanti to Zulu: African Traditions* (Musgrove, 1976), who depict African life much like Philipe Dupasquier, illustrator of *A Country Far Away* (Gray, 1989). Collectively, illustrated books on life in the United States, especially European American culture, portray characters in varied, promising, and exciting situations. See, for example, *The Man Who Walked Between the Towers* (Gerstein, 2003), *Mirette on the High Wire* (McCully, 1992), and *The Relatives Came* (Rylant, 1985).

Tacitly and explicitly, illustrators, text book writers, film directors, advertisers, and so on teach viewers about the real world through their fiction and nonfiction texts. However, as educators, we must help students learn to read illustrations and other visual texts as critically as they do written texts and begin to unlearn codes, or details, that keep cultures static. Studies of culture in picture books (Native American, African American, European American, Asian, African, etc.) provide strong examples of how culture is visually portrayed, and how illustrators teach viewers about cultures outside their own. When students critically read visual texts, they learn to speak to and against the text (Britzman, 1995). That is, they learn not only to ask, "What does this text mean?" but, more important, to ask, "Who am I becoming and how am I thinking about the world with this reading?" Such thinking offers an opportunity to shake up traditional views of culture and helps students relearn and question their own and others' assumptions about culture. They notice, analyze, and reflect on visual and written aspects of text. Reading the underpinning structures that make up visual texts (such as areas of canvas, perspective, use of color, design, center point of attention) will offer students strategies for critically reading all aspects of text in more depth and with an understanding of the artist/designer's intention.

Critically Interpreting Visual Representations in ELA Classes

Like professional illustrators, students share their visions and beliefs about the world through their visual texts. As you read your students' visual texts, look for visible information such as art principles and design, canvas orientation, perspective, composition, as well as tacit messages they are sending. Such readings will help you develop a critical approach to reading visual texts.

Reading Gender

Study the four images in Figures 7.10 a, b, c, and d. What details do students include? How have these students used space? What is their orientation? How are

Figure 7.10a *Francis's visual representation of* A Lesson Before Dying, *high school.*

Figure 7.10b *Sara's visual representation of* Their Eyes Were Watching God, *high school.*

Figure 7.10c *Patrick's visual representation of personal interest, middle grades.*

Figure 7.10d *Terese's narrative representation of revenge, high school.*

subjects portrayed in these images? Now, think about the gender of each of these artists. Which one(s) are created by males? Females? What makes you think so?

Figures 7.10b and 7.10d were created by females while 7.10a and 7.10c were created by males. Did you guess correctly? Both girls emphasize relationships in their images, and do so symbolically and descriptively. In Figure 7.10d, Terese illustrates an original narrative in which the main character, the girl in the center, intends to seek revenge on a friend who has done her wrong. She thinks of two rumors she can spread: her friend is going out with the "dorkiest guy," and that she has flunked algebra. She establishes a relationship with her friend, her friend with a boy, and her friend with a school subject. Terese uses a vertical orientation; the main character's ideal–actualizing revenge–lies in the upper two quadrants, while the real–her present position in a classroom–appears in the lower two. She uses soft pastel colors of reds, lavenders, blues, and pinks to convey her message. Within this representation, Terese has clear visions of how "dorky" males look: round black horn-rimmed glasses and a crew cut. Tacitly, Terese suggests that any girl who would go out with a dorky guy must also be dorky. As such, she illustrates her friend with pigtails, her perception of "dorky" for girls, and this image represents the way in which her friend's reputation would be ruined. Also notice how Terese targets algebra as the subject her friend will flunk. Tacitly, Terese conveys the message that subjects like math are difficult for girls. Because girls are known to enjoy literature and reading, this young artist may unconsciously understand that her friend would probably not fail English.

In Figure 7.10b, Sara chooses to use nature and flowers, in particular, to symbolize the quality of relationships that Janie, the main character in *Their Eyes Were Watching God* (Hurston, 1998) had with her three husbands. Like Terese, Sara demonstrates the significance that females place on relationships, good or bad. Figure 7.10b has a horizontal orientation, and reads from left to right. The given, or the first relationship that Janie had, was problematic, stale, and lifeless, as depicted by the stalk without the bloom. But, the far right flower burgeons with love and growth, and signifies Janie's satisfaction with her third husband Tea Cake. Tacitly, females are attracted to bright colors, and often use them in their visuals (Albers, 1996; Albers & Cowan, 2006b; Tuman, 1999). Terese uses colored pencil, and pastel reds, lavenders, and blues, while Sara uses similarly colored construction paper, with dark colors symbolizing unhappiness and bright pink flowers with yellow and red centers signifying happiness. Both artists convey a narrative; Terese illustrates an original story of revenge, while Sara tells a metaphoric story of Janie's loves over her lifetime. Both place significance on relationships, whether dorky or loving.

Figures 7.10a, a pen-and-ink drawing by Francis after reading *A Lesson Before Dying*, and 7.10c, a visual representation of Patrick's interest in golf, respectively, are in stark contrast with those created by the girls. While the girls choose to represent relationships, the boys represent individuals in their visual texts. In Figure 7.10a, Francis presents Jefferson in the electric chair as half hog and half human. Francis's representation of Jefferson is schematic and shows Jefferson's evolution ambiguously; Jefferson is literally split down the middle, the hog on the left and the human on the right. For Francis, Jefferson's evolution from animal to man is incomplete at his execution. Interestingly, Francis shows evidence of his inquiry into executions of the time. The skull cap, the wiring, the slatted chair—all are details in the design of early electric chairs. Furthermore, Francis's interest in the actual execution is like Aaron's in Figure 6.3; both boys choose to represent the violent ending in the novel. The use of pen and black ink further add starkness to Francis's interpretation. Lack of color adds to the intensity of the violence. Patrick's image of a golfer, Figure 7.10c, has similar traits to Francis's. Both boys choose to represent single males as the focus of their representations. Patrick, located on the right of the canvas, is by himself, enjoying a round of golf. Both boys use dark colors to highlight details (Francis's) or as a background (Patrick's). Unlike Francis's image, however, Patrick's image is narrative; viewers can imagine details surrounding the golfer. Unlike the girls, Francis and Patrick illustrate their subjects as independent: Jefferson is alone in the electric chair like the golfer is alone on the golf course.

How children become socialized toward gendered ways of visual representation is important when reading images critically (Albers, 1996; Albers & Cowan, 2006b; Boyatzis & Eades, 1999). Early on, girls and boys learn to read messages that are often directed toward them as gendered beings. In a recent launch of paint colors for children, Home Depot of Canada introduced a palette of yellow, pink, and lavender for girls in the shape of princess's shoes. The girl in the advertisement wears a tiara and is surrounded by pink flowers in her room. For boys, the palette of rich red, Mediterranean blue, and black takes the shape of Mickey Mouse heads. The young boy has a huge smile on his face, and has a sparsely decorated room, Children learn to read these codes, and learn to represent them in their own drawings and in their own interpretations of texts. Read Figure 7.2 again and compare it to Figure 7.11. What do you notice about the composition of each? The details? The orientation? Does it surprise you that a boy drew Figure 7.2 and a girl drew Figure 7.11? In work that Kay Cowan and I did in 2005, we asked students in grades 3 through 5 to draw as if they were the opposite sex. We wanted to know if children had more progressive ideas about the roles of females and males. We found out that young boys have learned that girls

Figure 7.11 *Third-grade girl draws with a boy's perspective.*

like the arts such as ballet or dance, like to dress up in high heels, like purses, and have nicely coiffed hair. Furthermore, they have learned that girls like specific animals such as rabbits and unicorns. They also visually represent girls in relationship with someone or something. Even when the girls are alone, as shown in Figure 7.2, they are performing in front of an audience. On the other hand, young girls visually represent boys as sports-minded, in conflict or at war, and interested in animals, specifically reptiles such as snakes or arachnids such as spiders. They also have learned that boys are interested in technology, especially video games and science.

As they grow older, boys and girls continue to internalize and build memory images of what it means to be a man or woman. Recall Figure 2.11 (see chapter 2, page 28), a pencil drawing of Romeo by a ninth-grade male. Even though this boy had seen two film versions of *Romeo and Juliet* in which Romeo is of slight build, this student chooses to represent him with bulging superhero-like muscles. Blair and Stanford (2004) suggest that boys often "morph" features of one character onto others. Tom Newkirk (2002) continues, "Boys almost never reproduce in their writing what they've seen in movies or TV–they transform it, recombine storylines, from various media, and regularly replace themselves and their friends as the heroes" (p. xviii). This boy visually renders an extremely strong and muscular Romeo who represents toughness, bravery, and competition in the fictional world, and made visible by the sword on his hip and the vial of poison in his hand. Similar expectations for boys emerge in popular culture texts, film, television, literature and so on, and this knowledge, both tacit and explicit, leads to gender socialization. Action, violence, and adventure are aspects of written texts that young boys find interesting (Wilhelm, 2001), interests that appear in this rendition of Romeo, while families, home life, and romance are aspects of written and visual texts that young girls find interesting (Gilbert & Taylor, 1991), and which emerge in their visual texts (Albers, 1996).

Reading Race

At the same time that students' visual texts suggest tacit knowledge about gender that has been learned and retranslated visually, their visual texts also show ideologies or beliefs about race, religion, and adolescence. In Figure 7.12, a 10th-grade girl from Korea, in the United States for three years, represents her interpretation of *Lord of the Flies* (Golding, 1959) and titles it "Fear of the Unknown," connecting this theme in the novel to

Figure 7.12 *Korean girl's representation of beauty and race.*

her life in the city. Like Terese and Sara in the previous section, Jayoung chooses pastel colors, and has learned what is beautiful about a teenage girl: flowing blond hair, blue eyes that look directly at the viewer, and a mouth that seems determined. The straight and thick lines that compose the buildings, associated with logic, science, progress, and order, also appear to confine the subject. Her interpretation of one of the novel's themes is nicely represented with the female in the foreground and the buildings in the background. Yet, problematic is Jayoung's representation of herself. Unlike the girl in the illustration, Jayoung is Korean, with shoulder length black hair and Korean facial features. The fact that she represents herself as European American rather than Korean is troubling. Although she cannot change her physical appearance to look European American, she can, and does, in illustration. By changing her own physical features, Jayoung has learned how to more easily assimilate and blend into the adolescent community at school.

One of the most troubling representations of race emerged during research I did in graduate school in which a sixth-grade boy retranslated his beliefs about

Figure 7.13
Conrad's representation of race.

race in three-foot papier-mâché sculpture (Figure 7.13) (Albers, 1996, 2004a; Albers & Murphy, 2000). A European American, Conrad, who was quiet and unassuming in class, built an African American male figure, and from his use of color and facial features, he retranslated his supremacist beliefs through art. Conrad painted the entire canvas black, representative of African American skin color. With a thick brush, he painted a swath of red across the neck, and large red circles at the shoulders. Both of these elements indicate mutilation: a slashing of the throat and the dismemberment of the arms. In addition, Conrad painted a red tongue that hangs out of a smiling mouth outlined in blue. In essence, Conrad created an image of a figure who smiles at its own mutilation. Through art, Conrad was able to represent his vicarious experience with lynching. Where this boy lives, an image like this is not contested. Hatred for people of color and hate speech are not reprehensible beliefs or behaviors for European Americans.

Reading Other Ideologies

Figure 7.14 *Sixth grader's representation of religious beliefs, cross in wire.*

Other representations of beliefs are retranslated through various art forms, as well. In the visual text shown in Figure 7.14, this 12-year-old girl, working in wire, is able to both represent her ability to work with this medium as well as convey her strong religious beliefs. Wire is a medium that has strength and stability. The blue wood on which the wire cross is placed functions as a support for the wire cross, but also symbolically represents Christ's wooden cross. Wire and wood are apt media for this student to represent her beliefs. When she was asked about this sculpture, she remarked that she was active in her church youth group, and wanted to make an image that represented this part of her life.

In one class, seventh-grade students were offered opportunities to illustrate for extra credit. Stephanie created an anti-cigarette ad, a clear indication of her beliefs about tobacco (see Figure 7.15). Notice how the image is one of demand. The hands crushing the cigarette pack are in the center of the canvas and demand that the viewer take to heart this message. Other visual texts also carry meanings and stances that adolescents bring to the classroom. Figure 7.16 represents seventh grader Andy's interest in car racing. He understands how cars are transported but also acknowledges that such sports are sponsored by beer companies. Notice the detail with which he inscribes the van that carries the race cars. Andy brings his inquiry to the visual text, and the visual text conveys his complex understanding of 18-wheelers. Genevieve, in Figure 7.17, shares her commitment to killer whales–to their environment and the need to protect this species. The sun represents the ideal–killer whales living peacefully and without threat of harm beneath the ocean.

Figure 7.15
Seventh-grade student Stephanie's anti-cigarette ad, color markers.

Figure 7.16 *Seventh-grade student Andy's representation of his love of racing, pencil drawings.*

Figure 7.17 *Eighth-grade student Genevieve's representation of her commitment to wildlife and environment.*

Unlearning: Critical Interpretive Analysis

Students' visual texts can be lovely images in which harmony prevails, but not all texts are tidy representations of students' learned knowledge. In fact, every visual text gestures toward and makes visible beliefs that adolescents have about the world. Close and critical readings bring to the surface beliefs, often invisible in other communication systems. Critical examination in all facets of education continues to be explored, and so must critical analysis of visual texts produced in ELA classes be done. As much as we often believe that visual texts are creative, innovative, and demonstrate perspectives in a new way, and that they release the imagination (Greene, 1995), they also show a failure of the imagination, explicit and tacit knowledge that students have learned that must be unlearned.

Critical discussions can lead to students' awareness of what they have learned, and with dialogue, they can unlearn beliefs that tend to stabilize culture, gender, race, and ideology. As Wink (1997) suggests, unlearning necessitates a shift in philosophy, beliefs, and assumptions. When students talk more substantively about the visual texts they make, they become aware of their learned knowledge. In this exchange, Sara explains her visual text (Figure 7.10b) that she made in response to *Their Eyes Were Watching God*, followed by the class's discussion of marriage:

Sara: I used the stages of life in flowers to represent her marriages and her search for happiness. The first stage represents her marriage to Logan. She never loved him and never wanted to marry him; she was forced to. The second stage represents her marriage to Joe, a happily bloomed flower. I think she thought she loved him at first, but realized that he allowed her no freedom to experience life. The third stage is a fully bloomed flower which represents her marriage to Tea Cake. She found happiness and love with him. I colored the flower pink and yellow, because she finally found freedom in him.

Teacher: Do you think if you are in a relationship that you lose a certain amount of freedom, Sara? So when that relationship is over, then you've got total freedom?

Sara: There are things in life that you would do if you weren't married. Being married or in a relationship can hold you back. There are just too many times that you aren't able to do the things you want to do. And when you are wanting to do something, or let's say you are making plans about something, you've got to include that person because of your commitment.

Teacher: Do you think Janie would have become the person that I think most of you think she became if she had not met Tea Cake? Was Tea Cake a needed catalyst for Janie to become the woman that I think we think she became at the end of the book?

Wes: She went through a change when she met him; she was a better person. She did things a little bit different. She had much more maturity when she was with him. It didn't necessarily have to be Tea Cake; it could have been somebody else.

Lisa: I don't know, when I think about their 'perfect love' and this great experience. Tea Cake, in reality, smacked her around and made her go out and work long hours. It seems that everyone here seems to think that they had this perfect great thing that helped Janie become this wonderful strong person. It seems like we are giving Tea Cake too much credit for something that Janie did.

Sara's visual text generated an interesting conversation about how this group of adolescents interprets Janie's character in relation to her husband Tea Cake. The teacher, Darriel Ledbetter, encourages his students to articulate their interpretations, their beliefs, so that they learn that when new ideas are introduced, they can change their minds, or unlearn their present assumptions. Sara rethinks what she believes about love providing freedom, while Wes reconsiders whether one person can help another achieve maturity and strength. Lisa, a young feminist in the group, challenges others to consider that women alone can become strong.

Visual texts created alongside readings of literary texts can prompt strong dialogue, and you can take advantage of these conversations to help students unlearn and relearn assumptions about gender, race, diversity, and other social issues. Such a move pushes students to be active in their learning, rather than passively accepting internalized beliefs that often control representation of the world.

Relearning: Focus on Shifting Perspectives

Examining visual texts from a critical perspective encourages us as educators to consider questions of responsibility and obligation. For instance, we must be prepared to talk with students who share gendered perspectives on how females and males live and work in the world. We must be prepared to talk with students who bring troubling beliefs about immigration, race, culture, and homosexuality. We now know how to applaud and praise positive visual texts, but how can we address visual texts that raise troubling issues?

First, we must acknowledge that no text resides in isolation; all texts are informed by previously encountered ones. Given students' assumptions about art, and their identifying particular colors and art media with specific genders, we can begin a democratic process by inviting them to consider the assumptions they hold about gender. We can talk with students about color choices that males and females make in their visual texts. Females can use bold and dark colors, and males can use pastels, without inferences placed upon these choices. We can also discuss the roles of males and females in society. We can discuss how males have become more involved in childcare and women more involved in their careers.

Such conversations invite students to consider the range of roles that men and women play in present-day society.

Second, we must encourage participatory-centered classrooms (Murphy, 1995) in which students engage in lively discussions about interpretations. Greene (1995) supports such conversations because "to get students' imagination moving in response to a text...may well be to confront the students with a demand to choose in a fundamental way, to choose between a desire for harmony along with an easy answer and a commitment to the search for alternative perspectives" (p. 129). Therefore, conversations about race, religion, stereotypes, relationships, gender, culture, and sexual orientation that emerge in visual texts and written texts can help students transform learned knowledge into more informed and relearned perspectives. In Darriel's high school English classes, students welcomed conversations that addressed difficult topics in literature that they read. They also created visual texts that furthered their understanding of these topics. Below is a short excerpt of my interviews with several of Darriel's high school juniors:

Peggy: Do you think high school students should engage in discussions that address critical topics like race, gender, religion, and sexual orientation?

Matt: Yes, I think they are needed. You can't just go on what you think about these topics. Everybody has a different view about them, and everyone needs a chance to talk about their ideas.

Lisa: I agree. I think that these discussions are extremely important because it teaches you how to think on your feet. You learn to voice your opinions coherently instead of sitting down like a student, and doing book work, and writing essay after essay. We need to hear everyone's opinion.

Peggy: Have these discussions helped you become better thinkers?

Matt: Yes, definitely. I have to stop and think every time somebody makes a point that I wouldn't have thought of at all, and think about why they would say something like that.

Lisa: We learn to connect literature with our personal lives. Without that personal connection, literature isn't relevant. When you read something, a topic that the author brings up, and apply it to your life, that's the goal in literature. I'm more open-minded than I use to be; I was always right in my mind!

Joe: If you want people to listen to you, you've got to listen to them.

Peggy: You also created visual texts in response to literature. What did you think of these engagements?

Matt: I think that artworks are very important. When people can actually see something and relate to it, it's more likely that they are going to understand what you are saying.

Lisa: I did a poster of a horizon because I think the horizon is one of the main themes in the book. I also did a poem written from Janie's point of view. The horizon is something that teenagers always have to think about. Adults always ask us, "Where are you going to college? What are you going to do after you graduate?" Like Janie, who set her sights on the horizon, I also set my eyes toward the horizon.

Students understand the significance of conversations that emerge around literature as well as the visual texts created in response to it. These conversations enabled Matt and Joe to share their insights on literature but also shaped their perspectives based upon what others say. Lisa learned to articulate her ideas and to understand that others' ideas are important to consider. She and Matt both recognize the importance that visual texts play in helping others "understand what you are saying."

Third, crucial to any representation are the choices that are made available in light of the medium. For example, Conrad's racial beliefs about African Americans may not have come to light had he been offered only pencils, paper, and markers. The 3-D properties of papier-mâché afforded him the potential to demonstrate his strong and firm belief in white supremacy. When such visual texts emerge, in whatever form, students must answer any challenges that arise. Once something is said or rendered visually, the student must be open for interrogation and contestation, especially when the belief is troubling for some.

Reflection on Critical Interpretation of Visual Texts

Continual work with the visual arts will enable students to develop their abilities to read, interpret, and communicate visually. As students learn to communicate visually, their visual text may encourage the class community into discussions about human nature, life, and their perceptions about it. Furthermore, when teachers and students both learn to read art, discussions can focus on critical visual readings of visual texts that make visible learned assumptions about gender, race, class, and other social issues. Over time, as students become more conscious of what and how they visually represent their beliefs, these texts then become the source of future teaching and learning.

ELA teachers can begin to introduce and study texts that present a range of perspectives and ways of living. For example, you and your students can bring in texts that illustrate and describe cultures and races not only as they are represented historically, but also as they exist in the present. You can create classroom space in which, for example, Native American life is presented and studied from the perspective of contemporary authors and illustrators. Be thoughtful and critical readers of picture books, historical texts, paintings, sculptures, and texts that cut across media and language. For instance, to study Augusta Savage's sculpture "Lift Every Voice and Sing" (1939) (http:// northbysouth.kenyon.edu/1998/art/pages/savage.htm) alongside James Weldon Johnson's (1900) writing of the African American anthem of the same title (www.english.uiuc.edu/maps/poets/g_l/johnson/poems.htm) offers learners a way of synthesizing and analyzing these two texts together. To study Africa and the culture of its many countries through art, picture books, news articles, magazines, and photographs encourages students to see a present-day Africa comprised of diverse cultures, languages, and experiences.

Critical readings of visual texts encourage students to build a less narrow and more complex view of culture and experience. As you begin to read visual texts more critically, share these insights with your students. In this way, they will read illustrations more critically and will present their perspectives in more thoughtful and less static ways.

CHAPTER 8

Designing and Implementing an Arts- and Inquiry-Based Curriculum

- *How do I design a flexible ELA curriculum that supports the visual arts and also addresses ELA concepts, strategies, and standards?*

- *How can I build in multimedia projects that support literacy and language learning?*

- *How do students' interests inform my curricular decisions?*

Born to Be an Artist: A Teacher's Story
by Nicole Manry Pourchier

I was born to be an artist—I was "in my own world," my parents said: a world where I was in charge and chaperoned only by my mind. I had very little sense of real and imaginary, thoroughly convinced my dramatic play was none other than the real thing. In my bedroom, the Metropolitan Museum displayed exquisite paintings and charcoals by an artist named Nicole, an old pal of Monet's, at least so she thought. My creative mind rewarded me with an impressive repertoire of real life experiences, all by the mere age of 10. (Figure 8.1 shows one of my "early works.")

My father is the most talented artist I have ever known, but he has never adopted the artist's lifestyle. Perhaps this is why I so admired our artist

neighbor, Ms. Mary. At home, I always tried to emulate my time spent at Mary's. Not only was Mary an artist like my father, but her lifestyle was an art in itself. The architecture of her home, the rock and herb gardens, the nature trails winding through the surrounding woods, the rare Ginkgo tree so meticulously planted outside her front door, the books lining the shelves in her hallways, the baskets hanging from the ceiling of her kitchen, and the looming branch that doubled as a Christmas tree in December, appearing to be suspended in midair above her couch. Oh, how I longed to be within the

Figure 8.1 *Nicole's artwork, age 7.*

walls of her world and how I treasure each moment spent there.

When I think about art and what it means to me, I go back to the afternoons we spent in Mary's window-lined studio. Mary saw herself in nature and when in her studio she was surrounded by it, perfectly situated in an open meadow, her only company being the woods and its inhabitants, along with a few nosy cows. If I could capture a single moment in a bottle to relive as often as I'd like, I'd choose the winter day my grandmother and I joined Mary in her studio for an introductory lesson in collage. Collage was Mary's medium of choice, and over the years she seemed to master it with her own unique flavor. As we sat at her table pouring over a collection of images, sifting through to find those that "spoke" to us, snow began to fall, covering the gentle slopes of the meadow in an icy blanket of purest white. It was an artist's dream, both young and old. Mary knew how to stop and enjoy life, and she relished in everything beautiful. Every Christmas, my family was invited for tea and gifts. I can still see my clumsy grandfather, whose art was machinery and dirt, moving through her house like a bull in a china shop, making genuine attempts at "cultured talk." But Mary loved my southern outdoorsman of a grandfather and his humorous talk, for she saw everyone as a magnificent work of art.

Despite my meticulously constructed museum-bedroom, somewhere along the way I became estranged from the artist's life. I began to have little time for art, and when I reached middle school, art was not deemed cool by my peers. By the time I reached high school I missed art but would never register for an art course because I felt insecure of my abilities. My experiences with art were now limited to the caricatures I drew as a cheerleader in charge of football banners. In college, I often walked by the art building wishing my schedule would lead me inside, or cast an envious gaze toward the art supplies in the back of the campus bookstore.

Being the overachiever that I am, I pursued my master's degree before seeking my first teaching job. This was the best decision I have ever made. I was able to participate in the National Writing Project. Surprisingly, this experience became a turning point in my career as a teacher and artist. Writing became art to me and, in turn, so did literature. My inspiration came from the works I created, and I was finally able to throw those confining graphic organizers out the window in exchange for collage. Art led me to my own writing and reading processes, and permitted me to break free from the formulaic reading and writing I was accustomed to.

Nicole's story reinforces the important role that the arts must play in ELA curriculum planning and design. For Nicole, early art experiences with her neighbor, and her father's own talent in art were instrumental in her own work as a fourth-grade teacher who fully integrates art into her curriculum planning, especially in writing. Other teachers with whom I have worked, including Mark Fishburn (chapter 6) and Tammy Frederick (chapter 7), keep in contact about their integration of the arts. Mark writes, "We just finished an art project for *Of Mice and Men* [Steinbeck, 1993]. The students really enjoyed it. I realized that in their work and presentations of their projects, they formalized what they had learned and what had impressed them about the novel. It came out in their art." Mark was unaware of the potential of the visual arts to develop literacy, until he took a course with me in semiotics and multimodality. In this course, he learned how to draw, use color, work in 3-D, and read art, both artistically and critically, and he integrated this knowledge into his own curriculum design. Now, he understands that students are "formaliz[ing]" their learning and thinking about literature as they construct English projects.

Like Mark, Tammy, and Nicole, you have learned a number of art techniques and how to read artworks both artistically and critically. In this chapter, you will learn to design ELA curriculum and classrooms with the arts and inquiry in mind. In particular, the Focused Study, as a curriculum design, allows for flexibility, inquiry, and support of all sign systems as students study the English language arts. You'll find in Appendix C two Focused Studies that address Immigration and the Dust Bowl, topics that are taught across grade levels. (See also Albers, 2006a, for a recently published Focused Study on the Harlem Renaissance.) These curricula are meant to support your own thinking and inspire you to generate your own ideas about how to imagine the arts and media-rich engagements in your teaching.

Designing Inquiry-Based Curriculum From a Visual Arts and Media-Rich Perspective

After experiencing media-rich engagements, teachers who work with children of all ages design projects that invite students to share learning across media. For example, first-grade teacher Heidi created a PowerPoint on animals for her students who "really got into all the animal noises and the pictures!" Fourth-grade teacher Jennifer had her students create PowerPoint presentations on social studies topics they study. Chantrise, a high school English teacher, invited her students to create visual projects that connected their heritage to a core novel they studied. Middle grades teacher Mel integrated video, still images, sound, and music into his ELA content presentations. And Rose Mary invited her high school students to create papier-mâché masks and write poems about their favorite characters from classic literature.

Greene (1995) suggests that art-based expressions (including film, plays, artworks, music, photography) encourage students to think alternatively about the fictional world of literature and the real world around them. Darriel and Alli, both high school English teachers, discovered that videotaping literature discussions helped them reflect upon their work with students in literature discussions.

Students, too, viewed their literature discussions and retrospectively analyzed their conversations. Alli was surprised at what she saw in her videotaped discussions:

> The vertical team system that we have in place in my English department mandates that we include several seminar-type discussions in our classrooms across the board. Most of my students trickled in from tenth honors classrooms and felt comfortable discussing the text. However, we discovered that they rarely took the discussion to the universal level—or connected to it.... On the whole, we felt that the conversation circled around itself. We discovered that we would like to see a much higher level of discussion the next time. Next time, I think that I will make the environment a little less stifling by imposing fewer restrictions on the subject matter of our discussions.

By studying videotaped discussions, Alli noticed the superficial level and circuitous nature of her class's literature discussions and effected change in her own practice. Designing an inquiry-based media-rich curriculum that emphasizes reflective learning suggests a shift in thinking. Rather than study print-based texts primarily, educators reconsider how multimedia have the potential to support strong literacy learning (Albers, 2006a; Albers & Cowan, 2006a).

Grounded in semiotics, an arts- and inquiry-based curriculum has as its core the importance of learners' interests and experiences. According to Burke (2004), learners bring knowledge and experience to their learning, and it is this personal inquiry that drives their interest in a subject or topic. As Short and Burke (1991) suggest, learners are actively involved in their own learning and cannot learn something that they are not already involved in thinking about. Learners are offered flexible opportunities to engage in research that interests them and express meaning in a range of media. For example, in Figure 8.2, Klea, a preservice teacher, researched both *Frankenstein* (Shelley, 2004) and his personal heritage. He started his presentation with a movie that he and his brothers made 10 years earlier to show his interest in writing and performing contemporary gothic tales. He created a meaningful semiotic text that includes visual, musical, and linguistic systems that, together, expressed his connection to this novel.

Figure 8.2 *Klea's semiotic connections to Frankenstein.*

Focused Study: An Arts- and Inquiry-Based Curriculum Design

I teach classes at my university for K–12 teachers that focus on theories of literacy learning as well as ELA curriculum design, teaching literature, integrating the oral, dramatic and visual language arts, and ELA assessment. At the same time that teachers study concepts and methods of teaching English, they participate in media-rich inquiry-based curriculum designed around topics and themes that they may teach: The Great Dust Bowl, Harlem Renaissance, Immigration, and Social Issues. The Focused Study, developed by Carolyn Burke (2004) and implemented by Beth Berghoff (1995, 2000) is a design that I believe offers space for flexibility in planning, teaching and learning, and many opportunities for media exploration, interpretation, and representation.

The Focused Study, illustrated in Figure 8.3, is a unit of curriculum that concentrates on a particular topic or issue, involves a community of learners, and operates under two assumptions: (1) Teachers are knowledgeable curriculum designers who make decisions based upon the lives, interests, and experiences of their students, and (2) curriculum is grounded in current theory and practice (Albers, 2006a). The flexibility and generative nature of the Focused Study enables teachers to develop confidence in their own subject matter expertise, and pushes them to design media-rich content and engagements that move away from or in tandem with a teacher's guide (if they use one).

Figure 8.3 *The Focused Study, a curricular framework.*

Furthermore, in this framework, teachers themselves become active inquirers— always searching out resources and materials that will push them to present content in media-rich ways, and who encourage such interpretations and responses from their students. They become curriculum designers who plan-to-plan (Watson, Burke, & Harste, 1989). They design a curriculum with ideas for instruction and learning in mind, but are flexible enough in their planning to enact changes based upon students' responses. They develop lists of potential texts (such as poems, songs, videos, nonfiction and fiction texts, picture books) to teach content, and integrate a large number of texts into their teaching to inspire further inquiry into the text or theme being studied (Albers, 2006a). Six components commonly make up a Focused Study: Initiating Engagements, Demonstrations, Text Study/Literature Study, Invitations for Inquiry, Opportunities for Sharing and Organizing Learning, and Reflective Action Plans (Albers, 2006a). These are defined and explained in the following section, in the context of a Focused Study on Immigration.

Immigration: A Media-Rich Focused Study in Action

To understand the design of a Focused Study, teachers participate in an Immigration Focused Study which serves as a semester-long demonstration on how to design, organize, and implement a media-rich and inquiry-based curriculum. Because ELA curricula are often built around themes, topics, or core texts, I organize this Focused Study around several core texts: Na's *A Step From Heaven* (2003) and Jiménez's *The Circuit* (1997) and *Breaking Through* (2002). Because of the growing population of immigrants to the metro Atlanta, Georgia area, teachers find this Focused Study significant because it offers them sustained inquiry into a variety of texts by and about immigrants.

A Focused Study begins with an inquiry question or questions general enough to allow for flexibility and student interests: "What does it mean to be an immigrant?" Other questions complement the overarching question: "Who is an immigrant?" "How are immigrants portrayed in various types of texts?" and "What are the experiences of immigrants?" From these questions, teachers develop pedagogically oriented questions that address the six components of the Focused Study with multimedia and visual arts integration in mind: How can immigration be introduced to build upon students' personal experiences? What demonstrations or strategy lessons will further develop students' knowledge about immigration? What texts will extend students' learning and engage their interests? What projects will emerge from this study? How will students organize and share their learning in a variety of ways? And, finally, how does this Focused Study support students' reflection on their learning?

To initiate teachers into thinking and working with a range of media in this Focused Study, I require that they keep an arts-based response notebook in which they capture and reflect on ideas they learn in both professional and literary texts (such as the one pictured in Figure 8.4), an idea inspired by Towson University (Towson, Maryland, USA) art educator Ray Martens. Although all teachers find arts-based note-taking difficult initially, they have learned how to read differently. As Lorraine put it, "I look for ideas rather than details, and try to symbolize across ideas. I also notice that my colors are becoming more vibrant, and my use of symbol more apparent." This is a particularly important shift in teachers' thinking about the role of arts-based thinking and learning. Lorraine continues, "I think [taking notes in this way] encourages students to develop metaphoric and symbolic thinking and synthesis across texts."

Figure 8.4 *Arts-based notetaking.*

In all Focused Studies, learners must have uninterrupted time for reading and writing across media. Such opportunities invite learners to explore alone or with others texts related to the Focused Study. Students learn to value this time

Figure 8.5 *Teacher presents inquiry into Sandra Cisneros.*

and learn that studying a range of texts extends their understanding of the focused area of study. In our immigration study, teachers have uninterrupted opportunities to study a range of topics within immigration and share and present their learning in a range of ways. One teacher studied Sandra Cisneros and her texts *Woman Hollering Creek* (1992) and *The House on Mango Street* (1991). The visual text pictured in Figure 8.5 shows her interpretation of Cisneros's house, and with people who live there and in the neighborhood presented within each window.

Initiating Engagements

Initiating engagements introduce the focus of the study and help participants reflect on their personal experiences and knowledge. They prompt learners to consider connections between the study and personal experiences, and set the stage for the upcoming learning. Within each Focused Study, I introduce four initiating engagements to build background knowledge to support future reading and thinking about the topic: (1) a self-running PowerPoint presentation on immigration; (2) a Gallery Walk of artists, politicians, historians, writers, and philosophers who are a part of the study; (3) a Book Pass; and (4) a newsletter.

Before we study any texts or have any discussion about the Focused Study on immigration, I ask learners, "What do we know about immigration?" This question *initiates* our study of immigration and the experiences and background they bring. I then dim the lights and a self-running six-minute PowerPoint presentation begins. With Neil Diamond's (2001) "America" playing in the background, the PowerPoint starts with photos and artworks of Native Americans before European settlement, followed by images of immigration at Ellis Island. The presentation shifts in tone and in content and Woody Guthrie's (1997) "This Land Is Your Land" plays in the background. Images stream across the screen of present-day immigration, cartoons, illegal border crossings, references to the English Only movement, and immigrant children caught in the political battle of who is American. The last slide invites learners to pose questions for further inquiry. Following this presentation, learners share their experiences, thoughts, and questions that emerge from this viewing.

After this PowerPoint presentation, teachers are invited to take a Gallery Walk among the authors, artists, musicians, politicians, and so on that they will study throughout the semester. Learners simply take a walk around the room where photographs and sample texts of various people who will be studied are posted on the wall as in a gallery. Learners stop and read the visual and written texts to acquaint themselves with names and texts they will study. This engagement introduces learners to cross-disciplinary connections significant to the study of immigration; prompts connections to other writers, artists, musicians, and historians whom they may already know; and sets the stage for future learning and reading. We then discuss issues that we believe will emerge in the texts that we study.

To connect their lives to immigration, we then do a book pass, which is a timed engagement in which learners each quickly peruse a text on the focus topic (such as picture books, poetry, short stories, art books, CDs, nonfiction texts) for a minute, after which the teacher prompts them to pass the book. This continues until all texts have been passed around the group. Each learner selects one text and shares her or his connection with the rest of the group. We then reflect upon themes, questions, and concepts that are raised from these texts. The book pass introduces learners to a large range of texts in a short time. This engagement also encourages them to consider questions about the Focused Study. As a literacy teacher, I learn about my students' interests and notice how they peruse texts (front, middle, end, inside or back covers, photos, illustrations), and to what aspects of texts they attend.

As a group, we now discuss the issues we notice across texts and across engagements. What questions, issues, and ideas emerged in the PowerPoint? In the book pass? In the Gallery walk? We discuss the issues that cut across these three engagements and generate questions that learners might want to investigate. Following these experiences, I hand out a newsletter that introduces the core texts, *A Step From Heaven* (Na, 2003) and *The Circuit* (Jiménez, 1997) and *Breaking Through* (Jiménez, 2002). The newsletter contains information on the authors of the core texts, a brief timeline, cartoons, historical, artistic, poetry, and other texts we may study. The newsletter also presents questions and issues about immigration that may prompt future investigation.

In one two-hour class, learners engage in a range of multimedia experiences that initiate, prompt, and build learning about immigration. In my education course, we then reflect upon the pedagogical implications of such engagements. We discuss the importance of building background context, the significance of multimedia to introduce learning, and the flexibility of these engagements. How can students create PowerPoint presentations to demonstrate their learning at the end of a study? How does the integration of music, art, image, and video support all students' language experience? How are multiple perspectives introduced in media-rich engagements? Teachers in the course build these engagements into their own curricula.

Demonstrations

Demonstrations are large-group, teacher-conducted, short strategy lessons intended to show students a concept, technique, or features of a text. Demonstrations often derive from students' questions about the content of the Focused Study or concepts important to an in-depth understanding of a text. Teachers often have ideas in mind for demonstrations before the Focused Study begins. However, they are flexible, especially when students have questions about a technique or strategy or want to know more about aspects of the Study. In my planning for this immigration-themed Focused Study, I considered presenting demonstrations that focused on conducting strong literature discussions, engaging students in studying poetry, helping students understand how to read narrative and expository texts, and interpreting meaning represented through visual art such as paintings, drawings, film, sculptures, and music.

One of my demonstrations invites teachers to consider how to engage students in poetry study, a genre that challenges many students. Inspired by Oscar Hernandez and Pam Smith, high school reading/literature teachers in the Fresno, California, area, I work with Tupac Shakur's (2000) "The Rose That Grew From Concrete," a contemporary poem/song by a rapper with whom students identify. To start, I invite learners to share information that they know about Tupac. I then project Tupac's poem on a screen. We talk about the title and what they think the poem means based upon this information. I layer the experience by reading the poem aloud, followed by deeper analysis. Learners then read, listen to, and engage in a self-running media-rich PowerPoint presentation with Tupac's poem set to music, sung by his mother, and narrated by Nikki Giovanni. We discuss the poem again, and especially note how interpretations evolve with every reading and across media. Learners illustrate their interpretation of Tupac's text and their illustrations are then pulled together into a quilt (see Figure 8.6 for an example).

Not all demonstrations are planned before a Focused Study starts, but arise from learners' questions. For example, in May 2006, millions of immigrants and advocates across the United States protested proposed immigration laws. Fresno, California, area teachers Oscar Hernandez, Yadira Gonzalez, and Jason Roach, all ninth-grade reading teachers, interrupted their current plans because their students wanted to study why such laws could be imposed. These teachers initiated a focused study on immigration in which they studied the writings of Gary Soto (1997), Francisco Jiménez (1997), and

Figure 8.6 *Visual interpretations of Shakur's poem.*

Sandra Cisneros (1991) alongside local, state, and national newspapers. Students wrote letters to the editor of their local paper, and several students' letters were published. They also drew political cartoons based upon their learning. Oscar Hernandez (2006) created a short movie (like those described in chapter 5) titled "Walkout RHS" in which he integrated music, still photos, and raw interview and walkout footage and posted it on the popular website, YouTube (http://www.you tube.com/watch?v=hsYf7SLI1dA).

Media-rich demonstrations, especially driven by learners' questions, encourage teachers to think in creative ways, and to consider the questions that learners bring to a Focused Study. Harste (2005) states, "We live in a world that is increasingly informed by the screen, computer, film, and television—including video games. We need to work with a number of media—including drama, clay, painting, watercolor, rap, hip hop, photography and so on—as we talk about and teach literacy."

Text Study/Literature Study

In a media-rich inquiry-based curriculum, time must be given for students to engage in text study. As Robert Scholes argues, "To put it as directly, and perhaps as brutally, as possible we must stop teaching literature and start studying texts" (cited in Pirie, 1997, p. 17). Scholes, as well as Applebee (1996) and Langer (1995), encourage ELA teachers to focus students' attention on interpretation and analysis, not only of a single text but across texts. ELA instruction, they argue, is more than a rearticulation of plot. Students should raise issues in literature, grapple with them, and resolve questions through discussion (see chapter 7 for samples of such student discussions).

In our Focused Study on immigration, learners study and talk about fiction and nonfiction texts in small groups. Not all groups study the same texts. Rather, based upon their interests, they choose from a number of *text sets* that may include news articles, picture books and novels, professional articles, art books, music, magazine articles related by theme, author, illustrators, or time period. For example, a text set focused on the concept of home and how are we shaped by home might include: *The Dream Jar* (Pryor, 1996), *A Very Important Day* (Herold, 1995), *Momma, Where Are You From?* (Bradby, 2000), and *Dragonwings* (Yep, 1977). Learners form their own small study groups and are encouraged to make explicit and implicit connections across and within texts. To share their studies, groups generate and illustrate a symbol that conveys their interpretation of a concept that connects all texts. Surrounding this, they choose a single character in one of the texts, and identify and illustrate six key events in this character's life. This engagement encourages the group to identify through discussion a character's journey and negotiate among one another events that affect this

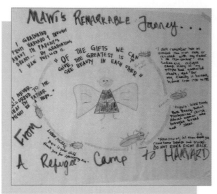

Figure 8.7 *Teachers' visual interpretation, text/literature studies.*

character's life. Figure 8.7 presents one group's visual representation of *Of Beetles and Angels: A Boy's Remarkable Journey From a Refugee Camp to Harvard* (Asgedom, 2002). High school teacher Carol reflects on the significance of text sets:

> I found that to be able to incorporate other novels, picture books, and articles and relate them to the core text was valuable. I also realized, for the first time, that picture books have a deeper message than I thought, and that they can be integrated into instruction in a meaningful way. I will begin to implement them into my class to teach literature concepts.

Such cross-textual and arts-based analyses encourage learners to identify and synthesize issues and themes their readings raise.

Invitations for Inquiry

Invitations, a literacy strategy designed and developed by Carolyn Burke (see Harste, Short, & Burke, 1988), and explored in depth by Katie Van Sluys (2005), support deeper learning, more in-depth study of smaller topics within the larger framework of the Focused Study. Invitations are experiences in which learners come together to engage in an activity of mutual interest. Within this activity, learners collaborate, share perspectives, raise questions, and respond to their learning in a variety of media-rich and visual arts ways. Invitations are just as the word implies: experiences that learners can accept or decline. Invitations are written from a semiotic perspective, or a perspective that values the many ways in which language is used (art, music, language, drama), and allow students with varying degrees of language experience to participate in the learning. For example, within the larger context of a unit on the Harlem Renaissance, learners may engage in smaller studies of artists and their artworks, women writers, poets, politicians, historical photographs, and so on. Along with at least one other person, learners present their learning in many different ways: short dramas, Readers Theatre, visual texts, poems, combinations of these. By providing learners with a range of ways to read and respond to topics within the Harlem Renaissance, all have the opportunity to participate in the learning, regardless of their language ability. Invitations are grounded in six key principles (Burke, 2004):

1. Attention is on meaning making.
2. Learning environment is social and collaborative.
3. The experience is open to learners of varied language flexibility.

4. The experience is consistent with knowledge about semiotics and disciplines.

5. The experience is open to alternate and media-rich responses.

6. Invitations should have the potential to generate future inquiry.

A number of varied texts are introduced within each invitation (such as picture books, poems, music, written texts, short stories, photos), and encourage a more complex view and understanding of the Focused Study.

Over the course of the semester, I learn about my learners' interests and questions, and design invitations with this knowledge in mind. Some are interested in more in-depth study of poets, photography, music, art, authors, historians, others in computer games, and others in drama and music. Together with at least one other person, learners work through one or more invitations. Two sample invitations are presented below:

Immigrants' Initial Experiences
- Read the interview with Li Keng Wong, (http://teacher.scholastic.com/activities/asian-american/angel_island/interview.asp), a Chinese immigrant who came to the United States many years ago. What does she remember about her early experiences? What other questions would you like to ask her?
- Read Baseball Saved Us (Mochizuki, 1995). What were the experiences of the Japanese Americans in the U.S. during WWII?
- How do these two stories differ? How are they similar?
- In your sketchbook, create a visual representation of your insights on immigration.

Political Shapers of Hispanic Culture: United Farm Workers and Cesar Chavez
- Cesar Chavez and his daughter Lisa Chavez shaped the political climate for the Hispanics in this country, and they were able to draw large crowds when they spoke.
- Read about their work and the influences they had on farm workers across the country.
- Working with materials in front of you, create a poster that illustrates their causes and that would draw a crowd of listeners.

Like initiating engagements, demonstrations, and text/literature studies, invitations encourage thinking and learning about immigration within an arts-integrated perspective. Learners perform, create, respond to, and generate new texts from their investigation with others on various interests within the Focused Study.

Opportunities for Sharing and Organizing

As teachers, we are held accountable for the learning of our students. We must be diligent about providing them with a range of ways and opportunities to document the course of their study, to organize and share their discoveries, and to

Figure 8.8 *Learning wall.*

Figure 8.9 *Fourth-grade student's Modigliani-like autobiographical painting.*

Figure 8.10 *Sarita's visual and linguistic interpretation of poem.*

address local, state, and national standards. Although written documents are often those most valued in school, ELA teachers must also consider integrating nonwritten texts such as visual artwork, music, multimedia presentations, tri-fold display boards, learning quilts (such as in Figure 8.6), and learning walls (see Figure 8.8) as part of their overall assessment of students' learning. Organizing their learning through a range of media encourages students to notice relationships—whether they be artistic, linguistic, electronic, or musical—and demonstrates complex and deep learning.

For instance, to create the visual text shown in Figure 8.9, a fourth-grade student has studied the abstract minimalist painter Amedeo Modigliani, then paints her own stylized image based upon her inquiry. Along with this art text she writes an autobiographical piece. Eisner (2002a) suggests that noticing such relationships matters and demonstrates complex thinking on the part of the learner. In another instance, ninth-grade English-language learner Sarita demonstrates a complex interplay between both written language and art (see Figure 8.10). Because Sarita recently immigrated to the United States and did not have a firm grasp on the English language, she was unable to communicate her strong understanding through writing. Marta, Sarita's teacher, encouraged her English language students to interpret texts through a variety of media. After studying a poem about how looks can be deceiving, she writes, "In my picture, there is a woman who believe [sic] in a man who looks nice and friendly; this man wasn't what he (aparento) and abuses her. The man controled [sic] her." Sarita's pencil drawing of the female clearly shows fear, both in her thoughts (bottom right hand corner), and in reality (riding in the carriage). Even though the female in the poem lives a life of affluence, the physical and emotional abuse that she suffers by the sophisticated man in a horse-driven carriage cannot be accepted.

In our particular Focused Study on Immigration, learners are offered a range of ways in which they shared their learning through literature studies, picture book

186

writing, art-inspired life cycles of characters, text sets to share with others, mask-making and poetry writing, class discussions, arts-based note-taking, response journals, and postmodern books (as well as others). Some wrote postmodern books while others wrote traditional picture books. Further, how they interpret these projects is often located in their experiences and confidence with representing through visual and linguistic means. Some arts-based notebooks contain complex images, while others are simple line drawings. The ways through which educators invite learners to share their learning is limitless, yet many students remind us that they have learned only to respond through writing, essays, and journals. As such, they rarely develop a more complex way to respond, and are often tentative in sharing their understanding in ways other than writing.

Two of my learners' favorite ways to respond are through transmediation and their writing of postmodern books. Transmediation is a semiotic process in which learners retranslate their understanding of a text, idea, or concept through another medium. After she has studied a range of texts, Geeta represents what she understands of the strengths that immigrants bring to the United States with color and language (see Figure 8.11). She transmediates her concept of immigration into art. Her bright use of colors suggests to viewers the possibilities that emerge from the voices and experiences of immigrants. Discussion surrounds each presentation. Before Geeta explains her representation, the class engages in a strategy called "Save the Last Word" [for the artist], adapted from "Save the Last Word" [for the author] (Harste, Short, & Burke, 1988). The class interprets Geeta's transmediation: "Geeta's piece is so energetic with the bold reds, greens, and yellows." "She seems to suggest the strong contributions that immigrants offer through their skills, experiences, and language." "The language texts are very different, some larger than others, and individual letters stand out, just like individual people and their stories." Geeta, then, has the last word:

Figure 8.11 *Geeta's transmediation.*

> I wanted to capture the essence of immigration–their contributions and the opportunities afforded [immigrants]. My great-grandparents immigrated to the U.S. and we still carry on some of our traditions, especially certain recipes that were handed down. The language, like Emiliano mentioned, is both a celebration and a barrier. The words that I have chosen express the positive nature of immigration, yet at the same time, I wanted to show how much language can prohibit immigrants from participating in basic everyday life. As you can see, language covers nearly one half of my picture. Language is a real challenge for immigrants, especially in this country.

Teachers find that transmediation helps learners organize their overall meaning, and invites a collective meaning, generated from the group's comments.

Creating postmodern books, or books written in nontraditional ways, is another favorite media-rich project. Based upon their inquiry into a topic, learners create a fiction or nonfiction book. They write books on sea turtles, friendship, the Elizabethan age, the Harlem Renaissance, teenage challenges, and the Civil Rights movement. These books demonstrate their learning and challenge them to consider how best to represent their learning. They plan out the shape of the book, consider materials they will use, and figure out how to bind the book. Jennifer's inquiry was on sea turtles, and she wrote a nonfiction interactive postmodern book to relay her learning (see Figures 8.12 a, b, and c). Her book cover, made from modeling clay, enabled Jennifer to easily create a soft,

  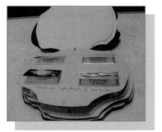

Figure 8.12a Jennifer's postmodern book, Sea Turtles, cover.

Figure 8.12b Jennifer's postmodern book, Sea Turtles, title page.

Figure 8.12c Jennifer's postmodern book, Sea Turtles, interior page.

pliable surface on which she could paint the colors of a sea turtle's shell. The title page is made from a piece of decorative and textured brown paper that resembles water, and she presents the eight different sea turtles, complete with a picture and some information about each, within the small cards on the page. She even used transparencies to show the digestive system of the sea turtle. Creating a postmodern book of this complexity posed many problems that Jennifer needed to solve, from the book's binding, to the transparencies, to the written text, to the interactive nature of the book. Not only did she learn more about sea turtles through her inquiry, she challenged herself to study how books are produced. Her book created quite a stir among her colleagues, and initiated a number of questions about its content and its making. They were especially interested in the social action element at the back of the book which invited readers to get involved in saving the sea turtle from extinction. Jennifer writes about this experience: "I learned that I have great ideas and creative ways to create a text my students would enjoy. I also learned what authors and illustrators go through everyday when creating a children's book." Other learners reflect on this multimedia project as Nicole does:

> Something I learned is that books aren't all linear. Everyone's books were so different and creative. I learned a lot about how to show information in new and fun ways. It was such a great project. Thanks for letting us do something that challenged us and pushed us to our limits.

Heather comments on the standards that are met when such projects are included to show student learning: "I really loved Hannah's Harlem Renaissance box. Watching her go through the symbols had me thinking of ways to use a project like this to assess students and to develop their critical thinking skills." Creative and media-rich projects encourage learners' to see themselves not just as writers or artists, but as creators of multi-media texts. They gain confidence in both art and language, and learn to understand how art has potential to communicate certain parts of the message while language communicates another part.

Another way to organize and share their learning lay within learners' own heritage. Learners in this Focused Study read immigrant stories, interviewed and collected their own stories of immigration, and wrote "I Am..." poems, such as Alli's (see Figure 8.13). Atop photographs of her family members, she layers her writing: "I hear my great-grandmother reading her Bible in her Irish accent/I see the beauty of Scottish hills, the Isle of Sky and I feel proud to be a part of them." Such media-rich texts demonstrate how learners communicate in complex ways. The text of Alli's poem is transformed as she adds elements of photography, font styles, and spatial layout.

Figure 8.13 Alli's poem, I Am.

To culminate our Focused Study of Immigration, learners create a cultural heritage project, a semiotic representation of their connections to a novel or major text that they studied. My ELA teachers initially struggle with this project, asking, "How can I connect my life to..." *Of Mice and Men* (Steinbeck, 1993), or *1984*(Orwell 1992), or *Buried Onions* (Soto, 1997). In effect, they ask the same questions that their students ask of them when they read such assigned literature. Once learners reflect on the elements of this project, they begin their journey by talking with family members, looking through old photo albums and letters, making favorite recipes and foods, collecting favorite family clothing, or even bringing in treasured memorabilia like locks of hair and funeral programs (see Figure 8.14 for

Figure 8.14 Cultural heritage projects.

examples). For Gramika, this project was an emotional journey, and offered her a way to organize her life artifacts alongside those which constituted her inquiry into *The Pearl* (Steinbeck, 1945):

> Creating the cultural heritage project was very emotional. My mother and I sat together and picked the different pictures that are included in my display. We laughed and cried together while we picked the pictures. After I read John Steinbeck's novella, *The Pearl*, there was no doubt that my cultural project would involve my family. Like Kino, the main character, my family is the most important thing in the world. We are so close that it seems like they are in my life everyday. My joy is my family's joy; and my happiness is theirs also. This project was too much fun and emotional. Creating my project was an absolute duplication of my feeling while reading *The Pearl*. I am glad that I am able to share how the book impacted me, and what I've learned from a 90-page novella by John Steinbeck.

These cultural heritage projects are always extraordinarily moving because through this media-rich text teachers realize the power of literature to connect deeply to their lives and experiences.

Crucial to learning is an opportunity for learners to reflect on their experiences over the course of a Focused Study, nine-week period, or semester. Learning walls, or audit trails (Harste & Vasquez, 1998; Vasquez, 2004), are generated from artifacts collected over the course of a study, and placed on the wall as reminders of student learning. At the end of a study, students reflect on their learning, connect it to past learning, and generate ideas to future learning. Patrick reflects on his class's learning wall:

> This [learning wall] reminds me of the many multimedia experiences we had. Students are constantly exposed to music, music videos, movies, and computer games outside of class. To better connect their learning in school with what they are most interested in, multimedia can frame their learning in activities and engagements that students don't normally consider learning activities, but fun, cool things that they do on their own time.

Reflective Action Plans

Reflective action plans provide learners with opportunities to purposefully apply their learning and demonstrate their understanding of new ideas, discoveries and connections. They prompt learners to revisit previous beliefs and knowledge and to summarize new understandings and beliefs. They also call on learners to "make a difference" to do something to change attitudes and/or practices (Albers, 2006a). After students have worked through a number of engagements, inquired personally and collectively within the Focused Study, and shared their learning, they generate ideas about their future learning: What went well? What would help us next time to better inquire? What do we want to learn next? What will we change? What will I do next? Students can reflect on their learning and writing, as does Cora, a sixth-grader:

> I think for us who really want to become writers...be yourself and write about what you think is best. You might have a great idea but someone says, "I don't think that's going to work." But just keep it and write it for yourself because even though other people don't like it, it's you who should be the critic.

Cora lays out the plan for her future as a writer; she will keep her writing ideas to encourage future writing. Cora generates a reflective action plan. Marcus, a fourth grader, reflects on the importance of art in his writing: "We explore a lot with art, especially when we sculpted our faces in our mask poems. We acted our emotions, and then we looked for words that expressed them. We studied our faces to see how our emotions look. We did everything." Marcus's reflective action plan includes art to help him develop descriptive language.

Just as students make reflective action plans, so teachers consider such questions as What went well? How did media-rich experiences support all learning? How will the learning in this study connect to future learning? These questions drive teachers to think about how they will approach the teaching of a text or theme in light of the whole Focused Study. Amy states, "I like invitations and want to start my Focused Study with these. They will give my students an introduction to the Focused Study, and I'll be able to see what areas interest them." Sam, a high school teacher, reflects on how she plans to begin her Focused Study with *House on Mango Street* (Cisneros, 1991) as the core text:

> pictures of Mexican communities, individual people, women, and groups of friends are placed on tables around the room. Students venture from table to table in search of different pictures while writing short responses to them in journals. I don't want to give students an introduction or structured lesson prior to this experience. We will then share responses—what do these pictures remind you of? How do they make you feel? What picture made you feel the worst/best and why? What about these pictures made you feel happy/sad/scared? Through these questions, students will be able to better understand the realities to Cisneros's novel as well as begin to consider the universal themes found within.

By using reflective action plans, you can learn several important features of designing strong curriculum:

- Engagements must be flexible and serve potentially different functions within a Focused Study.
- Media-rich engagements take time and must be carefully considered, organized, and managed.
- The Focused Study must engage students at all levels and experiences.

Such inquiry into ELA instruction pushes teachers to think more broadly about arts-based instruction and its potential for meaning making in their classrooms.

Creating Environment for Quality Arts and Media-Rich Integration

The Focused Study is a flexible curriculum framework that can build upon what it is that you currently do or become part of what you do or have to do in your own school district. The keys to strong curriculum design are student interests and flexibility of engagements. So, how do you get started with creating curriculum from a semiotic perspective? This section briefly describes the significance of professional development, teacher as learner, finding time for inquiry, and imagining success.

Professional Development

Teachers must value professional development, whether it be in graduate school or through professional development units, as a way to keep informed about current and media-rich practices. Professional development invites new learning and new information about inquiry topics around which you are passionate. Local, state, and national conferences provide me with invaluable professional development, especially in the areas of the visual or media arts, and most recently, podcasting. My work has advanced because of my conversations with other professionals who are interested in semiotics, visual arts integration, and new literacies. My university students are another valuable professional development resource. They continue to inspire new ideas in my teaching and learning, and raise questions that encourage new inquiry. Another less formal learning space is at my local community arts center, which continues to energize me and push my own thinking, and offer resources that support and build upon my interest in media-rich ELA instruction. At the clay studio, I talk with others about how they throw particular forms, how they glaze to get an interesting finish, or what museums or galleries they find interesting.

Some of my most engaging professional development occurs at local coffee shops and through e-mail. When opportunity affords (conferences, home visits, etc.), I have coffee with colleagues and good friends with whom I studied in graduate school and talk about current issues and literacy teaching and learning. They inspire me to think about the potential of media-rich engagements and curricula and encourage me to look outside literacy journals for insights on semiotic learning. E-mail and online discussion groups also keep me informed about current issues in literacy. NCTE's Commission on Arts and Literacy (COAL) (see www.ncte.org) was formed because of our collective interests on how to integrate the arts and technology. NCTE and IRA also partner on a wonderful site called ReadWriteThink.org (www.readwritethink.org) in which teachers can access a range of ideas for creating lessons that are inquiry and arts based.

Professional development in technology started for me when I moved from overhead transparencies to PowerPoint presentations. As I mentioned previously, Mel Mann, one of my graduate students, was the impetus for my passion for the potential of technology in my teaching and learning. Most recently, Oscar Hernandez, a Fresno, California-area high school reading teacher, has inspired me to work with video production with students. My passion drives experimentation, and through trial and error, I have learned a great deal about technology, teaching, and ELA. This interest has led me to initiate a podcast for English teachers, which invites preservice and inservice teachers to share their best practices. Technology and the visual arts have revolutionized the way I teach, and also serve to demonstrate the potential of the arts and inquiry to engage our 21st-century students.

Teacher as Learner

Within this book, you have positioned yourself as a learner. You have "taken lessons" and hopefully learned techniques and ideas about drawing, color, technology, and 3-D. Like your students, you also are a learner, and it is important that you find inquiry topics that drive you to want to know more.

I believe that it is essential that we teachers always have some inquiry in progress, and find time to share these interests and passions with our students. I am an insatiable learner, and have ongoing inquiries into several areas: the Harlem Renaissance, the Dust Bowl, Immigration, video/podcasting, and pottery. These areas drive both my personal and professional interests. My office and home libraries are large and continue to grow. Because many teachers have tight budgets, local libraries are a wonderful source for postmodern books, nonfiction, and fiction texts that address areas of a Focused Study. To be engaged in our own inquiry is essential if we want our students to be lifelong learners. When we are excited about a topic—for example pottery, gardening, bell choir, or carpentry—we share our findings and our learning with others, raise questions with others who have similar interests, and begin to bring in examples of this learning to share with our students. Such learning serves as a demonstration to our students that learning is life-long and can shift and change whenever we find something that piques our interests or we have a need to know something.

Finding Time for Inquiry

Those who attend presentations that I make often remark, "Where do you find the time for studying art, pottery, and literacy?" My simple answer is that I make the time for the work that energizes me. Because there are so many other things that I have to do on a daily basis that drain my energy, I have to have interests that encourage me and move my thinking in directions I might not have before imagined. For example, each week, I take a three-hour class in pottery and spend time during the weekend in the studio. This six hours offers me the time I need to explore this medium, and relaxes my mind so that I can muster up energy for my job. I take my journals and books to the gym so that I can keep up with current ideas in this field while I exercise. Consider the ways in which you might do the same. How often do you find yourself offering students time to work on their projects, or waiting for your own children to finish up their activities? These are wonderful moments to steal time to read up on your area of interest. If you have an interest in art, invite the art teacher into your classroom and practice the techniques she or he teaches to your students. Or occasionally spend your preparation period in the art room to practice along with the students. Taking time to explore your own interests is essential to your own thinking and teaching. Such inquiry offers you insights on how to encourage your own students to find their own passions.

Imagining Your Success

Arts- and media-integrated classrooms will happen when you imagine the possibilities. Greene (1995) writes that the "function of art is to make people see" (p. 16). When content is studied through an arts approach, students are likely to see different perspectives and imagine new meanings. We should think of curriculum as opening public spaces for students to share their voices and visions, and learn to interpret and represent drawing upon the resources and media they access daily. To do so honors the literacies they bring from home and to school. To start, consider the following:

- Begin with a question. What do you want to know more about? Technical aspects (inserting images, sound, film)? Developing strong PowerPoint presentations? Building resources? Learning more about drawing? 3-D?

- Delve into personal inquiry into this area. Seek out others who have experience. Read, practice, and play.

- Talk with colleagues who have developed arts-based projects or techniques in their classes and invite them to help you generate ideas for your own classroom.

- Invite the art teacher into your class or go into her or his classroom to study some of the techniques or ideas that interest you or that you want to incorporate into your own class (such as papier-mâché, color theory, drawing).

- Read professional journals and books like this one; they contain a number of wonderful ideas for you to consider as you integrate the visual arts into instruction.

- Consider borrowing some of your school's technology equipment over the summer or other holidays to practice some of the technology ideas presented in this book. Build a basic PowerPoint presentation to present content, and use callout text boxes, inserted images, or music.

Classroom Environment and Setup

Setting up a class environment that shows your commitment to the visual arts is crucial. Students should experience the visual arts immediately upon entering the room and know that they will contribute their own media-rich texts. When I walked into Lisa's class (pictured in Figure 8.15a) and Beth's class (pictured in Figure 8.15b), I immediately saw the visual texts that their students made alongside their written texts. And as students work in these classrooms, they know that the arts will always be at the heart of their learning. Art covers Lisa's walls and

Figure 8.15a Lisa's media-rich classroom.

Figure 8.15b Beth's art-focused classroom.

ceiling with her students' language and art texts. She also runs a clothesline from one corner of the room to display more artwork. Lisa builds an art workshop into her reading/writing workshop. The arts, for her, present students' learning in a way that written and oral language cannot.

In Beth's class, each student has her or his own area in which they place their materials, and she has designated other areas of the room for working with art. Outside Beth's class is a very large, white-painted steamer trunk on which are a few images. Immediately, this object invoked questions about the learning in which students were engaged. On the hallway walls were photographs of her students exploring space, color, and image on their individual suitcases. The theme of travel was immediately evident inside Beth's room, as well. There were white-painted train cases and suitcases piled atop one another. In a geography

Figure 8.16 *Train case and student inquiry.*

study, each student chose a place they wanted to study, and designed and painted their suitcases based upon what they learned. One student played with spatial placement of the objects that will become a part of his suitcase (see Figure 8.16). The cost of these cases was minimal; parents donated them or Beth found them at thrift stores. Further, Beth cleverly uses space in her small classroom. She has turned a coat closet into her supplies room. She gathers paper, pencils, colors, paints, found objects, and environmental objects (branches, stones, leaves, etc.) and organizes them into boxes where students can easily find them when they need them.

Kay Cowan, a former elementary teacher, displays her students' artwork all around the room. Masks fill one wall, while small artworks cover the front of a

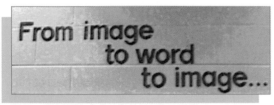

Figure 8.17 *Words that show commitment to arts.*

wooden podium, and other student paintings hang in other areas of the room. Prominently displayed on one wall are six very powerful words: "From image to word to image..." (see Figure 8.17). Students know that in Kay's classroom, they will be exploring literacy through the arts.

Overcoming Challenges: Time and Mess

Many teachers continue to ask me how they can integrate the arts when their curricula are so full. Consider the Focused Study as a framework for teaching. The arts can be integrated to support ELA concepts in demonstrations, invitations, text studies, and sharing and organizing through cultural heritage projects, transmediation, and multimedia presentations. The arts-based strategy lessons in Appendix B offer a good start. Strategy lessons in the visual arts will support students' learning to express meaning across media. As they respond in media-rich ways over time, they will become more proficient, and their artworks will be completed in a more timely manner. I do not let learners labor with their drawings. I want them to use fluid and loose lines to explain their thoughts; I want them to push themselves to think quickly through art. I want art to be a language that comes trippingly off their fingers as much as language comes trippingly off their tongues.

Art does take time to set up, organize, and finish. I did a workshop with a fifth-grade teacher on 3-D mask-building. Although we had nearly two hours, we had not anticipated that cutting out the eyes and mouths on 18 cardboard boxes would take as long as it did (rounded scissors do not help!). Unfortunately, we did not complete the masks that afternoon, and had to postpone finishing them until several weeks later. These things happen. However, that afternoon, students learned nuance in word choice, problem-solved aspects of mask-building, especially when noses or cheeks fell off, and most importantly, were introduced to looking at relationships between elements in the mask and their own experiences.

Art can be messy...if you let it. Working with paints, in particular, can be trying, yet when you take precautions—like putting down a dropcloth on the tables and on the floor (custodians are very concerned about clean floors)—clean-up is much easier. Also, students rarely should work directly on the desk surface; cover desks with newspaper or plastic for easy clean-up.

Although there are challenges in working with the arts in terms of time and mess, the benefits are worth every second of it. Students learn to pay attention to details and relationships, and they learn how to represent meaning because they have learned how not only to produce visual texts, but to read their texts.

Final Thoughts

You now have tools and techniques with which you can create a classroom in which the arts, inquiry, and technology enrich learning. You can read your students' work, and create a media-rich curriculum. I hope, too, that you have addressed any fears you might have had about teaching ELA with the arts, and moved forward many steps. This book cannot capture every detail of designing a media-rich ELA curriculum; however, you now have a flexible set of resources that will support you in your commitment to the arts and literacy. Your study of the visual arts, inquiry, and media-rich learning, once unfamiliar, is now more familiar.

I hope you will continue to explore the arts with your newly found talents, and perhaps, most importantly, your discovery that art truly does invite new perspectives on teaching and learning. And I hope that you continue to grow as an artist, and support your students as they learn to become more thoughtful and critical consumers and producers of texts.

Art Terms and Definitions

Acrylics: A type of paint (pigment suspended in a liquid); dries to form a hard coating

Additive: In 3-D, the method used by adding material to or combining materials

Aesthetics: A philosophy or study of art and its nature

Assembling: Joining multiple, often different, materials together

Bas-relief: A French word meaning "low-raised work"; this art is also known as relief sculpture

Blending: The gradual mixing of pigment or graphite to achieve a particular effect

Blind contour drawing: A drawing method done in one continuous line; the pencil continues moving while the artist's eyes are fixed on the object, never looking down at the paper

Carving: A sculpting method by which material is removed by cutting or chipping

Casting: A sculpting method in which liquid material is poured into a mold

Chalk: A drawing tool made from limestone and colored pigment

Charcoal: A drawing medium, available in black or white

Clay body: Type of clay, porcelain, earthenware, raku, stoneware; varies according to the geography of an area

Closed angle: A sharp angle in which the pencil is close to the surface of the paper

Collage: An arrangement of materials, cut or torn or found objects, pasted to a surface

Coil: A sculpting method in which long, round strips of clay are formed then molded together

Color spectrum: The distribution of colors produced when light is dispersed by a prism

Color wheel: An arrangement of colors in a circular format; representation of color

Colored pencils: A colored drawing medium

Colored markers: A colored drawing medium

Cool hues (colors): A family of related colors that range from greens through the blues; they evoke a "cool" feeling

Complementary colors: Colors that appear opposite each other on the color wheel

Composition: The content of an artwork

Contour line drawing: Drawing an object using one continuous line to show the outer and inner outlines of an object

Cross-hatch: A drawing technique; produced by lines crossing each other at angles more or less acute

Depth: The distance from the front of a composition to the back

Doodle: Seemingly haphazard drawing technique

Draping method: A sculpting method in papier-mâché used to cover large areas as in garments, landscapes

Dry pans: In watercolor; dry pigment, available in many colors, often used for outdoor work

Elements of shape: Basic shapes of all objects: line, dot, curved line, circle, angle

End run: In clay; the end run of one clay body is integrated into a new batch of another clay body

Eraser: Tool for removing unwanted marks; also used as a drawing tool to make white marks on composition

Fire: In clay; clay is heated to a range of degrees; the higher the degree, the harder the clay

Foreground: The part of a composition that appears to be in the front and nearest to the viewer; objects in foreground usually are larger in appearance

Form: An object that has height, depth, width

Gesture drawing: In drawing; a quick drawing that captures the energy and movement of the subject

Gradation: A gradual and smooth change from dark to light, such as from white to black or red to light pink

Gradated wash: In watercolor; a wash that is light at one end of the paper where less pigment is applied, and gradually becomes darker, where more pigment is applied

Graphite: Pencil; a drawing medium

Highlights: Area where light is strongest; centers attention through use of color or light

Horizon line: A line where the sky meets the ground

Hue: A color's name

Intensity: The brightness or dullness of a hue

Intermediate hues: Colors made by mixing primary and secondary hues together

In the round: Three-dimensionality of an object

Kiln: In clay; oven that is used for hardening, burning, or drying pottery

Knead: To work and press a medium, like clay or papier-mâché, into a malleable mass

Layer: In drawing, color; to add pigment or graphite on top of pigment or graphite

Light source: Where the light hits strongest or weakest; considered with highlights and lowlights

Lowlights: In drawing, color; deep or dark areas where the light does not reach

Medium: A material used to create a work of art: clay, watercolor, colored pencil, etc.

Middle ground: Part of the canvas that lies between the foreground and the background

Modeling: A sculpting method in which a soft medium, like clay or papier-mâché, is built up and shaped

Open angle: A wide open angle in which the tip of the pencil is the closest to the paper

Palette: A tray on which color is placed; a set of colors that an artist uses to create an artwork

Papier-mâché: Shredded paper mixed with liquid glue to create 3-D images

Perspective: Using lines and space to show depth in a composition.

Pigment: A finely ground colored power that gives paint its color

Pinch method: A sculpting technique used to give shape to clay or papier-mâché

Primary hues (colors): Yellow, red, and blue; colors from which all other colors are said to be made

Proportion: A principle of art that addresses the relationships of one part to the whole and of one part to another

Pulp method: A papier-mâché method of creating 3-D images

Score: To make thin, criss-crossed grooves into a surface; used to join clay surfaces

Secondary hues (colors): Made when primary colors are mixed equally

Self-portrait: An image of the artist made by the artist

Semi-liquid tube: In watercolor; wet pigment, for indoor work, available in many colors

Severe angle: An angle of the pencil that is very close to the paper

Shade: Black is added to darken a hue

Shape: An outline of an object

Slab: A sheet or slice of clay

Slab method: A sculpting technique used to form sheets of clay from a mass of clay

Slip: Liquid clay that acts as an adhesive to join two clay surfaces

Smudge: To blur a medium

Still life: A composition of arranged objects

Strip method: A sculpting method used to make 3-D images in papier-mâché; strips of paper are saturated with a liquid glue

Study: A series of drawings, paintings, sculptures, etc. in which an artist presents an object, person, or thing from different angles, positions, or perspectives

Stylized: An exaggerated image of a realistic object, person, or thing

Subtractive: A sculpting method in which material is taken away from the original material

Support: Any surface that holds a medium, such as paper, wood, canvas, fabric

Tempera: A type of liquid paint; available in multiple colors

Texture: Surface decoration in clay or how something looks like how it might feel

Throw(n): In clay; term used to describe work done on a pottery wheel; "throw a pot on the wheel"

Tint: White is added to lighten a hue

Three-dimension: Having height, weight, and depth

Tone: The darkness or lightness of a color

Triad hues: Three colors equally spaced on the wheel (i.e., yellow/blue/red, green/purple/orange)

Trompe l'oeil: French for "to trick the eye"; an art technique to create the optical illusion that the painted or sculpted objects are real

Two-dimension: Having height and width, but not depth

Value: The darkness or lightness of a color

Vanishing point: The point on the horizon line where parallel lines meet and then seem to disappear

Volume: Space occupied by 3-D objects

Warm hues (colors): A range of colors that evoke a warm feeling: yellows, reds, oranges

Wash: The background of a watercolor composition; thin, watery paint applied quickly with large brushstrokes

Watercolor: A painting technique using paint made of transparent colorants suspended or dissolved in water; describes a type of composition made with watercolors

Wedge: To knead clay into a malleable and workable mass

Arts-Based English Language Arts Lessons

The strategies listed in this section are meant to support and extend your work integrating the visual and media arts into ELA instruction.

Abstract Art...Abstract Writing

(IRA/NCTE Standards: 3, 6, 11)

Theoretical Position. Writers, especially poets, continually push readers to consider abstract concepts through their word choices, their settings, and their characters. William Carlos Williams's poem "The Red Wheelbarrow" (Ellman & O'Clair, 1976) is one of the most well-known abstract poems; readers have offered a range of meanings for this text, none definitive. e.e. cummings also created a stir with his nontraditional way of writing poetry. His "[plato told]" (Ellman & O'Clair, 1976) reflects the tragedies of war, and serves as an invitation for students to contrast the historical and contemporary aspects of war. Medieval morality plays used personified abstractions to represent human vices and virtues. Abstract art, like abstract writing, does not depict objects in the natural world, but instead displays shapes and colors in ways in which reality is altered or reduced in a way that simplifies reality. Georges Braque, Pablo Picasso, and Mark Rothko are considered abstract artists who have challenged viewers to see the world through shapes and colors—and make sense of them. Teaching students to read and analyze shapes and colors in this way supports their own understanding of abstract ideas in written texts, or abstract qualities in humans, especially English learners or those who struggle with written language.

Procedure. Students will create an abstract painting, sculpture, or drawing, and a written text to accompany it. A choice of media should be available, as abstractness spans across art forms. Students choose an abstract term, concept, or idea from texts they are reading or topics they are studying.

1. Independently through inquiry studies or as a group, students study texts of a range of writers (such as Sylvia Plath, Mem Fox, Sandra Cisneros, Nikki Giovanni, William Carlos Williams, e. e. cummings, and others), as well as artworks by various artists (such as Georges Braque, Pablo Picasso, Georgia O'Keefe, William Johnson, Jackson Pollack, Aminah Robinson, and others). Discuss these questions: What abstract concepts do these authors and artists try to embody in their work? How do they make the abstract more concrete through images, words, symbols?

2. Students choose an abstract concept they wish to study and around which they want to create a visual text. They research the concept, phrase, or idea to see how it is represented in various disciplines and art forms.

3. Students design a visual text, 2- or 3-D, that they believe embodies the abstract concept or idea they wish to convey. Using limited language or unconventionally written language, students write a piece that represents their art, and the art represents their language.

4. Students create a gallery of visual and verbal texts, look across texts, and reflect upon the concepts represented.

Further Inquiry. Invite students to create a semantic map, or table, that enables them to identify aspects that cut across art and language texts. Running horizontally across this map, students write the titles of the art works and writings. Running vertically, students write characteristics that they noticed which comprise the concept of abstractness.

LESSON RESOURCES

cummings, e.e. (1976). In R. Ellman & R. O'Clair (Eds.), *Modern poems: An introduction to poetry* (p. 220). New York: Norton.
Falconer, I. (2000). *Olivia*. New York: Atheneum.
Perry, V. (2005). *Abstract painting: Concepts and techniques*. New York: Watson-Guptill.
Williams, W.C. (1976). The red wheelbarrow. In R. Ellman & R. O'Clair (Eds.), *Modern poems: An introduction to poetry* (p. 111). New York: Norton.

Color, Consumerism, and Critique

(IRA/NCTE Standards: 10, 11, 12)

Theoretical Position. Within inquiry-based learning, compositions located within learners' lives generate interest and focus. When they understand color theory, learners begin to notice how shades of color also inform shades of meaning and viewer response. Repetition in art, as in writing, emphasizes elements or concepts. Working with Andy Warhol's technique of repetition and color, learners discuss commercial icons that are significant to them, and how and why such products (including humans as objects of beauty) are "must haves." Helping students to critique advertisements and use repetition and color to emphasize the significance they have on our thinking and consumerism can help us meet another educational goal: to encourage students to take a stand on social issues.

Procedure. In this project, learners are invited to work with a particular product (such as hamburger chain restaurants, clothing, music icon) and find a number of images that represent this product. Invite them to discuss how this product is represented across magazines, billboards, or newspaper ads. What features are accented? Which colors are used? After creating a collage of this product, invite students to choose one of these images, photocopy it 9 or 12 times, and then color or decorate each of the frames. This engagement teaches learners to study how repetition in art, as in writing, serves distinct purposes and conveys intentions.

1. Students study Andy Warhol's technique of repetition, his intention behind painting well-known subjects such as Marilyn Monroe, a Campbell's tomato soup can, and Jackie Kennedy. Discussion may center on the purpose behind writers', artists', musicians', etc. use of repetition in their compositions: Why is repetition used? What purpose does it serve the viewer/reader/listener? Independently, students can further inquire into other artists and their use of repeating colors.

2. Discuss how advertisers often target young children and teens as significant consumers; students look across magazine ads and choose a product or a company they on which they wish to focus. Invite students to find this product in a variety of magazines, and ask them to make a statement about how this product is represented differently and for different audiences. For example, "Burger King [Nike, Old Navy, Gameboy, etc.] advertises differently in *Transworld Skateboarding* than they do in *Time* or *Newsweek*.

3. Students choose one of these images and make 9 or 12 black-and-white photocopies of this product.

4. Using markers, colored pencils, oil pastels, or tissue paper, students layer various colors onto each of the images and decorate their images with other media. Students tape together their images to create a Warhol-like collage, and share their art and intentions with their class. (See chapter 3 for an example of a Warhol-like collage.)

5. Students write a statement about their art, the product, and consumerism in general, and share these with the class. Post the images around the room, school, and hallway to make a collective statement on consumerism.

Further Inquiry. Based upon this collage, learners think like the advertisers, and create their own original ad for a product. In this project, they write original text around a visual object. They present this product to the rest of the class as if they were marketing this product for a particular audience. Ask students to consider the following questions in their presentation: How did this art project inform their word choices? The style of the ad? And how did such building of image help them to better design their writing? How does such repetition function in music, art, language, dance? Why is repetition important to meaning?

LESSON RESOURCES

Rodley, C. (Director). (2003). *Andy Warhol–The complete picture*. Richmond Hill, ON: Bfs Entertainment.

Staff of Andy Warhol Museum. (2004). *Andy Warhol 365 takes: The Andy Warhol Museum collection*. New York: Harry N. Abrams.

Autobiographical Drawings/Figures

(IRA/NCTE Standards: 1, 2, 8, 12)

Theoretical Position. Autobiography is an important genre for ELA learners both to read and respond, and write and respond. Autobiography, however, is not solely located in language, but lives are also made significant through pictures, paintings, photographs, and artifacts. Inviting students to study artifacts from their own lives, listen to and record stories of family members, and remember events in their lives that have meaning supports writing as inquiry (Harste, Short, & Burke, 1988).

Procedure. To accompany autobiography or memoir, students draw themselves in situations, settings, or with objects that have significance.

1. As a class and in small groups, read excerpts from several good autobiographies and biographies, then as a class discuss autheticity, voice, and detail. Stories from Sandra Cisneros's *Woman Hollering Creek* (1992) or *The House on Mango Street* (1991), Ken Mochizuki's *Baseball Saved Us* (1993), Francisco Jiménez's *The*

Circuit (1997) and *Breaking Through* (2002), Ji-li Jiang's *The Red Scarf Girl: A Memoir of a Cultural Revolution* (1998), Nikki Giovanni's *Rosa* (2005), and Gary Soto's *Living Up the Street* (1992) are strong examples. Who writes with more conviction? How are similar details rendered across a biography and an autobiography written about or by a person? Invite a critical reading of such texts.

2. Invite students to gather artifacts from home, collect statements from family members, interview, and bring important objects to think through their own meaningful life experiences. Encourage them to reflect on the stories that make the object or picture or interview personally significant.

3. Students write up short vignettes for several artifacts.

4. As students are writing their stories, invite them to create a life-size image of themselves, using what they have learned about figure drawing, paint it and problem-solve how they will keep it upright. Invite them to draft their autobiographical image before they cut it out of cardboard or Styrofoam or other materials. Encourage them to reflect on how their stories may change from this construction, or how this construction may change because of their stories. (Figure B.1 presents an example of a life-size figure.)

5. Students share their life-size images with each other and perform one of their favorite stories. Invite them to reflect on how the full-size image encourages different thinking than the small images that often accompany such writings.

Figure B.1 *Life-size figure.*

Further Inquiry. Children of all ages come into our classrooms with a wealth of experiences. As ELA teachers, we want students to notice their world, recognize the significance of these experiences, and to value the lives they bring into the classrooms. Autobiographical writings and life-size images of our students give significance to them in all their fullness. Whenever possible, support students' learning and thinking with life-size projects, projects that may not fit into the classroom, but are the lives represented within and around the school.

LESSON RESOURCES

Aldrin, B. (2005). *Reaching for the moon*. New York: HarperCollins.
Borg, M. (1998). *Writing your life: An easy-to-follow guide to writing an autobiography*. Fort Collins, CO: Cottonwood Press.
Bridges, R. (1999). *Through my eyes*. New York: Scholastic.
Cisneros, S. (1991). *House on Mango Street*. New York: Vintage.
Cisneros, S. (1992). *Woman hollering creek: And other stories*. New York: Vintage.

Giovanni, N. (2005). *Rosa*. New York: Holt.

Jiménez, F. (1997). *The circuit: Stories from the life of a migrant child*. Albuquerque: The University of New Mexico Press.

Jiménez, F. (2002). *Breaking through*. Boston: Houghton Mifflin.

Jiang, J. (1997). *Red scarf girl: A memoir of the cultural revolution*. New York: HarperCollins.

Mochizuki, K. (1993). *Baseball saved us*. New York: Lee & Low.

Mochizuki, K. (2003). *Passage to freedom: The Sugihara story*. New York: Lee & Low.

Soto, G. (1992). *Living up the street*. New York: Laurel Leaf.

Transmediation

(IRA/NCTE Standards: 4, 5, 9, 10, 11, 12)

Theoretical Position. Transmediation is a process in which we realize that we can make meaning in many sign systems. Transmediation, more specifically, is the movement of meaning from one sign system to another. By taking what we know in one sign system and recasting it in another system (music, math, art, drama, movement, written language) new signs and new forms of expression are created, and new knowledge is generated. Transmediation is a fundamental process to becoming literate (Harste, Short, & Burke, 1988). Such engagements encourage students to go beyond a literal understanding of what they have experienced. Furthermore, students who are reluctant to take risks or who have disparate notions of language see that not everyone has the same response to a selection. Although much of the meaning is shared, variations in interpretation add new meanings and new insights. Often, as students use art to construct meaning, they generate new insights of their own. With art as a second language, they often come to understand the text at a different level than when they first read the book. Response through art necessitates a different reading and representation of a text than a written response. Figures B.2a and B.2b present two examples of students' transmediations of the book *Bridge to Terabithia* (Patterson, 1987).

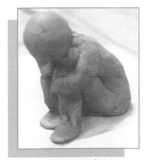

Figure B.2a *Student's transmediation*, Bridge to Terabithia.

Figure B.2b *Student's transmediation*, Bridge to Terabithia.

Procedure. Transmediation requires that students have a variety of media with which to express interpretation of a text.

1. Students work in small groups of four or five. Ask them to first read the selection, individually or as a group.

2. After reading the selection, students think about what they read and then use the materials to transmediate their understanding. Encourage students to move beyond a literal interpretation of the story to one which invites metaphorical thinking. Ask them to think about the meaning of the story and see if they can find a way to visually sketch that meaning. It also helps to ask students to draw their own connections to the story. Explain to students that there are many ways to express the meaning of an experience and they are free to experiment with their interpretation. Students should not be rushed but be given enough time to read, create artworks, create dramas, etc.

3. When the sketches are complete, each person in the group shows her or his sketch to the others in that group. The group participants study the sketch and say what they think the artist is attempting to say.

4. Once everyone has been given the opportunity to present an interpretation, the artist gets the last word and describes his or her intentions to the group. Sharing continues in this fashion until all group members have shared their artworks. Each group can then identify one project to be shared with the whole class.

LESSON RESOURCES

Eisner, E.W. (2002). *The art and the creation of mind.* New Haven, CT: Yale University Press.
Pugh, S.L., Hicks, J.W., Davis, M., & Venstra, T. (1992). *Bridging: A teacher's guide to metaphorical thinking.* Urbana, IL: National Council of Teachers of English.

Illustrated Life Cycles

(IRA/NCTE Standards: 7, 8)

Theoretical Position. Illustrated Life Cycles support students' ongoing interpretative strategies. Significant in the teaching of literature is to encourage students to examine events that are life-changing for characters in a story. Events are not merely discussed in terms of plot, but rather, students must consider how these events had an impact on a character. Illustrated Life Cycles, informed by Linda Rief's (1992) idea of positive-negative graphs, often express more than essays and talk can so they become an important part of knowing and understanding characters, connecting with events in the novel that the character

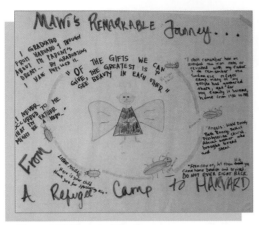

Figure B.3 *Character life cycle.*

experiences, and sharing and celebrating each others' insights on literature. (See Figure B.3.)

Procedure. Students can work individually or in small groups of no more than four. Invite students to create a life graph that represents important events in a character's life. When the life graph is presented on a wall, students can look across events, study, and negotiate which six events most affect the character's decisions and actions. Such discussion encourages deep (as opposed to superficial) interpretation of text.

Furthermore, such visual representations enable students to see a character's range of experiences.

1. Students study a major or minor character's life in a text, and identify and list the 10 most important events in that character's life.

2. Students then discuss among themselves, and trim these ten events to six. Together, they write a short statement about how and why each event affected this character's life.

3. On large newsprint or construction paper, students create a life cycle for this character, illustrating the important events in their lives. Using large sheets of newsprint is important to this engagement because it allows students to read and view the events more clearly, and encourages confidence when representing their ideas. Students then tape their life cycles on the wall for others to see.

4. Students share their thinking about why they selected the events they did and the details surrounding these events. These presentations help students focus on the storyline as well as character analysis because as they identify the six events, they must also explain why these events are significant in the character's life.

5. Students use this life cycle graph to create a character analysis essay or an essay that addresses critical issues of importance to readers.

Further Inquiry. Students can create cycles or graphs for a number of engagements: (1) students create and illustrate their family history shown through pictures, illustrations, and short stories accompanied by short captions for each image/event; (2) students generate their own life cycle or graph, and use this text as a springboard for future writing pieces; (3) students create a life cycle around individual authors they study, then compare and contrast the authors' lives with their own; 4) students analyze and synthesize sociological/natural events to see how they influence the writing, art, music, etc. of the time.

LESSON RESOURCES

Rief, L. (1992). *Seeking diversity: Language arts with adolescents*. Portsmouth, NH: Heinemann.
Rosenblatt, L.M. (1995). *Literature as exploration*. New York: Modern Language Association of America.

Color, Inquiry, and Purpose in Art

(IRA/NCTE Standards: 1, 3, 7, 12)

Theoretical Position. Art can offer students opportunities to explore their interests across disciplines. For instance, how can their study of animals be integrated into other ways of learning? How do art and math work together? How do art and reading engage students in inquiry? Harste (1994) argues that sign systems, or communication systems, cut across disciplines, and that we must be able to recognize this when we define literacy.

Procedure. Lisa Siemens, a Winnipeg, Manitoba teacher and her students build an inquiry focused on roosters and chickens. They study artists and writers who create texts around these birds. They then make a calendar, featuring students' artwork, to sell them at their school as a fundraiser. See Figure B.4 for an example.

Figure B.4 *Calendar, based on student inquiry into chickens and roosters.*

1. Based on student interest and with your students' input, choose an animal, creature, or idea to study; gather as many resources, including music, photographs, art, and so on, as possible and make these available for students to study. The focus of this study can be centered on the animals of a country or continent, or a variety of different species or breeds of the same animal.

2. In their sketchbooks, students do studies of the animals, creatures, or ideas and make decisions about how they want them to appear on the canvas. They make notes about what they learn about the animal, creature, or idea. They place these notes alongside their drawings, just like da Vinci and Michelangelo did.

3. They begin to draft their animal, each person choosing ways that they want to represent it. They draw and paint on a support (such as paper, cardboard, newsprint, canvas, fabric) which is then posted on the wall for all to see.

4. Take a digital photograph or scan each of the students' artworks, and create a calendar format using Microsoft Publisher. Feature the artwork of an individual student for each month of the year. With large classes, you can make several calendars, or make a collage of two or three images per month. Invite students to talk about calendars, their purpose, time and timelines, various ways in which time is recorded, and so on. In this way, art, writing, inquiry, and math operate together to support students' learning.

5. Calendars can be sold as fundraisers or become class calendars.

Further Inquiry. Working with inquiry and art offers creative opportunities for students to consider various types of professions that support art, inquiry, and writing. Furthermore, students can begin to think about how their artwork can support causes they believe in, such as raising money to help people affected by Hurricane Katrina. Such fundraisers not only raise money for important issues, but they also become strong learning engagements in which students understand the importance of research and representation.

LESSON RESOURCES

Damerow, G. (1995). *Storey's guide to raising chickens: Care/feeding/facilities.* North Adams, MA: Storey Books.

Galdone, P. (2006). *The little red hen.* New York: Clarion Books.

Landström, L., & Landström, O. (2005). *Four hens and a rooster.* New York: Farrar, Straus & Giroux.

Poole, A.L. (1999). *How the rooster got his crown.* New York: Holiday House.

Scarry, R. (1963). *The rooster struts.* New York: Golden Books.

Ward, H. (2003). *The rooster and the fox.* Minneapolis, MN: Carolrhoda.

Conceptualizing Concept With Contour Lines

(IRA/NCTE Standards: 1, 3, 4, 12)

Theoretical Position. In content area literacy, we continually challenge our students to get a sense of the whole idea or concept studied. Sometimes this is done through diagrams or through graphic organizers. The art technique of contour drawing can support students as they internalize the concept of getting the main idea or getting a sense of whole by investigating the details. Furthermore, with contour drawings, students can learn to visualize connections between the whole and the parts.

Procedure. In this engagement, students generate a contour drawing of one of the concepts in their text—perhaps it is as simple as an apple in their study of botany or an outline of Shakespeare's Globe Theater—to get a sense of its components. Such drawings help students visualize the whole concept and investigate to get a sense of details that support the concept. In Figures B.5a and B.5b, the student has done a contour drawing of the apothecary scene from *Romeo and Juliet*. Notice how she starts with a simple contour drawing in Figure B.5a, then integrates her knowledge through inquiry to create a more complete rendering of the times in Figure B.5b.

Figure B.5a *Contoured drawing, apothecary scene,* Romeo and Juliet.

Figure B.5b *More detailed drawing, apothecary scene,* Romeo and Juliet.

1. Consider a concept your students are studying. Invite them in small groups of no more than four students or individually, to read several texts (print, nonprint, or electric) on the concept, and construct a contour drawing of what they understand about the concept. Each group or individual can create a contour drawing of this concept, as well.

2. Students share their contour drawings with the class and talk about what they understand generally about the concept.

3. Students return to their inquiry and begin to read closer for information important to the concept, and begin to fill in their contour drawing. Encourage students to revise their contour drawings based upon their evolving knowledge about the concept.

4. Students post their drawings on the wall, then all look across the drawings and discuss what they learned from these drawings about the overall concept. Each group or individual then shares their drawings with the class.

Further Inquiry. Students can also sketch outlines of fiction or nonfiction pieces they wish to write. Developing an understanding of the idea they want to investigate will help them look for supporting details and be more critical about which texts to consult.

LESSON RESOURCES

Moline, S. (1995). *I see what you mean: Children at work with visual information.* York, ME: Stenhouse.

Contoured Characters and Celebrities

(IRA/NCTE Standards: 3, 4)

Theoretical Position. Connecting learning with our own interests is very important in teaching (Short, Harste, & Burke, 1996). Students must be vested in their learning in order to get the most out of it. Inviting students to explore the details of a character or celebrity of their choosing will enable them to connect with a topic relevant to their lives. Doing contour line drawings of such characters or celebrities invites students to look at characters from a new perspective (Greene, 1995).

Procedure. Students choose a favorite character from a story they are reading, or a celebrity they are investigating for a research project. They reconstruct their image of this character or celebrity based upon their readings.

1. Review the elements of shapes with students, and build their knowledge about the use of shape to convey emotion and relationships among characters. Invite them to consider drawing the contour outline first before adding details.

2. Invite students to consider important details about the character or the celebrity they are drawing. What aspects do they think are important? Which ones are unimportant? From this reflection, they gather the information then begin to add details to their contour drawings.

3. Invite students to do more than one drawing so they can show their understanding of how the character changed across time in the novel or story or the celebrity changed across his or her lifetime.

4. Ask students to share their finished drawings with other students, generate collective ideas about the character or celebrity, and write a narrative or nonfiction text with the drawings as illustrations.

Further Inquiry. As students continue to build their knowledge about art principles, they will also learn to notice details that make a person who she or he is. For example, John Lennon's round glasses are almost iconic to images that portray him (see Figure 2.20 in chapter 2). Encourage students to consider just those details that make the character or celebrity unique.

LESSON RESOURCES

Greene, M. (1995). *Releasing the imagination: Essays on education, the arts, and social change.* San Francisco: Jossey-Bass.

Hodge, A. (1991). *Drawing.* New York: Gloucester Press.

Rappaport, D. (2001). *Martin's big words: The life of Dr. Martin Luther King, Jr.* New York: Hyperion Books for Children.

Redman, L. (1984). *How to draw caricatures.* Chicago: Contemporary Books.

Consumerism, Consciousness, and Product Labels

(IRA/NCTE Standards: 3, 5, 10)

Theoretical Position. Critical literacy encourages thoughtful and conscious readings of all texts, visual, written, musical, movement, etc. Product labels and packaging are written to entice the consumer into buying products. The visual and verbal texts on packaging express concepts, ideas, and ideologies of marketers, advertisers, and sellers of that product. According to Harris (2001), marketers and advertising aim to make products aesthetically pleasing to consumers, and vicariously engage in the scene, image, or text they create. Becoming aware of the messages sent to consumers, young and old, is particularly of importance in schools because schools are sites in which critical discussion of consumer messages can take place in the context of learning about how language works as a tool of communication.

Procedure. In this engagement, students will learn to critically read, analyze, and discuss the visible and invisible messages sent to consumers on product labels and packaging.

1. Invite students to bring in a range of everyday texts, especially product packages, product labels, interesting materials used to package products advertisements (cereal boxes, candy wrappers, body lotion bottles, etc.).

2. Students present these texts and place them on the floor or table so that all texts can be studied collectively. Students discuss images, words, phrases, and concepts, that span across various texts, answering questions such as: What are the common words, colors, concepts used in these texts? What do those who

created this packaging try to explicitly say to the consumer? What messages are visible to the consumer? What invisible messages are being sent to the consumer?

3. Students divide the texts into categories that make sense to them (food, music, cosmetic, electronic, etc.). In small groups, students study the everyday texts within one category, and identify visible messages sent within these categories. They share their findings with the rest of the groups.

4. Students can collectively create a large visual text based on their analysis and findings, or in small groups, students can create a visual text around the everyday texts within a specific category. The finished visual text is displayed on the wall.

5. Students reflect in writing or through art their response to the role of art in advertising in everyday texts.

Further Inquiry. Examining everyday texts can lead to inquiry into the role of advertising in the lives of young children and adolescents. Students can collect television commercials to study how directors use visual imagery, special effects, music, etc. to entice the young consumer into buying products. Students may want to study the advertisements in magazines targeted for girls and those for boys. Invite them to look across these images to see the messages, visible and invisible, that advertisers send to readers.

LESSON RESOURCES

Gunter, B., & Furnham, A. (1998). *Children as consumers: A psychological analysis of the young people's market.* New York: Routledge.

Harris, D. (2000). *Cute, quaint, hungry and romantic: The aesthetics of consumerism.* New York: Basic Books.

Kenway, J., & Bullen, E. (2001). *Consuming children: Education-entertainment-advertising.* Buckingham, England: Open University Press.

Vasquez, V. (2004). *Negotiating critical literacies with young children.* Mahwah, NJ: Erlbaum.

Community Building Through Illustrated Life Graphs

(IRA/NCTE Standards: 7, 8)

Theoretical Position. Building community in a classroom is vital if classrooms are to be democratic places where all students' experiences, backgrounds, and voices are supported and heard. Illustrated life graphs are evolving nonprint-based representations of the lives and experiences of the students we teach. Illustrated life graphs, informed by Rief's idea of positive-negative graphs (1992), often express more than essays and talk can and, therefore, they become an important part of knowing each other, and sharing and celebrating each others' lives and experiences. Invite students to create a life graph that represents important events in her or his life, then display their graphs on the classroom wall. Students should be encouraged to visualize the group's set of life graphs to see the range of experiences that each brings to the classroom. This engagement fully supports the importance of diversity at all levels, bringing to the foreground aspects of culture that are rarely represented in literature.

Procedure 1: Personal Life Graphs

1. Invite students to generate the 10 most positive and negative experiences in their life on paper and write a statement about why these experiences come to mind.

2. On graph paper, ask students to create a life graph of their experiences, rating the experience from 1 (most positive) to 5 (most negative).

3. Students illustrate their life graph with photographs, drawings, or clip art that represents each of these experiences.

4. Students share their timelines in small groups to introduce themselves to others in the class.

5. Students' life graphs can be posted on the wall for others to see.

6. Students examine the life graphs, noting similarities and differences among their classmates.

7. This timeline is placed in their writing folders and becomes a source of future writing.

Procedure 2: Authors'/Characters' Life Graphs

1. Students study an author's life and create 10 most important events in that author's life; or students read a text and create a life graph of important events that occur in a character's life.

2. On graph paper, students create a life graph for this author or character, illustrating the important events in his or her life.

3. Students can present their life graphs as part of a research project/multimedia project or as an author or character study.

4. Students use this life graph to write a critical essay or essay about their connections (or lack thereof) to the characters.

Further Inquiry. Students can draw from this personal or collective life graph to create a longer multi-genre autobiographical work. In this writing, students choose a range of media (such as photographs, fabrics, artworks, objects) and write short pieces using a variety of genres (poems, captions, news articles, narratives) to describe the significance of these media to their lives.

LESSON RESOURCES

Bridges, R. (1999). *Through my eyes*. New York: Scholastic.

Giovanni, N. (2004). *Rosa*. New York: Henry Holt.

Krull, K. (2003). *Harvesting hope: The story of Cesar Chavez*. San Diego, CA: Harcourt.

Rappaport, D. (2001). *Martin's big words: The life of Dr. Martin Luther King, Jr.* New York: Hyperion Books for Children.

Rief, L. (1992). *Seeking diversity: Language arts with adolescents*. Portsmouth, NH: Heinemann.

Fingerprints, Characters and Stories

(IRA/NCTE Standards: 3, 5, 10)

Theoretical Position. As potter Warren McKenzie said once, a person's hands are his or her most important tools. The meanings that we can make with our hands —fingers, palms, fingernails, knuckles—as tools are endless. Ed Emberley (2000) demonstrates this concept in his book *Fingerprint*. Even with few art skills, students of all ages can create or imagine a number of different characters, or create landscapes, all with the tips of their fingers, and a few basic lines. Fingerprints are both physical—as in fingerprints left on objects we touch—and figurative—as in leaving a mark on others' lives. Fingerprints play very strongly in Julia Alvarez's poem, "Dusting," in which the narrator responds to her mother's removal of her fingerprints she makes on furniture. In this engagement, students use their fingertips to create figurative fingerprints of characters, scenes, or visual imaginings in published or original stories.

Figure B.6 *Student's fingerprint drawing,* Romeo and Juliet.

Procedure. Students study both color and shapes to create a scene from a story, poem, or their own lives. Students use their fingertips as the primary tool by which to create characters. They press their fingers into various hues and in different configurations to create their own characters. Add contour lines and elements of shape to create lively and interesting characters in published or original stories. (See Figure B.6 for an example of a student's fingerprint drawing.)

1. Students read stories with interesting characters and talk about the features that make these characters interesting to them.

2. Generate discussions about the use of colors, mixed colors, and how these help to create meaning for us. For example, if a mouse were pink in a story instead of brown, how does that change the meaning we make? Such discussions help students understand how authors often make particular points with the use of color.

3. Introduce Emberley's book on fingerprinting to demonstrate how a number of ideas can emerge at students' fingertips when making meaning.

4. Invite students to practice making characters, settings, and objects with their fingertips using various colors. What characters emerge in these artworks? In Figure B.6, this student created the balcony scene from *Romeo and Juliet*. Notice elements of the play that appear in the visual text.

5. Students choose a character from a published or original story that they would like to create using Emberley's technique. Share these illustrations and talk about their generative nature in terms of drama and writing.

Further Inquiry. As students learn the language of art, they can begin to envision artworks retranslated by using a number of different techniques, such as fingerprinting. They can take van Gogh's *Starry Night* (1889), for example, and retranslate it into a fingerprinting painting. How does it change? They could move one of their favorite illustrations in a book, *Lon Po Po* (Young, 1989), for example, into fingerprinting. How does fingerprinting encourage a different reading? How does it encourage a different type of writing? Students can play with a number of different tools, including sponges and Styrofoam to notice how texture works in illustration, and how these textures also suggest different interpretations and expressions of meaning. Students learn that such details are intentional and play different roles in their composing, and from this, they become more discriminate about the choices they make as artists and writers.

LESSON RESOURCES

Alvarez, J. "Dusting." http://mailman.depaul.edu/pipermail/teach-poetry/2004-February/000060.html

Emberley, E. (2000). *Fingerprint*. Boston: Little, Brown.

van Gogh, V. (1889). *The starry night*. New York: Museum of Modern Art. Retrieved February 26, 2007, from http://www.ibiblio.org/wm/paint/auth/gogh/starry-night

Young, E. (1989). *Lon po po*. New York: Philomel.

Illustrations and Comprehension

(IRA/NCTE Standards: 3, 10)

Theoretical Position. Eisner (2002a) describes several forms of thinking that are important in learning. Helping students notice relationships between an image's details and its whole will support them as they learn to notice relationships between details in a written text. Furthermore, helping students read across the two language systems and notice details encourages a more complex way of thinking about texts. English learners often depend on illustration to make sense of a story they read, and to express their interpretation of texts, as Mei Lu's representation of homelessness demonstrates (see Figure 1.7 in chapter 1). Studying image as it relates to text is an important strategy when supporting all students' learning.

Procedure. After reading several picture books or illustrated texts, discuss ways in which the images and the text are in direct relationship to generate meaning.

1. Read *Willy el Timído* (Browne, 1993), a text written in Spanish, to your class. Ask students to talk about what they learned about this story. Invite them to generate the strategies that they used to make sense of this text (such as pictures, Spanish words similar to English words, syntax, dialogue cues, etc.). Now read *Willy and Hugh* by this same author (Browne, 2003). Invite students to notice the relationships between both books, especially as they relate to Willy and other gorillas in the texts.

2. Encourage your students to notice the relationship between the illustrations and the written text in and between books. What do they notice between these two language systems in Browne's stories? How do the illustrations express meaning that the words do not? How does the written language express meaning that the illustrations do not? How do they both operate together to construct a more complex interpretation of the text?

3. Invite students to remember what they have learned about basic shapes, contour lines, value, and gradation. Ask students to tell stories graphically, by drawing, painting, or mixing media to tell a story without words. They then share these stories with the class.

Further Inquiry. Students can learn to study images as they do text. They notice the marks on the canvas in the same way that they notice a writer's use of metaphor or simile. To take this inquiry further, students can study photographs or illustrations in their textbooks to consider why the images are appropriate (or not). Do the illustrations fit the story that is being told?

LESSON RESOURCES

Browne, A. (1993). *Willy el tímido*. Mexico: Fondo de Cultura Economica.

Browne, A. (2003). *Willy and Hugh*. Cambridge, MA: Candlewick.

Kiefer, B.Z. (1995). *The potential of picturebooks: From visual literacy to aesthetic understanding*. Englewood Cliffs, NJ: Merrill.

Illustrating Story, Creating Story

(IRA/NCTE Standards: 3, 4, 11)

Theoretical Position. Reading and writing narratives are important to understanding how story works, and why we read and create story. Kress & van Leeuwen (1996) talk about the significance of the marks on a page that identify our interests. Students' illustrations, at any age, can support their writing and reading stories. These same stories, then, indicate to teachers students' interests and ideas. When students choose particular features of an object, person, or animal, they show which aspects of the literary text they find interesting. (See Figure 6.4 in chapter 6, a student's interpretation of a scene in *Animal Farm* [Orwell, 1996].)

Procedure. This engagement invites students to illustrate their interpretation of a text. They look across the illustrations of other class members, note which aspects are commonly drawn, and those which are less representative.

1. Use a story or text that is currently a part of your study and invite students to respond to this text through drawing. Remind them of basic shapes, composition, shading, and line and how these elements help them visually represent their interpretation.

2. When students are finished, place all the illustrations on the wall, and do a Gallery Walk. Students study one another's drawings, and make notes of common events or aspects of characters captured. Silently, they choose one of the illustrations, and create a different story in which this illustration might fit.

3. Students discuss the visual representations, and share their own stories. They place their writings under the illustration they chose. Students then discuss the relationship between visual and written texts. Such discussion leads to insight into the transaction between the reader and the writer.

Further Inquiry. As students become more comfortable with working in the arts, they will rely on the arts to help them generate ideas. This semiotic relationship, or an intimate relationship between the two language systems, is what we want our students to achieve. When students begin to think through art, their work becomes qualitatively different. They notice the relationships. Invite students to compare their early artworks and stories to those created later on and reflect on their growth as storywriters.

LESSON RESOURCES

Orwell, G. (1946). *Animal farm*. New York: Harcourt.

Rosenblatt, L.M. (1996). *Literature as exploration*. New York: Modern Language Association of America.

Response, Reflection, and Mixed Media

(IRA/NCTE Standards: 3, 5, 10)

Theoretical Position. Every mark and every decision in an artwork is intentional, suggest Kress and van Leeuwen (1996). When students are invited to create mixed media responses to literature, nonfiction texts, artworks, etc., the choices they make are not haphazard but deliberate. Wendy, the student artist who created the mixed media artwork pictured in Figure B.7, has created a work that represented her response to Jiménez's novel, *The Circuit: Stories From the Life of a Migrant Child* (1997).

She recognizes in her artwork the role that diversity plays in her own life, as well as how it is represented in the novel. The objects she uses—from the cotton ball attached to the simple command "dare to dream," to the blackboard made from craft sticks, chalk and black magazine paper—signify and celebrate diversity and immigration. Objects, like craft sticks, take on new functions when mixed media is considered. Students learn the potential of everyday objects to explain complex ideas.

Figure B.7 *Wendy's response to* The Circuit, *mixed media.*

Procedure. In this engagement, students create mixed media texts in response to a written, visual, or musical text or a concept that they wish to display artistically. Consider the number of media that can represent this learning and thinking: photographs, written text, craft sticks, textured papers, cotton, magazine paper, etc. The purpose is to experiment and challenge students to consider how objects in one space take on very different meanings in another. Students should consider design, how white space plays out in the design, and how and why images or objects overlap.

1. Students make a list of people, objects, places, ideas, and events that symbolize the text(s) to which they are responding. What objects, ideas, people, words, or phrases come to mind?

2. Students look through magazines, newspapers, photo albums, candy wrappers, etc. to find images that support their interpretation. They also look for and gather other "found objects" around the house, in school, or outdoors. They speculate on the objects' new function in their mixed media text.

3. Invite students to consider texture in their mixed media artwork. How does adding cotton, sandpaper, stones, or foam add to the interpretation?

4. Students select the objects and images they wish to use, design their project, and build it. Although Wendy's image is on sketch paper, students should be encouraged to think three-dimensionally.

5. Students share their mixed media with others, students comment on one another's visual texts, and each artist is given the last word on his or her work. Visual texts are displayed on the wall for closer analysis and, perhaps, future discussion. Students may wish to write reflective comments on their process, their intended meaning, and their learning from others who read and analyzed their visual text.

Further Inquiry. Mixed media can inspire students to consider objects in different spaces and places. When they are encouraged to construct visual texts with branches, leaves, discarded coffee cups, etc., students begin to learn the potential of a medium in meaning-making. Invite students to select one medium, for example, a discarded coffee cup, and encourage them to use it in a number of different ways to create another text. Such thinking inspires students to consider how language can be used in a number of different ways, in the same way as the discarded coffee cup.

LESSON RESOURCES

Day, B. (2001). *Mixed media*. Oxford, England: Oxford University Press.
Jiménez, F. (1997). *The circuit: Stories from the life of a migrant child*. Albuquerque: University of New Mexico Press.
Michel, K. (2005). *The complete guide to altered imagery: Mixed-media techniques for collage, altered books, artist journals, and more*. Gloucester, MA: Quarry Books.
Taylor, B. (2006). *Mixed media explorations: Blending paper, fabric and embellishment to create inspired designs*. Stow, MA: Quilting Arts.

My Town: Writing With Strong Imagery

(IRA/NCTE Standards: 2, 3, 8)

Theoretical Position. Inquiry-based curriculum has as one of its central tenets the importance of learner's interests and experiences (Harste, Short, & Burke, 1988).

Further, in literacy classrooms, writing is one of the communication systems learners must know well (Murray, 1991). Writers must feel the *need* or obsession to write, and have *faith* in what they say is significant. These qualities enable students to develop a "craft of ease—without guilt" (Murray, 1991, p. 19). In addition, students should write fast, and use genre as a pattern for writing, in order to know how to write well. *Uptown* by Collier (2000) is a memoir of the author's growing up in Harlem, New York, and is filled with wonderful language and imagery. Students will study his text and create their own illustrated book based upon their own community, town, or city.

Procedure. Students create a collective book based upon their experiences in the community, city, or town in which they live. They read and study Collier's *Uptown* (2000), and write a short statement, illustrate it, and perform the collective book through Readers Theatre. (Figure B.8 presents a sample artwork created through this activity.)

Figure B.8 *A-Town illustrated page, inspired by* Uptown, *tempera paints.*

1. Read Collier's *Uptown* (2000) to the class, showing the illustrations. If possible, place this book on overhead transparencies or on PowerPoint so all students can see the text on a screen. Students reread the text, each student taking a turn to read one page. Discuss as a class Collier's use of collage, and his use of strong literary devices, in particular, metaphor and simile.

2. Inform students that the class will write its own collective book based upon their own town, city, or community. Students generate ideas for a title of their book. Once their title is generated, students write their own extended metaphor or simile based upon their town, city, or community: "A-town is a warm summer night. I love to drive my black mustang down Peachtree St." Several students volunteer to read their texts. They spend another few minutes finishing up their written texts.

3. Students then illustrate their metaphor or simile, using a range of media (pencils, markers, magazine images, paints).

4. Students hold up their illustrated pages and read their impression of their city, town, or community. They read these texts again, only on the second reading, students gather in different configurations around the room to read their pieces (twos, threes, singles). Everyone reads the first words: "A-town is..." and the student finishes reading his or her page.

5. For the next day, digitally scan the students' books, and create a PowerPoint presentation. While each page is projected onto the screen, students read their texts. Another option is to create a self-running PowerPoint book and set it to music. Students watch and read their book as if it were a movie.

6. Students reflect on their learning, respond to the different ways the book was read, and the various aspects of their city, town, or community they appreciate.

Further Inquiry. This engagement can lead to a study on community, family, or experiences that make a community unique. Students focus on the positive aspects of community, and share ideas for making their community even stronger.

LESSON RESOURCES

Collier, B. (2000). *Uptown*. New York: Henry Holt.
Kalman, B. (2000). *What is a community? From a to z*. New York: Crabtree.
Robinson, A.B.L. (1997). *A street called home*. San Diego, CA: Harcourt.

Language Strategy Lessons Using Colors

(IRA/NCTE Standards: 5, 6, 10, 12)

Theoretical Position. Recognition and use of symbol and metaphor are complex concepts that we, as ELA educators, hope to foster in our students. Thinking metaphorically and representing symbolically push students to think from new perspectives and in sophisticated ways (Gardner, 1991; Greene, 1995). Furthermore, these two concepts are often associated with the arts or aesthetic, and when art and language are fused in this way, students understand the relationships that exist within communication. No text is just art, and no text is just language. There is a semiotic relationship between the two (Albers & Cowan, 2006b).

Procedure. To support students' understanding of descriptive, figurative, colorful language, we often turn to heavily worded passages expecting that students will be able to mimic such language. Yet this is not always the situation. To demonstrate how language is playful and figurative and can support the teaching of literary elements, secure a copy of Nordine's *Colors* (2000) CD and book. His creative venture into the personification of colors can support students learning language through language (Halliday, 1978). Just as artists use shades of color or hues in their artworks, so writers use shades of meaning in their words.

1. Invite students to name as many colors as they can and examine these words and what they mean to them.

2. Hand a set of paint swatches from a local home improvement or hardware store to small groups of students. Invite them to talk about the names of the colors and shades of color within this set of colors. Encourage them to talk about why colors are continually remixed to express just that right emotion, feeling, or information.

3. Introduce Nordine's *Colors* (2000), and invite students to listen and read along (several times) as he personifies each of the colors for which he was commissioned to write short jingles. Initiate a discussion of the actual texts and his intonations. How does he create character from colors? How does he introduce dialogue to make these colors seem real? How does he use shades of meaning to distinguish among and between colors? How, for example, does he distinguish among lavender, indigo, purple, and magenta—all colors from the same family?

4. Invite students, in small groups, to create a color that would fit into their own set of color swatches. Invite them to think of a story or a poem in which that color plays an important role. How did they think about and conceptualize shades of meaning, both in art and language?

5. Invite students to mix a set of colors, create their own jingles, and compile them into a class book.

Further Inquiry. When students understand the significance that words have in various texts, they become aware of the importance of diction, or word choice, in the texts they write. They understand that "yellow" may not be the exact word they want, but it may be "sunburst." Attention to representation and choosing just the right languages through which to communicate are essential as students continue to grow as writers. They will draw upon these shades of meaning in their short stories, poems, narratives, and even expository texts.

LESSON RESOURCES
Nordine, K. (2000). *Colors* [CD]. New York: Asphodel.
Nordine, K. (2000). *Colors*. San Diego, CA: Harcourt.

Paper Sculpture Forms

(IRA/NCTE National Standards: 3, 6, 11)

Theoretical Position. The arts invite awareness of aspects of the world that perhaps we had not noticed before (Eisner, 2002a). For example, when we look at a paper sculpture, can we envision it as made of something else? And, if so, how does this pose a type of problem worth resolving? As Eisner (2002a) suggests, the arts liberate us from the materiality of an object, and enable us to step into the world of others and experience their thoughts vicariously. An artist's communication often baffles the viewer, but with inquiry into techniques, we can often see how to recast an artist's idea into another medium and make it our own. This engagement invites students to consider how the simple and common material of paper can be worked to create lovely works of art, and generate strong writing.

Procedure. Using large sheets of paper and scrap papers (such as wrapping papers, newspapers, textured papers, various types of boxes, egg cartons, etc.), students create their own paper sculptures. They learn to experiment with how the paper folds, how it twists and turns, how it responds to the edge of scissors as it is run against the grain of the paper, how it takes color, and how designs on papers work together. Figure B.9 shows an example of a paper sculpture.

1. Invite students to interpret a story, poem, or set of texts and then sculpt it using large sheets of colored papers, different textures of papers, and different thicknesses. Encourage them to generate ideas about the story and what they thought were important concepts.

Figure B.9 *Teacher's 3-D paper sculpture, inspired by ancient Egyptian headwear.*

2. Now, suggest that students investigate what these concepts mean through Internet or library research. How might they represent, for example, the concept of hope? With some investigation into this concept, along with their story, poem, or set of texts they initially interpreted, students build more complex understandings of this word. Invite them to sketch images of what they learn through their inquiry.

3. Introduce students to paper art or sculptures that are made from all sorts of materials. (Images of such artworks can be found by doing a Google image search. Or, consider taking photos of artworks, especially sculptures, displayed in public settings such as banks, schools, libraries, businesses, hospitals, and around towns and cities.) Invite students to read the art and think about what the artist is saying. Then, ask students to think about how they might recast, for example, Frank Stella's bronze sculpture into paper? Henry Moore's bronze sculptures into paper? Wooden masks (African, Native American, Australian, etc.) into papier-mâché? What do they want their sculpture to represent? How do they want it to look? What colors are important in this representation? Think, too, about design. What problem-solving techniques might they need to draw upon? How might they have to consider the three-dimensionality of their work? How will they be able to hang the piece?

4. Invite students to explore the cutting and tearing of the various types of paper. Then, encourage them to glue down edges on all sides so that the sculpture becomes 3-D. Invite them to record their thoughts in their sketchbooks. What do they notice about how paper tears? How it rests on other paper? How various colors can be combined to create interest?

5. Invite students to choose a 3-D sculpture, like Frank Stella's, that closely represents the concept they wish to represent and recast it into paper. How can they create 3-D shapes and sizes to represent this concept?

Further Inquiry. Students notice shapes, media, and concepts presented in public art, as well as art in their textbooks. Invite students to study artworks in a medium and retranslate them into another medium. How does the meaning change for the viewer? For the artist?

LESSON RESOURCES
Frank Stella. http://www.artseensoho.com/Art/GAGOSIAN/stella97/stella1.html
Pablo Picasso. http://www.henry-moore-fdn.co.uk

Writing and Illustrating Postmodern Books

(IRA/NCTE Standards: 1, 4, 5, 6, 8, 12)

Theoretical Position. Inquiry-based curriculum has as one of its central tenets the importance of learner's interests and experiences. According to Burke (2004), learners bring knowledge and experience to their learning, and this personal inquiry drives their interest in a subject or topic. Learners are actively involved in their own learning (Short & Burke, 1991) and cannot learn something that they aren't already involved in thinking about. Within an inquiry-based curriculum that supports a multimedia perspective, learners are offered flexible opportunities to engage in research that interests them and express meaning using a range of media. Postmodern books are especially valuable to learners of varied experiences and language abilities because such books offer a direct connection to the communication potential of the visual image, which allows learners to participate in ways that support their ongoing learning. (See Figure B.10 for a sample of a postmodern book about Shakespeare.)

Figure B.10 *Postmodern book from inquiry into Shakespeare, mixed media.*

Procedure

1. Students spend time looking at a number of different nonfiction books written with nontraditional formats. As a class, they discuss elements that they like and do not like about these books in terms of illustration as well as written text.

2. Students select an animal, insect, reptile, bird, etc. to research, both through narratives and through expository texts. They gather information about their subject and think about a text that they would like to design, develop, and illustrate.

3. Students illustrate their information to show relationships between the written text and the illustrated text. For example, they show the life cycle of a frog through image as well as written text.

4. Elements of shape become an important framework for students as they think about the shape of the book that they would like their research to take. They create "postmodern" books, or books that do not take on traditional shapes. For example, if they want to research birds, perhaps their text takes the shape of a birdhouse, or a tree, or the habitat in which their researched topic lives. One teacher made a book on sea turtles (see Figures 8.12 a, b, and c in chapter 8). She made a turtle shell for the cover and inside pages filled with images and limited text for her second grade students.

5. Students present their books at a book fair and then share readings of their work. These books become a part of the class library.

Further Inquiry. Encourage students to consider how text is changing shape every day from a traditional book, to Internet texts (such as hyperlinks), to postmodern books. How do they understand the function of each of these texts? How does a postmodern book challenge readers to think about the art concepts as they are linked to their inquiry? How do postmodern books encourage students to think outside the confines of the squares and rectangles that traditional books suggest?

LESSON RESOURCES

Bamford, R.A., & Kristo, J.V. (1998). *Making facts come alive: Choosing quality nonfiction.* Norwood, MA: Christopher-Gordon.

Bang, M. (2000). *Picture this: How pictures work.* New York: SeaStar Books.

Murphy, C. (2006). *Graceland: An interactive pop-up adventure.* Philadelphia: Quirk Books.

Peterson, G. (1994). *Greg Hildebrandt's book of three-dimensional dragons.* Boston: Little, Brown.

Sabuda, R. (2003). *Alice's adventures in Wonderland.* New York: Little Simon.

Reading and Writing Collage: An Artist's Study

(IRA/NCTE Standards: 1, 3, 7)

Theoretical Position. Children's books offer wonderful examples of the various art techniques used by artists to express their interpretation of the written text. Think, for example, about some of your favorite books and why you engage with them so much. What do the artists do that is different? Unique? Expressive? Artworks often generate questions about their making. How do artists construct the artwork? What media do they use? How do the media help them express their messages? Part of learning to read visual texts necessitates that learners be able to read the structures that underpin these texts. This process involves learners' attention, recognition of technique, and interpretation of the visual image (Kiefer, 1995).

Procedure. Invite students to study the various collage work in picture books or artworks illustrated by collage artists David Wisniewski, David Diaz, Eric Carle, Aminah Robinson, and Romare Bearden.

1. Gather a number of books in which collage is the illustration technique. Invite learners to discuss or pose questions about the illustrations. What elements do they use to create their collages? How do artists create the artwork? What effect do real objects have on our interpretation of the story and the image?

2. Invite learners to choose their favorite artist and study the artist, his or her illustrations, and the stories in and across his or her books. Encourage students to generate theories about how the artwork is done, how well they think that the artist communicates his or her ideas through art, and record this synthesis of information into their journals. Invite students to write about how they believe the artwork is done.

3. When learners have studied their texts, invite them to try the technique of the artist whom they studied, and create a page or two that would accompany one of the texts they read. Encourage them to write down the process by which they constructed their pages. What do they like? What do they think was the most challenging?

4. Invite learners to place their visual text on the wall; others study and respond to these texts. Engage learners in a reflective discussion on the role of art, technique, and expression.

Further Inquiry. How artists express meaning is equivalent to how writers use words. Artists, like writers, create their pieces based upon their knowledge of what the medium allows them to say. Students should keep all of their visual texts from throughout a nine-week period or a semester, study the techniques that span across their own visual texts, and try to explore new ways of responding.

LESSON RESOURCES

Brown, K. (1995). *Romare Bearden*. Broomall, PA: Chelsea House.

Bunting, E. (1999). *Smoky night*. San Diego, CA:Voyager Books.

Carle, E. (2000). *Dream snow*. New York: Philomel Books.

Carle, E. (2002). *The art of Eric Carle*. New York: Philomel Books.

Greenberg, J. (2003). *Romare Bearden: Collage of memories*. New York: Harry N. Abrams.

Hartfield, C. (2002). *Me and Uncle Romie*. New York: Dial Books for Young Readers.

Robinson, A.B.L., & Genshaft, C.M. (2002). *Symphonic poem: The art of Aminah Brenda Lynn Robinson*. Columbus, OH: Columbus Museum of Art, in association with Harry N. Abrams.

Whipple, L. (1991). *Eric Carle's animals animals*. New York: Putnam.

Wisniewski, D. (1996). *Golem*. New York: Clarion Books.

Wisniewski, D. (1999). *Sundiata: Lion king of Mali*. New York: Clarion Books.

Revising Story, Revising Art

(IRA/NCTE Standards: 5, 10, 11)

Theoretical Position. Revising writing is a part of the process that we strongly encourage in our writers because we know that attention to detail, mechanics, and content all contribute to strong writing (Graves, 1983). Often, such attention to revising illustrations is not afforded students; however, visual texts that accompany written texts are texts in and of themselves, and revising them can offer students an opportunity to add detail or content that might not have appeared otherwise. (See pencil sketches of Olivia, for example, in Figure 2.28 in chapter 2.) Students learn that revision occurs across language systems and that all language systems contribute to the students' overall meaning (Kress & van Leeuwen, 1996).

Procedure. Using the techniques of basic shapes, contour line drawings, value, curved, and cross-hatched lines, and smudging, invite students to redraw one of their favorite characters to create the illusion of depth. Also encourage them to consider details that they may not have considered before and how this changes the nature, personality, or physicality of their character.

1. Invite students to draw a favorite character or scene from an event or experience that is meaningful to them.

2. After they have completed the illustration, invite the class to comment on the illustration in terms of what they like, what is missing, or what would add to the illustration, much like they would do to in a writer's workshop.

3. After this discussion, encourage students to revise their illustration, and suggest that they reflect on this revision, and if it relates to a written text, how this revision supports a stronger written text. Invite students to notice how image and word support one another in the composing process, and encourage students to continue to revise illustrations alongside their written stories.

Further Inquiry. As students continue to grow in their reading and writing, strongly encourage visual representations to accompany their writing or their interpretation of written texts. When students push meaning into symbolic or aesthetic texts, they become aware of how they their thinking always involves metaphor (Pugh et al., 1992). Through metaphorical thinking, divergent meanings or meanings that are varied across learners become evident and supported in ELA classrooms. Students quickly learn that meanings are multiple and dependent upon their own experiences, knowledge, and backgrounds.

LESSON RESOURCES

Pugh, S.L., Hicks, J.W., Davis, M., & Venstra, T. (1992). *Bridging: A teacher's guide to metaphorical thinking.* Urbana, IL: National Council of Teachers of English.

Same Story? Different Illustrations!

(IRA/NCTE Standards: 3, 4, 7)

Theoretical Position. Being able to synthesize and analyze across texts is a valued strategy for all learners. Reading across images, as well as across written texts, enables students to develop a more complex strategy of synthesis and analysis. Students learn that images have particular structures (Kress & van Leeuwen, 1996), different details, and these lead to a better understanding of the illustrator's and author's view of the story. Rather than merely compare and contrast elements in a written story, students analyze written texts in relation to the images that accompany it. Fairy tales, a common genre studied across ages, provide a good example of how the same story is told, but often with different illustrations.

Procedure. This engagement invites students to look across versions of the same story, and study the different illustrations. There are a number of fairy tales that have several versions: Snow White, The Three Pigs, Cinderella, Rumplestiltskin, etc. Gather several versions of several fairy tales. Read the artwork in the different versions and discuss as a class the choices that the artists make. Discuss which story is more enjoyable and why. Do more realistic illustrations inspire more in-depth responses? Are they taken more seriously? Are stories illustrated with less realism taken less seriously?

1. Students discuss the basic storylines of well-known fairy tales or folk tales. Invite students to study the images and the text relationships. How do the images support the written text and how does the written text support the illustrated text?

2. Read a second version of this same story and look at the illustrations. How does, for example, Trina Schart Hyman's (Heins, 1979) illustration of the wicked stepmother differ from Nancy Ekholm Burkert's (Jarrell, 1987)?

3. Invite students to consider the importance to the story of how an artist illustrates characters. Which of these two illustrators' works is more inviting? Which of these appeals to different audiences? Which ones are taken more seriously than others?

Further Inquiry. Encourage students to investigate the relationships between their impressions of each story and the illustrations that accompany it. Invite them to look at some of their content area books and notice the illustrations or pictures that accompany the written texts. Which do they believe are accurate and interesting? To which do they pay little attention and why? And if they could change the illustration, what might they consider in the place of the original?

LESSON RESOURCES

Jarrell, R. (Translator). (1987). *Snow White and the seven dwarfs*. New York: Farrar, Straus & Giroux.

Heins, P. (1979). *Snow White*. New York: Little, Brown Young Readers.

Datlow, E., & Windling, T. (Eds.). (1993). *Snow white, blood red*. New York: Eos.

Grimm, J., Grimm, W., & Heins, P. (1974). *Snow White*. Boston: Little, Brown.

Time and Place: Mixed Media Collage and Papier-Mâché

(IRA/NCTE Standards: 2, 3, 4, 12)

Theoretical Position. As Robert Scholes argues, "To put it as directly, and perhaps as brutally, as possible we must stop teaching literature and start studying texts" (cited in Pirie, 1997, p. 17). In other words, students must begin to analyze texts, not merely fact-find details in a text for the purposes of multiple choice tests. When students express their interpretation of texts through art, and in this engagement, 3-D art, they must study the information provided by the author to interpret and reconstruct their interpretation in more complex ways.

Procedure. This engagement invites students to create a 3-D collage that visualizes the time and place of the story they are writing or reading or a place they have visited or would like to. For example, if they read Lester's *From Slave Ship to Freedom Road* (1998), what types of materials would they put together to suggest this time and place? Wood, tea-stained newspaper, cloth? If they wanted to represent a place they would like to visit what would it be? Any text with a strong setting can be interpreted through mixed media and papier-mâché, and offers students more insight into the challenges of the environment about which they read.

1. Students inquire into a place and space that they would like to represent. They search for both information and objects that might represent this place. Encourage students to think about using text in various types of sizes to add to their image. Students in one teacher's classroom were invited to use mixed

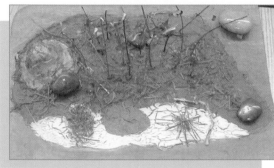

media to represent their understanding of the environment of Golding's *Lord of the Flies* (1959). The student whose work is shown in Figure B.11 uses papier-mâché as a base, paints the wooden canvas, covered in a light papier-mâché, blue for the water, adds actual sand and nettles from his yard, and other media to recreate this harsh setting. Notice the details that indicate her understanding of the text and shown through this visual text.

Figure B.11 Student's mixed-media representation of Lord of the Flies.

2. As they inquire, students think critically about the objects they have chosen, the shapes that they make through papier-mâché, and how these art elements represent the place and people or space.

3. Encourage students to write about how they designed the image. Where did they place the images? Why did they do so? How do they want the reader/viewer to read this image? (Review the image in Figure 6.6, which shows a different student's interpretation of the themes in Golding's novel, survival. Like the other student, Soje uses written texts and magazine images to demonstrate her understanding of the environment, the time and place, of this novel.)

4. Students display their images as in a gallery, and like art experts, they share their story with the viewers/readers of their artwork. Family and friends or other classes may be invited in to tour the gallery. With journal paper placed at each of the visual texts, students are encouraged to write something to the author or illustrator of the text.

Further Inquiry. Students are in a number of different places and spaces in a given day. How do these spaces inform their actions? Their talk? Encourage students to consider how settings act on them and how they act upon their settings.

LESSON RESOURCES

Day, B. (2001). *Mixed media.* Oxford, England: Oxford University Press.

Dye, S. (2004). *The mixed media sourcebook: Techniques for successfully combining painting and drawing mediums.* New York: Watson-Guptill.

Golding, W. (1959). *Lord of the flies.* New York: Perigee.

Lester, J. (1998). *From slave ship to freedom road.* New York: Dial Books.

Sample Focused Studies: The Great Dust Bowl and Immigration

A Focused Study (Burke, 2004) is a unit of curriculum that concentrates on a particular topic or issue and involves a community of learners. Throughout the study learners are provided opportunities to reflect on what they know, to bring their own experiences and questions to bear on the focus of study, to construct new understandings, and to use those new understandings in support of further learning.

Focusing Question: What was it like to live during the Great Dust Bowl (GDB)?

Initiating Experiences

Help students reflect on their personal experiences and knowledge. These engagements introduce the focus of the study and trigger connections between the study and personal experiences, setting the stage for the upcoming learning. Everyone involved—those that write the curriculum and those that work with it—shares responsibility for contributing ideas and questions.

Great Dust Bowl Multimedia Presentation. What do we already know about this time in our country's history? Introduce this historical period through a multimedia presentation of Dorothea Lange's photographs, Woody Guthrie's "The Great Dust Bowl," maps, and timelines. Learners jot down ideas and share the connections made.

Great Dust Bowl Book Pass. Before the Focused Study begins, gather a number of books focused on the GDB (see Comprehensive Text Set that follows). Students choose one they believe represents their interest. The Book Pass begins with each student perusing her or his chosen book, then passing it after one minute. This continues until all books have been passed. Students select one book from which to draw personal and Focused Study connections.

Uninterrupted Opportunities for Reading and Writing

Following the introduction of the study, invite learners to explore related texts, both on their own and through read-aloud selections, Readers Theatre, or Web-based information. Invitation and choice are key and learners are encouraged to contribute suggestions.

Text Sets for Studying the Great Dust Bowl. Set up the library of GDB books around the room, with texts separated into smaller text sets. Make available at least 40 books related to the GDB and the Great Depression for reading and studying throughout the Focused Study. A comprehensive list of resources can be found at the end of this section.

Text Study/Literature Study

These activities support in-depth learning of related content and concepts. One text or multiple texts might be used. Learners work together in small groups to set the course of their reading and discussions. Small-group conversations allow for the active participation of everyone in the group.

Possible Core Texts for Studying the Great Dust Bowl

Hesse, K. (1997). *Out of the dust*. New York: Scholastic.

Steinbeck, J. (1940). *The grapes of wrath*. New York: Heritage.

Stanley, J. (1993). *Children of the dust bowl: The true story of the school at Weedpatch Camp*. New York. Crown.

Literature Discussions. Learners respond in small-group and large-group settings to the text(s) read and the strategies learned. Based upon these readings and discussions, learners learn more about the context of the time period, as well as text structures and features.

Intertextual Analysis. Students study several media-rich texts and discuss the nature of how migrants were perceived and/or lived during the GDB. Students choose from music by Woody Guthrie, news stories, books such as *The Dust Bowl* (Booth & Reczuch, 1996), and photographs of the GDB by Dorothea Lange and Walker Evans.

Invitations to Inquiry

Invitations support deeper learning on specific issues of interest. Encourage learners to work with a partner or small group to identify and pursue their questions.

Media-Rich Explorations of the Great Dust Bowl. Looking across the texts documenting this historical period—journals, photographs, music, literature— learners consider the following questions:

- How is life documented through art?
- How do musicians express personal experience through music?
- How do authors help us see life during this time?
- What aspects of life were captured through photography?

Creating Political Billboards of the Great Dust Bowl. In this invitation, students investigate the financial hardships endured by migrants and those involved in the GDB through assorted texts of the time. Students create a billboard appealing to politicians, which they believe will attract public attention, as well as political action.

Demonstrations

Demonstrations are large-group, teacher-conducted, short strategy lessons intended to show students a concept, technique, or features of a text. Demonstrations often derive from students' questions about the content of the Focused Study or concepts important to an in-depth understanding of a text.

The Main Idea. Demonstrate strategies for identifying the main idea in expository texts. Teach learners to read from general to specific and vice versa. Learners use this structure both to read and write expository texts.

Creating PowerPoint Projects. The teacher demonstrates how to build strong PowerPoint presentations. Based upon their personal inquiry into one of the GDB authors studied, students create a PowerPoint presentation integrating image, music, special effects, written text, and video.

Organizing and Sharing

Artifacts support the manipulation and preservation of accumulating information. These should highlight relationships being explored and should reflect the tools/methods of the knowledge domains being studied.

Audit Trail or Learning Wall. Artifacts produced during the study are placed onto an evolving wall. Learners write interesting and important comments made by the group onto the butcher paper, and include photographs of learners engaged in the experiences and any other learning artifacts.

Writing Visual Persuasive Essays. After reading one of the core texts, students write a visual persuasive essay. This essay includes a series of visual images (photographs, sketches, cartoons, etc.) that show the plight of the migrants and those affected by the GBD. In addition, they write an essay that supports the images, and appeals to politicians for action.

Culminating Experiences/Reflective Action

These activities help participants reflect upon and construct their understanding of the Focused Study. Provide learners with opportunities to purposefully apply their learning and demonstrate their understanding of new ideas, discoveries and connections. These engagements prompt learners to revisit previous beliefs and knowledge and to summarize new learning and encourage learners to "make a difference"–to do something to change attitudes and/or practices.

Public Service Announcements. At the end of the unit of study, students pull together, using Windows Movie Maker, a 30-second or one-minute public service announcement (PSA) that addresses an issue raised in their study of the GDB. For example, students may create a PSA on children forced to migrate without their families, or soup lines, or substandard housing.

Engagements Occurring Throughout the Unit

Uninterrupted Reading. Learners have time daily to read texts related to the topic provided by you or themselves. Include fiction and nonfiction picture books, poetry, magazines featuring the time period, nonfiction texts, websites, etc. (See text set that follows for possible texts for reading.)

Learning Wall. Create a student-generated wall of collected artifacts, comments, questions, and statements of learning to display throughout the Focused Study. This can include a timeline, images, photographs of learners, artworks, favorite quotations, etc.

Sketchbook. Learners collect artifacts, photographs, notes, music, etc. that address their interests in this Focused Study. These artifacts generate ideas for media-rich presentations.

Focused Study Resources. Learners collect resources that may be valuable in the study the topic.

TEXT SET ON THE GREAT DUST BOWL

Books

Andryszewski, T. (1993). *The dust bowl: Disaster on the plains.* Brookfield, CT: Millbrook Press.

Booth, D., & Reczuch K. (1996). *The dust bowl.* Toronto, ON: Kids Can Press.

Coombs, K.M. (2000). *Children of the dust days.* Minneapolis, MN: Carolrhoda Books.

Hamilton, V., & Pinkney J. (1992). *Drylongso.* San Diego, CA: Harcourt Brace Jovanovich.

Gregory, J.N. (1989). *American exodus: The dust bowl migration and Okie culture in California.* New York: Oxford University Press. (Companion website: http://faculty.washington. edu/gregoryj/exodus/index.htm)

Isaacs, S.S. (2002). *Life in the dust bowl.* Chicago: Heinemann.

Janke, K. (2002). *Survival in the storm: The dust bowl diary of Grace Edwards.* New York: Scholastic.

Low, A.M. (1984). *Dust bowl diary.* Lincoln, NE: University of Nebraska Press.

Meltzer, M. (2000). *Driven from the land: The story of the dust bowl.* New York: Benchmark Books.

Myers, A. (1992). *Red-dirt Jessie.* New York: Walker.

Porter, T. (1997). *Treasures in the dust.* New York: HarperCollins.

Raven, M.T., & Essley, R. (1997). *Angels in the dust.* Mahwah, NJ: BridgeWater Books.

Sandler, M.W. (2003). *America's great disasters.* New York: HarperCollins.

Stanley, J. (1992). *Children of the dust bowl: The true story of the school at Weedpatch Camp.* New York: Crown Publishers.

Steinbeck, J. (1992). *The grapes of wrath.* New York: Penguin Books.

Turner, A.W., & Barrett, R. (1995). *Dust for dinner.* New York: HarperCollins.

Worster, D. (1982). *Dust bowl: The southern plains in the 1930s.* Oxford, England: Oxford University Press.

Music

Guthrie, W. (1998). *Dust bowl ballads.* Cambridge, MA: Rounder Records.

Guthrie, W., & Lomax, A. (1988). *Library of Congress recordings.* Cambridge, MA: Rounder Records.

Photography

Ganzel, B. (1984). *Dust bowl descent.* Lincoln: University of Nebraska Press.

Lange, D., & Taylor, P.S. (1975). *An American exodus: A record of human erosion.* New York: Arno Press.

Rothstein, A. (1978). *The Depression Years.* New York: Dover Publications.

Video and Film

Blumofe, R.F., Leventhaal, H. (Producers), & Ashby, H. (Director). (2000). *Bound for glory* [Motion picture]. United States: Metro Goldwyn Mayer Home Entertainment.

Drain, M., Gazit, C., & Steward, D. (Producers). (1998). *Surviving the dust bowl* [Motion picture]. Alexandria, VA: PBS Home Video.

Lloyd, L.M. (1997). *Five great weather disasters* [Video recording]. Atlanta, GA: Weather Channel.

Lorentz, P. (Writer/Director). (1936). *The plow that broke the plains.* Washington, DC: National Audiovisual Center. Retrieved February 28, 2007, from http://www.archive.org/details/PlowThatBrokethePlains1

Zanuck, D.F. (Producer), Johnson, N. (Writer/Producer), & Ford, J. (Director). (1996). *Grapes of wrath* [Motion picture]. United States: Twentieth Century Fox Home Entertainment.

Websites

American Folklife Center. (1998). *Voices from the Dust Bowl: The Charles L. Todd and Robert Sonkin Migrant Worker Collection* . Washington, DC: Library of Congress. Retrieved February 19, 2007, from http://memory.loc.gov/ammem/afctshtml/tshome.html

California State University Bakersfield. (n.d.). *Dust bowl migration digital archives.* Retrieved February 19, 2007, from http://www.lib.csub.edu/special/dustbowl.html

EDSITEment. (2002). *Dust bowl days.* Retrieved February 19, 2007, from http://edsitement.neh.gov/view_lesson_plan.asp?id=300

National Drought Mitigation Center. (n.d.). *What is Drought?* Retrieved February 19, 2007, from http://www.drought.unl.edu/whatis/dustbowl.htm

Nelson, C. (n.d.). *About the dust bowl.* Retrieved February 19, 2007, from http://www.english.uiuc.edu/maps/depression/dustbowl.htm

Public Broadcasting Service (PBS). (n.d.). *The American experience: Surviving the dust bowl.* Retrieved February 19, 2007, from http://www.pbs.org/wgbh/pages/amex/dustbowl/

Schmidt, L.J. (2001). *From the dust bowl to the Sahel.* Retrieved February 19, 2007, from http://earthobservatory.nasa.gov/Study/DustBowl/

Texas Humanities Resource Center. (n.d.). *The Dust Bowl.* Retrieved February 19, 2007, from http://www.humanities-interactive.org/texas/dustbowl/

University of South Dakota. (n.d.). *The Dust Bowl.* Retrieved February 19, 2007, from http://www.usd.edu/anth/epa/dust.html

Focusing Question: How has immigration informed our national identity?

Initiating Experiences

Immigration Multimedia Presentation. What do we already know about immigration? What are our heritages? A multimedia presentation might introduce immigrant artists, authors, musicians, politicians, and activists and offers additional information about how immigration has evolved from Ellis Island to contemporary society.

Immigration Gallery Walk. Display photographs of key figures from the historical period on the wall accompanied by a brief biography and a text they created. This gallery introduces learners to the texts they will study or may choose to study.

Uninterrupted Opportunities for Reading and Writing

Partial Text Set for Studying Immigration. Set up the library for this Focused Study around the room, with texts separated into smaller text sets. At least 40 books related to immigration are available for reading and studying throughout the study. A portion of that is listed here:

Beatty, P. (2000). *Lupita mañana.* New York: Harper Trophy.

Bierman, C. (2005). *Journey to Ellis Island: How my father came to America.* New York: Hyperion.

Lawlor, V. (1997). *I was dreaming to come to America: Memories from the Ellis Island Oral History Project.* New York: Penguin.

Lasky, K. (2003). *My America: Hope in my heart, Sofia's Ellis Island diary, book one.* New York: Scholastic.

Ryan, P.M. (2000). *Esperanza rising.* New York: Blue Sky Press.

Sandler, M.W. (2004). *Island of hope: The journey to America and the Ellis Island experience.* New York: Scholastic.

Sinclair, U. (2002). *The jungle.* New York: Modern Library.

Tarbescu, E. (1998). *Annushka's voyage.* New York: Clarion Books.

Woodruff, E. (2004). *The memory coat.* New York: Scholastic.

Yin. (2003). *Coolies.* New York: Puffin.

Text Study/Literature Study

Possible Core Texts for Studying Immigration

Jiménez, F. (1997). *The circuit: Stories from the life of a migrant child.* Albuquerque: University of New Mexico Press.

Jiménez, F. (2002). *Breaking through.* Boston: Houghton Mifflin.

Na, A. (2003). *A step from heaven.* New York: Puffin.

Literature Discussions. Learners respond in small-group and large-group settings to the text(s) read and the strategies learned. Based upon these readings and discussions, learners learn more about the context of the Focused Study, as well as text structures and features.

Intertextual Analysis. To encourage complex study of the core text, introduce one or more texts that pose similar or dissimilar issues. Learners raise issues within these texts and discuss them in light of the core text. Such reading invites learners to synthesize meaning across, between, and among texts. Such readings push them to see connections that are not immediately known, but may become apparent through group discussion. Texts may include poems, prose, art, magazine ads, picture books, lyrics, etc.

Invitations to Inquiry

Media-Rich Explorations of Immigration. Make available for exploration texts on thinkers, artists, musicians, historians, authors, and photographers. Ask learners to consider key questions such as, What were some of the concerns of these greats? What key events occurred that affected their thinking? What did writers convey in their art? What might the clothing tell us about the time? What kinds of performances were featured? What aspects of life were captured through photography?

Readers Theatre of Immigration. After you demonstrate a Readers Theatre performance, invite learners to find favorite texts, music, and poems that address the Focused Study, excerpt them, and pull them together for a small-group performance. Encourage learners to develop the reading to include single and multiple voices to highlight their understanding of the texts.

Demonstrations

Taking a Stance. Learners engage in what it means to take an aesthetic stance and an efferent stance by examining three art objects and recording what they feel (aesthetic) and what information they retain (efferent). This experience enables learners to understand the importance of stances when reading narrative and expository texts.

Transmediation: Working in Clay. Present learners with a demonstration on three hand-building techniques in clay: pinch, coil, and slab. After this demonstration, invite learners to represent their understanding of a single text or the historical period. Keep in mind, clay is but one medium through which learners can recast their interpretation.

Organizing and Sharing

Exit Slips. At the end of each day, learners capture what's on their minds on exit slips, or three questions that they respond to visually and through writing: (1) Something I learned..., (2) Something I have a question about..., (3) My learning in sketch form. Read these slips to discover what students have learned and what you may need to re-teach or develop further.

Photography. Throughout the Focused Study, take photographs, and ask students to take photographs later in the term, to document student learning and study. Photographs allow students to revisit and study their learning over time.

Culminating Experiences/Reflective Action

Cultural Heritage Projects. After reading the core text, learners investigate their own heritage by conducting family interviews and examining family texts including photographs, letters, official and other documents. They connect what they find in their heritage to ideas and issues in the core text that they found interesting.

Engagements Occurring Throughout the Unit

Uninterrupted Reading. Learners have time daily to read texts related to the topic provided by you or themselves. Include fiction and nonfiction picture books, poetry, magazines featuring the time period, nonfiction texts, websites, etc.

Learning Wall. Create a student-generated wall of collected artifacts, comments, questions, and statements of learning to display throughout the Focused Study. This can include a timeline, images, photographs of learners, artworks, favorite quotations, etc.

Sketchbook. Learners collect artifacts, photographs, notes, music, etc. that address their interests in this Focused Study. These artifacts generate ideas for media-rich presentations.

Focused Study Resources. Learners collect resources that may be valuable in the study the topic.

APPENDIX D

Text Sets

Chapter 2: Inquiry Into Drawing

Children's/Adolescent Literature

Elements of Shape

Bang, M. (1999). *When Sophie gets angry–really, really angry.* New York: Blue Sky.

Benes, R.C. (2004). *Native American picture books of change: The art of historic children's editions.* Santa Fe: Museum of New Mexico Press.

Bergen, L. (2003). *Stanley: Daddy lion.* New York: Disney.

Henkes, K. (1993). *Owen.* New York: Greenwillow.

Moers, H. (1986). *Hugo the baby lion.* New York: Henry Holt.

Parr, T. (2001). *It's okay to be different.* New York: Megan Tingley.

Rathmann, P. (1995). *Officer Buckle and Gloria.* New York: Putnam.

Shannon, D. (1998). *No, David!* New York: Blue Sky.

Taback, S. (1999). *Joseph had a little overcoat.* New York: Viking.

Basic Shapes

Cronin, D. (2000). *Click, clack, moo: Cows that type.* New York: Simon & Schuster.

Lobel, A. (1980). *Fables.* New York: HarperTrophy.

Pinkney, A.D. (1998). *Duke Ellington.* New York: Hyperion.

Shannon, D. (1998). *No, David!* New York: Blue Sky.

Wiesner, D. (2001). *The three pigs.* New York: Clarion.

Value and Gradation

Caines, J.F. (1980). *Window wishing.* New York: HarperCollins.

Feelings, T. (1995). *Middle passage.* New York: Penguin. (See also his illustrated works *Moja Means One* and *Jambo Means Hello.*)

Greenfield, E. (2002). *Honey, I love.* New York: Amistad.

Hughes, T. (1978). *Cave birds: An alchemical cave drama.* New York: Viking.

Leodhas, S.N. (1989). *Always room for one more.* New York: Henry Holt.

Macaulay, D. (1981). *Cathedral: The story of its construction.* Boston: Houghton Mifflin. (See also his books *Pyramid*, *City*, and *Motel of the Mysteries.*)

McCloskey, R. (1941). *Make way for ducklings.* New York: Puffin.

Professional Resources

Borgeson, B. (1983). *The colored pencil: Key concepts for handling the medium*. New York: Watson-Guptill.

Jurstedt, R., & Koutras, M. (2000). *Teaching writing with picture books as models*. New York: Scholastic.

Shulevitz, U. (1997). *Writing with pictures: How to write and illustrate children's books*. New York: Watson-Guptill.

Chapter 3: Inquiry Into Color

Children's/Adolescent Literature

Atkins, J. (2000). *Aani and the tree huggers*. New York: Lee & Low.

Bartone, E. (1997). *Peppe: The lamplighter*. New York: HarperTrophy.

Bradby, M. (1995). *More than anything else*. New York: Scholastic.

Bruchac, J. (1995). *Native plant stories*. Golden, CO: Fulcrum.

Bunting, E. (1999). *Smoky night*. New York: Voyager.

Cooper, F. (1998). *Coming home: From the life of Langston Hughes*. New York: Penguin.

Duggleby, J. (1998). *Story painter: The life of Jacob Lawrence*. San Francisco: Chronicle.

Emberley, E. (2000). *Fingerprint drawing book*. Boston: Little, Brown.

Everett, G. (1991). *Li'l sis and Uncle Willie: A story based on the life & paintings of William H. Johnson*. New York: Rizzoli.

Grimes, N. (1999). *My man Blue*. New York: Dial.

Lawrence, J. (1993). *Harriet and the promised land*. New York: Simon & Schuster.

Leach, D.F. (2001). *I see you I see myself: The young life of Jacob Lawrence*. Washington, DC: The Phillips Collection.

Lorbiecki, M. (2000). *Sister Anne's hands*. New York: Penguin.

Miller, W. (1997). *Richard Wright and the library card*. New York: Lee & Low.

Nordine, K. (2000). *Colors*. San Diego, CA: Harcourt.

Quackenbush, R.M. (1995). *Here a plant, there a plant, everywhere a plant, plant! A story of Luther Burbank*. Santa Rosa, CA: Luther Burbank Home & Gardens.

Say, A. (1993). *Grandfather's journey*. Boston: Houghton Mifflin.

Shange, N. (1994). *I live in music*. New York: Welcome.

Tsuchiya, Y. (1997). *Faithful elephants: True story of animals, people and war*. Boston: Houghton Mifflin.

Young, E. (1989). *Lon po po: A red-riding hood story from China*. New York: Philomel.

Professional Resources

Andy Warhol Staff. (2004). *Andy Warhol 365 takes*. New York: Harry N. Abrams.

Barnes & Noble. (2001). *Watercolors: A step-by-step guide*. New York: Author.

Hellmuth, C. (2003). *Collage discovery workshop: Make your own collage creations using vintage photos, found objects and ephemera*. Cincinnati, OH: North Light.

Itten, J. (1973). *The art of color*. New York: Van Nostrand.

Leland, N. (1998). *Exploring color*. Cincinnati, OH: North Light.

Leland, N., & Williams, V.L. (2000). *Creative collage techniques: A step-by-step guide including 52 demonstrations and the work of over 60 artists.* Cincinnati, OH: North Light.

Linscott, C. (1999). *Watercolor: Project book for beginners.* Laguna Hills, CA: Walter Foster.

Chapter 4: Inquiry Into Three-Dimension

Children's/Adolescent Literature

Andrews-Goebel, N. (2002). *The pot that Juan built.* New York: Lee & Low.

Bunting, E. (1997). *December.* San Diego, CA: Harcourt.

Bunting, E. (1999). *Smoky night.* New York: Voyager.

Carle, E. (1998). *Draw me a star.* New York: Putnam.

Carle, E. (2002). *The art of Eric Carle.* New York: Philomel.

Fine, R.E. (2003). *The art of Romare Bearden.* New York: Harry N. Abrams.

Garland, S. (1983). *Potter brownware: A picture book.* New York: Scribner.

Ginsberg, M. (1997). *Clay boy.* New York: Greenwillow.

Greenberg, J. (2003). *Romare Bearden: Collage of memories.* New York: Harry N. Abrams.

Hartfield, C. (2002). *Me and Uncle Romie.* New York: Dial.

Park, L.S. (2003). *A single shard.* New York: Yearling.

Wisniewski, D. (1996). *Golem.* New York: Clarion.

Professional Resources

Bawden, J. (1995). *The art and craft of papier mâché.* San Francisco: Chronicle.

Chavarria, J. (1994). *The big book of ceramics: A guide to the history, materials, equipment, and techniques of hand-building, throwing, molding, kiln-firing, and glazing pottery and other ceramic objects.* New York: Watson-Guptill.

Clark, K. (1999). *The potter's manual.* Edison, NJ: Chartwell.

Fulton, R. (Producer). (1993). *Eric Carle: Picture writer.* United States: Searchlight Films.

Goldsworthy, A. (1990). *Andy Goldsworthy: A collaboration with nature.* New York: Harry N. Abrams.

Henry, S. (1997). *Cut-paper play! Dazzling creations from construction paper.* Charlotte, VT: Williamson.

Hopper, R. (1986). *Functional pottery: Form and aesthetic in pots of purpose.* Iola, WI: Krause.

Hopper, R. (2004). *Making marks: Discovering the ceramic surface.* Iola, WI: Krause.

Kenny, J.B. (1976). *The complete book of pottery making* (2nd ed.). Iola, WI: Krause.

McGraw, S. (1991). *Papier-mâché for kids.* Richmond Hill, ON: Firefly.

Michel, K. (2005). *The complete guide to altered imagery: Mixed-media techniques for collage, altered books, artist journals, and more.* Gloucester, MA: Quarry.

Mix. (1987). *Construction paper sculpture.* Portland, ME: J Weston Walch.

Perrella, L. (2006). *Alphabetica: An A–Z creativity guide for collage and book artists.* Gloucester, MA: Quarry Books.

Tourtillott, S.J. (Ed.). (2003). *The Penland book of ceramics: Master classes in ceramic techniques.* New York: Lark.

Warshaw, J. (2001). *The practical potter: A step-by-step guide.* London: Hermes House.

Williams, M. (1996). *Making your own papier mâché: Creative ideas for beautiful designs.* New York: Sterling.

REFERENCES

Albers, P. (1996). *Art as literacy: The dynamic interplay of pedagogy and gendered meaning making in sixth grade art classes.* Unpublished doctoral dissertation, Indiana University, Bloomington.

Albers, P. (1997). Art as literacy. *Language Arts, 74*(5), 338-350.

Albers, P. (2001). Literacy in the arts. *Primary Voices, 9*(4), 3-9.

Albers, P. (2002). Making the most of demonstrations. *Clay Times, 8*(6), 48-50.

Albers, P. (2004a). Literacy in art: A question of responsibility. *Democracy and Education, 15*(3-4), 32-41.

Albers, P. (2004b). Dancing platters. *Clay Times, 10*(6), 46-47, 49.

Albers, P. (2006a). Imagining the possibilities of multimodal curriculum design. *English Education, 38*(2), 75-101.

Albers, P. (2006b). Jerry Maschinot's large bottle-form vessels. *Clay Times Magazine.*

Albers, P. (2006c, December 2). *Visual discourse analysis: An artist's perspective.* Paper presented at the annual meeting of the National Reading Conference, Los Angeles, CA.

Albers, P., & Cowan, K. (1998). *The tensions and possibilities of integrating the arts: A study of seven elementary teachers and their curriculum.* Paper presented at the annual meeting of the National Reading Conference, Austin, TX.

Albers, P., & Cowan, K. (2006a). Literacy on our minds: A student-inspired symposium. *Language Arts, 83*(6), 514-522.

Albers, P., & Cowan, K. (2006b, November 29). *"I don't know why": A study of gender in children's artwork.* Paper presented at the annual meeting of the National Reading Conference, Los Angeles, CA.

Albers, P., & Murphy, S. (2000). *Telling pieces: Art as literacy in middle school classes.* Mahwah, NJ: Erlbaum.

Applebee, A.N. (1996). *Curriculum as conversation: Transforming traditions of teaching and learning.* Chicago: University of Chicago Press.

Arts Education Partnership. (2005). *Third space: When learning matters.* Washington, DC: AEP.

Ashton, D. (Ed.). (1972). *Picasso on art: A selection of views.* Cambridge, MA: Da Capo.

Bang, M. (2000). *Picture this! How pictures work.* New York: SeaStar Books.

Bayles, D., & Orland, T. (1993). *Art & fear: Observations on the perils (and rewards) of artmaking.* Santa Barbara, CA: Carpa.

Berger, K. (2000). *A theory of art.* New York: Oxford University Press.

Berghoff, B. (1995). *Inquiry curriculum from a semiotic perspective: First graders using multiple sign systems to learn.* Unpublished doctoral dissertation, Indiana University, Bloomington.

Berghoff, B., Borgmann, C.B., & Parr, C. (2003). Cycles of inquiry with the arts. *Language Arts, 80*(5), 353-362.

Berghoff, B., Egawa, K.A., Harste, J.C., & Hoonan, B.T. (2000). *Beyond reading and writing: Inquiry, curriculum, and multiple ways of knowing.* Urbana, IL: National Council of Teachers of English.

Blair, H.A., & Stanford, K. (2004). Morphing literacy: Boys reshaping their school-based literacy practices. *Language Arts, 81*(6), 452–460.

Boyatzis, C.J., & Eades, J. (1999). Gender differences in preschoolers' and kindergartners' artistic production and preference. *Sex Roles, 41*(7/8), 627–638.

Britzman, D.P. (1995). Is there a queer pedagogy? Or, stop reading straight. *Educational Theory, 45*(2), 151–165.

Burke, C.L. (2004). *Curriculum as inquiry.* Paper presented at the annual conference of the National Council of Teachers of English, San Francisco, CA.

Carger, C.L. (2004). Art and literacy with bilingual children. *Language Arts, 81*(4), 283–292.

Cowan, K.W. (2001a). The arts and emergent literacy. *Primary Voices K–6, 9*(4), 11–18.

Cowan, K.W. (2001b). *The visual-verbal connections of literacy: An examination of the composing processes of the fifth- and sixth-grade student.* Unpublished doctoral dissertation, Georgia State University, Atlanta.

Cowan, K.W., & Albers, P. (2006). Semiotic representations: Building complex literacy practices through the arts. *The Reading Teacher, 60,* 124–137.

cummings, e.e. (1976). In R. Ellman & R. O'Clair (Eds.), *Modern poems: An introduction to poetry* (p. 220). New York: Norton.

da Silva, K. (Ed.). (2001). Drawing on experience: Connecting art and language. *Primary Voices K–6, 10*(2), 2–8.

DuCharme, C.C. (1991). *The role of drawing in the writing processes of primary grade children.* Paper presented at the spring conference of the National Council of Teachers of English, Indianapolis, IN.

Dyson, A.H. (1988). *Drawing, talking, and writing: Rethinking writing development.* Berkeley, CA: Center for the Study of Writing.

Dyson, A.H. (2001). Relational sense and textual sense in a U.S. urban classroom: The contested case of Emily, girl friend of a ninja. In B. Comber & A. Simpson (Eds.), *Negotiating critical literacies in classrooms* (pp. 3–18). Mahwah, NJ: Erlbaum.

Eisner, E.W. (1982). *Cognition and curriculum: A basis for deciding what to teach.* New York: Longman.

Eisner, E.W. (1991). What the arts taught me about education. In G. Willis & W.H. Schubert (Eds.), *Reflections from the heart of educational inquiry: Understanding curriculum and teaching through the arts* (pp. 34–48). Albany: State University of New York Press.

Eisner, E.W. (1992). The misunderstood role of the arts in human development. *Phi Delta Kappan, 73*(8), 591–595.

Eisner, E.W. (2002a). *The arts and the creation of mind.* New Haven, CT: Yale University Press.

Eisner, E.W. (2002b). What can education learn from the arts about the practice of education? *Journal of Curriculum and Supervision, 18*(1), 4–16.

Eisner, E.W. (2003a). The arts and the creation of mind. *Language Arts, 80*(5), 340–344.

Eisner, E.W. (2003b). Artistry in education. *Scandinavian Journal of Educational Research, 47*(3), 373–384.

Ernst, K. (1994). *Picturing learning: Artists and writers in the classroom.* Portsmouth, NH: Heinemann.

Ernst, K. (1997). *A teacher's sketch journal: Observations on learning and teaching*. Portsmouth, NH: Heinemann.

Evans, W.R., Applewhite, A., Evans, T., & Frothingham, A. (2003). *And I quote: The definitive collection of quotes, sayings, and jokes for the contemporary speechmaker*. New York: St. Martin's Press.

Freire, P., & Macedo, D. (1987). *Literacy: Reading the word, reading the world*. South Hadley, MA: Bergin & Garvey.

Flynn, R.M. (2002). Shakespearean slide shows. *English Journal, 92*(1), 62-68.

Gardner, H. (1991). *The unschooled mind: How children think and how schools should teach*. New York: Basic Books.

Gilbert, P., & Taylor, S. (1991). *Fashioning the feminine: Girls, popular culture and schooling*. Sydney, NSW, Australia: Allen & Unwin.

Goldonowicz, J. (1985). Art and other subjects. *Art Education, 38*(6), 17.

Gombrich, E.H. (1994). *The image & the eye: Further studies in the psychology of pictorial representation*. London: Phaidon.

Graves, D.H. (1975). An examination of the writing processes of seven year old children. *Research in the Teaching of English, 9*(3), 227-241.

Graves, D.H. (1983). *Writing: Teachers and children at work*. Portsmouth, NH: Heinemann.

Greene, M. (1995). *Releasing the imagination: Essays on education, the arts, and social change*. San Francisco: Jossey-Bass.

Greene, M. (2001). *Variations on a blue guitar: The Lincoln Center Institute lectures on aesthetic education*. New York: Teachers College Press.

Greenway, W. (1996). Poems and paintings: Shades of the Prison House. *English Journal, 85*(3), 42-48.

Halliday, M.A.K. (1978). *Language as social semiotic: The social interpretation of language and meaning*. Baltimore: University Park Press.

Harste, J.C. (1994). Literacy as curricular conversations. In R.B. Ruddell, M.R. Ruddell, & H. Singer (Eds.), *Theoretical models and processes of reading* (4th ed.; pp. 1221-1242). Newark, DE: International Reading Association.

Harste, J.C. (2005, January 28). *How the arts enhance learning*. Keynote address delivered at the 2005 Georgia Read Write Now Conference, Atlanta, GA.

Harste, J.C., Short, K.G., & Burke, C.L. (1988). *Creating classrooms for authors: The reading-writing connection*. Portsmouth, NH: Heinemann.

Harste, J.C., & Vasquez, V. (1998). The work we do: Journal as audit trail. *Language Arts, 75*(4), 266-276.

Igoa, C. (1995). *The inner world of the immigrant child*. Mahwah, NJ: Erlbaum.

International Reading Association (IRA) & National Council of Teachers of English (NCTE). (1996). *Standards for the English language arts*. Newark, DE; Urbana, IL: Authors.

Itten, J., & van Hagen, E. (1973). *The art of color: The subjective experience and objective rationale of color*. New York: Van Nostrand.

Kajder, S. (2004). Plugging in: What technology brings to the English/language arts classroom. *Voices From the Middle, 11*(3), 6-9.

Katzive, B. (1997). Looking, writing, creating. *Voices From the Middle, 4*(3), 25-29.

Kiefer, B.Z. (1995). *The potential of picture books: From visual literacy to aesthetic understanding*. Englewood Cliffs, NJ: Merrill.

Kist, W. (2005). *New literacies in action: Teaching and learning in multiple media*. New York: Teachers College Press.

Kress, G., & Jewitt, C. (2003). Introduction. In C. Jewitt & G. Kress (Eds.), *Multimodal literacy* (pp. 1–18). New York: Peter Lang.

Kress, G., & van Leeuwen, T. (1996). *Reading images: The grammar of visual design*. New York: Routledge.

Kress, G., & van Leeuwen, T. (2001). *Multimodal discourse: The modes and media of contemporary communication*. London: Edward Arnold.

Kress, G., & van Leeuwen, T. (2006). *Reading images: The grammar of visual design* (2nd ed.). New York: Routledge.

Lambert-Stock, P. (2004). President's update: NCTE in the 21st century. *The Council Chronicle, 14*(2), 12.

Langer, J.A. (1995). *Envisioning literature: Literary understanding and literature instruction*. New York: Teachers College Press.

Langer, S.K.K. (1957). *Philosophy in a new key: A study in the symbolism of reason, rite, and art* (3rd ed.). Cambridge, MA: Harvard University Press.

Lankshear, C., & Knobel, M. (2003). *New literacies: Changing knowledge and classroom learning*. Buckingham, England: Open University Press.

Lark. (2003). *The Penland book of ceramics: Master classes in ceramic technique*. New York: Lark Books.

Lewis, D. (1991). *Warren Mackenzie: An American potter*. New York: Kodansha International.

Lyons, D. (1997). *Edward Hopper: A journal of his work*. New York: Whitney Museum of American Art, in association with W.W. Norton.

MacMillan, D. (2000). "Taking a line for a walk": The art of Paul Klee. *The Lancet, 356*(9238), p. 1361.

Macedo, D. (1994). *Literacies of power: What Americans are not allowed to know*. Boulder, CO: Westview Press.

Merriam-Webster. (1998). *Merriam-Webster's Collegiate Dictionary*. Springfield, MA: Author.

Miller, J. (2006). *Arts in education*. Denver, CO: Education Commission of the States.

Moxey, K. (1994). *The practice of theory: Poststructuralism, cultural politics, and art history*. Ithaca, NY: Cornell University Press.

Murata, R. (1997). Connecting the visual and verbal: English and art for high school sophomores, *English Journal, 86*(7), 444–449.

Murphy, S. (1995, July). *Celebrating communities: From wishes to actualities*. Paper presented at the 1995 International Whole Language Umbrella Conference, Windsor, ON.

Murray, D. (1991). One writer's curriculum. *English Journal, 80*(4), 16–20.

Newkirk, T. (2002). *Misreading masculinity: Boys, literacy, and popular culture*. Portsmouth, NH: Heinemann.

Noden, H., & Moss, B. (Eds). (1995). Nurturing artistic images in student reading and writing. *The Reading Teacher, 48*, 532–534.

Olshansky, B. (1994). Making writing a work of art: Image-making within the writing process. *Language Arts, 71*(5), 350–356.

Olshansky, B. (1995). Picture this: An arts-based literacy program. *Thrust for Educational Leadership, 53*(1), 44–47.

Olshansky, B. (1997). Picturing story: An irresistible pathway into literacy. *The Reading Teacher, 50*, 612–613.

Patterson, W. (2003). Breaking out of our boxes. *Phi Delta Kappan, 84*(8), 568-574.

Penrose, R. (1998). *Picasso*. London: Phaidon.

Pirie, B. (1997). *Reshaping high school English*. Urbana, IL: National Council of Teachers of English.

Piro, J.M. (2002). The picture of reading: Deriving meaning in literacy through image. *The Reading Teacher, 56*, 126-134.

Pugh, S.L., Hicks, J.W., Davis, M., & Venstra, T. (1992). *Bridging: A teacher's guide to metaphorical thinking*. Urbana, IL: National Council of Teachers of English.

Rabkin, N., & Redmond, R. (2005, January 8). The art of education success. *The Washington Post*. Retrieved January 9, 2005, from http://www.washingtonpost.com/wp-dyn/articles/A57870-2005Jan7.html

Rosenblatt, L.M. (1995). *Literature as exploration* (5th ed.). New York: Modern Language Association of America.

Shagoury, R. (1989). *Authors of pictures, draughtsmen of words*. Portsmouth, NH: Heinemann.

Short, K.G., & Burke, C.L. (1991). *Creating curriculum: Teachers and students as a community of leaders*. Portsmouth, NH: Heinemann.

Short, K.G., Harste, J.C., & Burke, C.L. (1996). *Creating classrooms for authors and inquirers*. Portsmouth, NH: Heinemann.

Siegel, M. (1984). *Reading as signification*. Unpublished doctoral dissertation, Indiana University, Bloomington.

Siegel, M. (1995). More than words: The generative power of transmediation for learning. *Canadian Journal of Education, 20*(4), 455-475.

Sonesson, G. (1988). *Methods and models in pictorial semiotics*. Retrieved February 12, 2007, from http://www.arthist.lu.se/kultsem/pdf/rapport3.pdf

Sonesson, G. (2004). *The quadrature of hermeneutic circles*. Retrieved February 12, 2007, from http://www.chass.utoronto.ca/epc/srb/cyber/Sonesson1.pdf

Steiner, W. (1995). *The scandal of pleasure*. Chicago: University of Chicago Press.

Thayer, H.S. (1981). *Meaning and action: A critical history of pragmatism*. Indianapolis, IN: Hackett.

Thayer, H.S. (Ed.). (1982). *Pragmatism: The classic writings*. Indianapolis, IN: Hackett.

Tuman, D.M. (1999). Gender styles as form and content: An examination of gender stereotypes in the subject preference of children's drawing. *Studies in Art Education, 41*(1), 40-60.

Van Sluys, K. (2005). *What if and why? Literacy invitations for multilingual classrooms*. Portsmouth, NH: Heinemann.

Vasquez, V. (2004). *Negotiating critical literacies with young children*. Mahwah, NJ: Erlbaum.

Watson, D., Burke, C.L., & Harste, J.C. (1989). *Whole language: Inquiring voices*. Markham, ON: Scholastic Canada.

Weaver, C. (2002). *Reading process and practice*. Portsmouth, NH: Heinemann.

Wilhelm, J. (2001). It's a guy thing. *Voices From the Middle, 9*(2), 60-63.

Williams, W.C. (1976). The red wheelbarrow. In R. Ellman & R. O'Clair (Eds.), *Modern poems: An introduction to poetry* (p. 111). New York: Norton.

Wink, J. (1997). *Critical pedagogy: Notes from the real world*. New York: Longman.

Winterson, J. (1995). *Art objects: Essays on ecstasy and effrontery*. New York: Vintage.

NOVELS/CHILDREN'S LITERATURE CITED

Ackerman, K. (1992). *Song and dance man*. New York: Dragonfly.

Anonymous. (1998). *Go ask Alice*. New York: Aladdin.

Asgedom, M. (2002). *Of beetles and angels: A boy's remarkable journey from a refugee camp to Harvard*. Boston: Little, Brown.

Baylor, B. (1987). *The desert is theirs*. New York: Aladdin.

Baylor, B. (1987). *When clay sings*. New York: Aladdin.

Bradby, M. (1995). *More than anything else*. Danbury, CT: Orchard Books.

Bradby, M. (2000). *Momma, where are you from?* Danbury, CT: Orchard Books.

Brown, D. (2003). *The da Vinci code*. New York: Doubleday.

Brown, M. (1982). *Shadow*. New York: Atheneum.

Bunting, E. (1999). *Night of the gargoyles*. New York: Clarion Books.

Carle, E. (1981). *The very hungry caterpillar*. New York: Philomel Books.

Carle, E. (1992). *Draw me a star*. New York: Philomel Books.

Chopin, K. (1982). *The awakening*. New York: Avon.

Cisneros, S. (1991). *The house on Mango Street*. New York: Vintage.

Cisneros, S. (1992). *Woman hollering creek: And other stories*. New York: Vintage.

Collier, B. (2000). *Uptown*. New York: Henry Holt.

Crane, S. (1990). *The red badge of courage*. New York: Tor.

Creech, S. (2003). *Love that dog*. New York: HarperTrophy.

Falconer, I. (2000). *Olivia*. New York: Atheneum.

Feelings, M. (1971). *Moja means one: A Swahili counting book*. New York: Dial.

Feelings, M. (1974). *Jambo means hello: A Swahili alphabet book*. New York: Dial.

Feelings, T. (1995). *The middle passage: White ships/black cargo*. New York: Dial Books for Young Readers.

Fox, M. (1998). *Tough Boris*. New York: Voyager Books.

Gaines, E.J. (1994). *A lesson before dying*. New York: Vintage.

Gerstein, M. (2003). *The man who walked between the towers*. New York: Roaring Brook Press.

Goble, P. (1978). *The girl who loved wild horses*. Scarsdale, NY: Bradbury Press.

Golding, W. (1959). *Lord of the flies*. New York: Perigee.

Gray, N. (1989). *A country far away*. New York: Orchard Books.

Greenberg, J. (2003). *Romare Bearden: Collage of memories*. New York: Harry N. Abrams.

Griffin, J.H. (2003). *Black like me*. New York: New American Library Trade.

Grimes, N. (1999). *My man Blue*. New York: Puffin.

Hawthorne, N. (1981). *The scarlet letter*. New York: Bantam Dell.

Herold, M.R. (1995). *A very important day*. New York: William Morrow.

Hesse, K. (1999). *Out of the dust*. New York: Scholastic.

Hurst, J. (1988). *The scarlet ibis*. Mancato, MN: Creative Education.

Hurston, Z.N. (1998). *Their eyes were watching god*. New York: Perennial Classics.

Jiménez, F. (1997). *The circuit: Stories from the life of a migrant child*. Albuquerque, NM: University of New Mexico Press.

Jiménez, F. (2002). *Breaking through*. Boston: Houghton Mifflin.

Johnson, S.T. (1999). *Alphabet city*. New York: Puffin.

Kids Discover. (1999). *Immigration*. New York: Author.

Lee, H. (1988). *To kill a mockingbird*. Boston: Little, Brown. (Original work published 1960)

Leodhas, S.N. (1965). *Always room for one more*. New York: Henry Holt.

Macaulay, D. (1979). *Motel of the mysteries*. Boston: Houghton Mifflin.

Macaulay, D. (1981). *Cathedral: The story of its construction*. Boston: Houghton Mifflin.

Macaulay, D. (1982). *Pyramid*. Boston: Houghton Mifflin.

Macaulay, D. (1983). *City: A story of Roman planning and construction*. Boston: Houghton Mifflin.

Martin, B., Jr. (1996). *Brown bear, brown bear, what do you see?* New York: Henry Holt.

Martin, B., Jr., & Archambault, J. (1987). *Knots on a counting rope*. New York: Henry Holt.

Martin, R. (1998). *The rough-face girl*. New York: Putnam.

McCully, E.A. (1992). *Mirette on the high wire*. New York: Putnam.

McDermott, G. (1986). *Anansi the spider: A tale from the Ashanti*. New York: Henry Holt.

McDermott, G. (1993). *Raven: A trickster tale from the Pacific Northwest*. New York: Voyager.

Mochizuki, K. (1993). *Baseball saved us*. New York: Lee & Low.

Muñoz Ryan, P. (1999). *Amelia and Eleanor go for a ride*. New York: Scholastic.

Morrison, T. (1970). *The bluest eye*. New York: Holt, Rinehart & Winston.

Musgrove, M. (1976). *Ashanti to Zulu: African traditions*. New York: Dial.

Myers, W.D. (1993). *Brown angels: An album of pictures and verse*. New York: HarperTrophy.

Myers, W.D. (2001). *Monster*. New York: Amistad.

Na, A. (2003). *A step from heaven*. New York: Puffin.

Nordine, K. (2000). *Colors*. San Diego, CA: Harcourt.

Orwell, G. (1946). *Animal farm*. New York: Harcourt Brace.

Orwell, G. (1992). *1984*. New York: Knopf.

Paschen, E., & Mosby, R.F. (2001). *Poetry speaks: Hear great poets read their work from Tennyson to Plath*. Naperville, IL: Sourcebooks MediaFusion.

Paulsen, G. (2002). *Woodsong*. New York: Aladdin.

Patterson, K. (1987). *Bridge to Terabithia*. New York: HarperTrophy.

Pryor, B. (1996). *The dream jar*. New York: William Morrow.

Robinson, A.B.L. (1997). *A street called home*. New York: Harcourt Brace.

Robinson, A.B.L., & Genshaft, C.M. (2002). *Symphonic poem: The art of Aminah Brenda Lynn Robinson*. Columbus, OH: Columbus Museum of Art, in association with Harry N. Abrams.

Rostand, E. (1950). *Cyrano de Bergerac*. New York: Bantam Classics.

Rylant, C. (1985). *The relatives came*. New York: Bradbury Press.

Rylant, C. (1996). *A fine white dust*. New York: Aladdin.

Salinger, J.D. (1951). *Catcher in the rye*. New York: Modern Library.

Say, A. (1993). *Grandfather's journey*. Boston: Houghton Mifflin.

Shakur, T. (1999). *The rose that grew from concrete*. New York: Pocket Books.

Shelley, M. (2004). *Frankenstein*. New York: Pocket Books.

Silverstein, S. (1964). *The giving tree*. New York: Harper & Row.

Silverstein, S. (2004). *Where the sidewalk ends*. New York: Harper & Row.

Soto, G. (1997). *Buried onions*. San Diego, CA: Harcourt Brace.

Steinbeck, J. (1993). *Of mice and men*. New York: Penguin.

Steinbeck, J. (1945). *The pearl*. New York: Viking.

Walker, A. (1992). *The color purple*. New York: Harcourt Brace Jovanovich.

Willems, M. (2004). *Knuffle bunny: A cautionary tale*. New York: Hyperion Books for Children.

Williams, T. (1999). *The glass menagerie*. New York: New Directions.

Wisniewski, D. (1996). *Golem*. New York: Clarion Books.
Wisniewski, D. (2005). *The wave of the sea-wolf*. New York: Clarion Books.
Yep, L. (1977). *Dragonwings*. New York: HarperTrophy.
Young, E. (1989). *Lon po po*. New York: Philomel.

ARTWORKS CITED

Savage, A. (1939). *Lift every voice and sing*. Retrieved February 28, 2007, from
    http://northbysouth.kenyon.edu/1998/art/pages/savage.htm
Schuster, O. (circa 1940). *Indian Canoeing*. Peggy Albers, personal collection.
Hopper, Edward. (1923). *House By the Sea*. Whitney Museum of American Art, New York.

MUSIC/AUDIO RECORDINGS CITED

Diamond, N. (2001). America. On *The essential Neil Diamond* [CD]. New York: Columbia.
Guthrie, W. (1997). This land is your land. On *The Asch recordings, vol. 1: This land is your land*
    [CD]. Washington, DC: Smithsonian Folkways Recordings.
Nordine, K. (2000). *Colors* [CD]. New York: Asphodel.
Santana (1998). Black magic woman. On *The best of Santana* [CD]. New York: Columbia
    Legacy.
Shakur, T. (2000). The rose that grew from concrete. On *The rose that grew from concrete*
    [CD]. Santa Monica, CA: Amaru/Interscope Records.

VIDEOS/FILMS CITED

Hernandez, O. (Producer). (2006). Walkout RHS.
    http://www.youtube.com/watch?v=hsYf7SLI1dA
Searchlight Films (Producer) & Fulton, R. (Director). (1993). *Eric Carle: Picture writer*. New
    York: Philomel.
Brown, D., Zanuck, R. (Producers), & Spielberg, S. (Director). (1975). *Jaws* [Motion
    picture]. Hollywood, CA: Universal Studios.

WEBSITES CITED

Allen Say quotation. Retrieved February 11, 2007, from http://www.vickiblackwell.com/
    lit/lonpopo.html
Aminah Robinson. Retrieved February 11, 2007, from http://www.enquirer.com/editions/
    2003/08/01/tem_frilede01artist.html
Andy Warhol's Marilyn prints. (n.d.). Retrieved July 24, 2006, from http://webexhibits.org/
    colorart/marilyns.html
Color wheel. Retrieved February 14, 2007, from http://www.siteprocentral.com/color_
    tutor.html
David Hockney. (n.d.). Retrieved June 22, 2006, from http://www.npg.si.edu/cexh/artnews/
    hockney.htm
The drawings of Leonard da Vinci. (n.d.). Retrieved February 28, 2007, from http://www.
    drawingsofleonardo.org
Goldsworthy, A. (n.d.). *Introduction to sheepfolds*. Retrieved June 22, 2006, from http://www.
    sheepfolds.org/html/info/info00.htm

256

Historical images. (n.d.). Retrieved August 12, 2006, from http://en.wikipedia.org/wiki/Public_domain_image_resources#Historical_images

Immigration. (n.d.). Retrieved September 6, 2006, from http://www.kidsdiscoverteachers.com/aspx/pDetail.aspx?ListGUID=5BF15E31-CB41-4441-832D-C7E9D796927B

Overview, Microsoft Office PowerPoint 2003. (n.d.). Retrieved February 20, 2007, from http://office.microsoft.com/training/training.aspx?AssetID=RC010713231033

INTASC Standards. Retrieved February 14, 2007, from http://www.ccsso.org/content/pdfs/corestrd.pdf

ISTE Standards. Retrieved February 14, 2007, from http://www.iste.org

Johnson, J.W. Lift every voice and sing. Retrieved February 12, 2007, from http://www.english.uiuc.edu/maps/poets/g_l/johnson/poems.htm

Mark Rothko. (n.d.). Retrieved August 18, 2006, from http://www.nga.gov/feature/rothko/classic2a.shtm

Pablo Picasso. (n.d.). Retrieved June 22, 2006, from http://en.wikipedia.org/wiki/Pablo_Picasso

Romare Bearden Foundation. (n.d.). Retrieved June 22, 2006, from http://www.beardenfoundation.org

Self-portrait with vanitas symbols. (n.d.). Retrieved June 22, 2006, from http://gallery.euroweb.hu/html/b/bailly/selfport.html

INDEX

Note. Page numbers followed by *f* indicate figures.